POOR SUPPORT

POOR SUPPORT

Poverty in the American Family

DAVID T. ELLWOOD

BasicBooks
A Division of HarperCollinsPublishers

Excerpts in chapter 6 from Leon Dash's articles "Children's Children," "Motherhood the Hard Way," "When Outcomes Collide with Desire," "Mario, I Want a Baby," and "Breaking the Hold of a 'Choke Chain' " copyright © The Washington Post. Reprinted with permission.

Library of Congress Cataloging-in-Publication Data

Ellwood, David T.
  Poor support.

  Includes index.
  1. Public welfare—United States. 2. Poor—
Government policy—United States. 3. Social
Security—United States. 4. Family policy—
United States. I. Title.
HV91.E453 1988   361.6'0973   87–47779
ISBN 0–465–05996–1 (cloth)
ISBN 0–465–05995–3 (paper)

96 97 98 99 RRD 20 19 18 17 16 15 14 13

To my parents

CONTENTS

PREFACE

In a strange way, this book developed out of the debate surrounding Charles Murray and George Gilder, two conservatives whose ideas held great sway in the Reagan administration. During that debate, others often cited my work in their attempts to refute conservative suggestions that the welfare system was the cause of great harm. With my work being used as ammunition in defense of welfare, I was naturally drawn in.

My colleague Mary Jo Bane and I had for some years been exploring the links between social welfare programs and poverty. We had found that some people were long-term poor, and it was obvious that family structures were changing rapidly. But somewhat to our surprise, welfare did not seem to deserve much blame for these phenomena. Indeed, the research suggested that welfare had done a lot to protect families and children, and the unintended negative effects were quite modest. Welfare seemed to do far more good than harm. I was called upon now to deliver that message to the public.

But the message didn't sell very well. People hated welfare no matter what the evidence. It wasn't just conservatives; liberals also expressed deep mistrust of the system, and the recipients themselves despised it. Each group disdained it for different reasons, but the frustration and anger with the present system were unmistakable. And frankly, I had to admit that even I, who had been asked to come to the system's defense, found much to dislike. Yet it was obvious that the vast majority of people I spoke with also believed that society ought to help the poor. The conservative proposal simply to cut welfare back sharply was not much more popular than welfare itself.

This book is my attempt to understand the widespread disdain for welfare that exists in spite of the professed desire of most Americans to help the poor. I now believe that welfare, by its very nature, creates conflict and frustration and tension because it treats the symptoms of poverty, not its causes. Yet this is not a pessimistic book. I find myself far more hopeful about society's ability to help the poor in ways that reflect our basic values than I was before I entered the debate. Having looked hard at the causes of poverty, I am convinced that nonwelfare policies exist that can support the poor by reinforcing and rewarding their efforts. Such policies ensure the security of families while increasing their control, responsibility, and independence.

My debt to others is extremely large. Indeed, one of my greatest fears is that many who have provided me with insights will see their ideas in these pages without the full credit they deserve. Without a doubt, my greatest intellectual debt is to Mary Jo Bane, who is now the director of the Center for Health and Human Resources at Harvard's Kennedy School of Government. Because so much of my work in this area has been with Mary Jo, and because I have benefited from so many conversations with her, whatever insights this book offers are hers as well. Irwin Garfinkel has probably done more than anyone else to convince a whole generation of politicians and intellectuals that child support ought to be a critical element in social policy. He certainly convinced me. I have also learned much from my association with Manpower Demonstration Research Corporation (MDRC), which has done a great deal of extraordinary work exploring what does and does not work in aiding welfare recipients. I particularly thank Judy Gueron, MDRC's president, for her many helpful insights. Robert Reischauer and Robert Lerman both were instrumental in my thinking about ways to help the working poor. William Julius Wilson's compelling ideas about America's ghettos have moved me with their clarity and depth. And my many discussions with Lawrence Summers taught me a great deal and helped me sharpen my vague early ideas. Henry Aaron, Gary Burtless, Sheldon Danziger, Greg Duncan, Robert Greenstein, Frank Levy, Glenn Loury, Rebecca Maynard, Daniel Patrick Moynihan, Richard Nathan, and David Wise, among many others, also have been influential in my thinking, and sources of encouragement.

The Ford Foundation Project on Social Welfare and the American Future offered generous financial support. It also sponsored a number of conferences, where I had a chance to air my ideas and hear those of many others who have worked in the field. I am particularly grateful for the moral and intellectual support of Gordon Berlin and Alice O'Connor. The U.S. Department of Health and Human Services has supported a number of my research efforts. I have found my association with many in the department, especially Daniel Weinberg, to be an important source of information and inspiration. Martin Kessler of Basic Books talked me into doing this book and provided help throughout.

Still, the people who struggled through this project with me in a day-to-day way deserve my greatest thanks. Tom Kane reviewed draft after draft, created and re-created tables and figures, even checked footnotes. Without his thoughtful reactions, his unfailing good humor, and his very hard work, this book might never have been completed. Naomi Goldstein, who participated in portions of this research, was an extremely careful reader and offered some of the most helpful comments I received. I am grateful to Regina Aragon and Jon Crane, who read drafts and offered insightful comments. I also thank my wonderful secretary, Sandra Metts, for all of her efforts.

The most important person of all, though, was my wife, Marilyn. She alone read every draft. She alone had the courage to say that a chapter was awful or that an argument was too complicated by half. But she always had an idea about how things could be fixed—and endured many a boring dinner conversation as I tried out yet another version of an argument. She provided true support.

I have dedicated this book to my parents. They taught me to value both compassion and rigorous thought. I hope that neither ambition nor academia have distorted those values too much.

POOR SUPPORT

1

Beyond Welfare

It was one of those poignant scenes that talk shows thrive on. On September 17, 1986, Oprah Winfrey was hosting an hour on welfare, and the most prominent guest was Lawrence Mead, who had recently finished a provocative book calling for mandatory work for people who are on welfare. But the action was in the audience. Two women were yelling, not at the host or the guest, but at each other. The women looked and even dressed similarly, but their antagonism was unmistakable. One said that even though she was working her tail off, trying to earn enough money to raise her family, she was hardly making it. But she certainly was not going to take any handouts. She deeply resented the mothers on welfare who were getting money, medical insurance, and food stamps while they were doing nothing. The other woman, who was on welfare, countered by saying that no lazy person could raise and clothe a family on the tiny amount that she was given for welfare and food stamps and that hers was a hard and often desperate struggle. Both women felt they were trying hard. Both felt they weren't making it. And both hated the welfare system.

Everyone hates welfare. Conservatives hate it because they see welfare as a narcotic that destroys the energy and determination of people who already are suffering from a shortage of such qualities. They hate it because they think it makes a mockery of the efforts of working people, such as the woman on the Oprah Winfrey show. Liberals hate it because of the way it treats people. The current system offers modest benefits while imposing a ridiculous array of rules that rob recipients of security and self-esteem. Recipients are offered no real help and have no real dignity.

The American public hates welfare, too. In 1984, according to a survey of the National Opinion Research Center (NORC), some 41 percent of Americans thought we were spending too much on welfare. Only 25 percent thought we spent too little. According to political scientist Hugh Heclo, "The general pattern has varied little since the New Deal: since 1935 a majority of Americans have never wanted to spend more on welfare."[1] Politicians would have to be out of their minds to campaign for expanded welfare benefits.

Why Does Everyone Hate Welfare?

Those who defend welfare in spite of its problems often claim that the critics of welfare lack compassion. This same lack of compassion, they say, can be seen in budget cuts for programs to educate and feed young children, in attempts to restrict medical protection, and in plans to limit job training programs. They wonder, where is the understanding and support for those who are less fortunate?

Defenders of welfare emphasize that social welfare policy is badly misunderstood. Most of the money spent to help people goes to the aged or disabled. Much is spent on medical care. When you look at how much money actually is targeted for cash, food, or housing for the young and healthy poor, you discover that the money represents less than 4 percent of the government's total expenditures and less than 1.5 percent of the national income. And there is little evidence that welfare has played a major role in changing the structure of the family or altering values. Even a conservative Reagan administration report on the family, which Senator Daniel Patrick Moynihan labeled "less a policy paper than a tantrum,"[2] acknowledged that "statistical evidence does not confirm those suppositions" that welfare is responsible for the high illegitimacy rates in some minority groups.[3]

Stinginess surely plays a role in attitudes toward welfare. Yet the current conservative bibles on the subject, Charles Murray's *Losing Ground* and Lawrence Mead's *Beyond Entitlement,* both profess a strong desire to help the poor. According to Murray, "When reforms do occur, they will happen not because the stingy people have won, but because generous people have stopped kidding themselves."[4] Mead argues, "The main problem with the welfare state is not its size, but its permissiveness."[5] And the American public, which is so unwilling to expand welfare, is strongly in favor of doing more to help the poor. When the phrase "assistance for the poor" was substituted for "welfare" in the NORC survey just mentioned, some 64 percent favored spending more, and only 11 percent said the country should spend less.

I doubt that a misunderstanding of social welfare policies is the real heart of the matter. It is not that Americans forget that a large share of "welfare" goes to the aged and disabled. They do not consider that money to be "welfare." Welfare, as the public uses the term and as I will use it in this book, means cash, food, or housing assistance to healthy nonaged persons with low incomes. That kind of welfare is what the public objects to, regardless of its size. The working woman on the Oprah Winfrey show would not have been comforted by statistics showing that we spend far more on Social Security than on welfare.

I believe the disdain for welfare reflects something much more fundamental than a lack of compassion or misinformation. Welfare is a flawed method of helping people who are poor and disadvantaged. Welfare brings some of our most precious values—involving autonomy, responsibility, work, family, community, and compassion—into conflict. We want to help those who are not making it but, in so doing, we seem to cheapen the efforts of those who are struggling hard just to get by. We want to offer financial support to those with low incomes, but if we do we reduce the pressure on them and their incentive to work. We want to help people who are not able to help themselves but then we worry that people will not bother to help themselves. We recognize the insecurity of single-parent families but, in helping them, we appear to be promoting or supporting their formation. We want to target our money to the most needy but, in doing so, we often isolate and stigmatize them.

Charles Murray's powerful indictment of the social welfare system implicitly emphasizes these contradictions. According to Murray, the very system that was designed to help the poor has created dependent wards by penalizing the virtuous and rewarding the dysfunctional. Much of Murray's book is a graphical and statistical discussion of what has happened to the poor in general and to the black poor in particular. The intellectual establishment, particularly the liberal intellectual establishment, has been quick to attack Murray's work, and these attacks have cast considerable doubt on the credibility of his conclusions. But what is often missed in this frenzy is that although Murray is almost certainly wrong in blaming the social welfare system for a large part of the predicament of the poor, he is almost certainly correct in stating that welfare does not reflect or reinforce our most basic values. He is also correct in stating that no amount of tinkering with benefit levels or work rules will change that.

Welfare inevitably creates these conflicts because it treats the symptoms of poverty, not the causes. People are not poor just because they lack money. They are poor because they do not have a job, because their wages are too low, because they are trying to raise a child single-handedly, or because they are undergoing some crisis. Worse yet, in treating the symptoms rather than the causes of poverty, welfare creates inevitable conflicts in incentives and values that undermine the credibility and effectiveness of the system.

Better solutions demand a better understanding of why people are poor and a set of social policies that respond to the causes. This book seeks to determine the causes of poverty in families with children. It is a book about policies that support people and help them cope with legitimate problems without turning to traditional forms of welfare. It is a book that seeks to help the poor in ways that reflect and reinforce our values.

Of Causes and Values

How can we decide on the causes of poverty? Obviously we cannot allow ourselves to become trapped into simplistic conceptions or conclusions. Two of the most fruitless directions over the years have been "proof by success" and "proof by failure." The former is the traditional conservative method and the latter is the one adopted by liberals.

Conservatives proclaim that anyone can make it in this country, and they cite the many successes as proof of their argument. Millions of immigrants arrived in the United States with little more than a determination to succeed. They did well, and their children did better. Conservatives remind us of Linn Yann, the young Cambodian who came to this country at age 9, knowing no English, and reached the National Spelling Bee finals just six years later.[6] There are jobs unfilled, the conservatives say, low-paying jobs to be sure, but jobs that could serve as the starting point for ambitious people. People can escape poverty if only they use some elbow grease. The poor are those who lack the determination to make it.

Liberals laugh at the suggestion that people would knowingly turn down a chance to have middle-class security for a life of poverty and dependence. They consider the failure of so many people to make it as proof of larger problems. The high rate of poverty, especially among children, is clear evidence that society has failed in some dimension or another. Liberals cite a long list of problems. There is a shortage of real jobs—jobs with a future. People are trapped by limited opportunities, poor education, discrimination, and historical and institutional patterns that limit the possibilities for success in our society. They are mistreated and misunderstood by policy.

Neither of these conceptions takes us far. That there are many successes surely does not prove that motivated people always succeed. That people fail does not tell us much about what might be the problem. What is required is something more than tired anecdotes and analogies that are used to debate the basic character of human beings. Such approaches seem fraught with hidden biases, agendas, and motivations.

But we also cannot expect to come up with a "scientific" reason for poverty in the same way that we could diagnose why an automobile isn't running well. Behind any determination of the reasons for poverty must lie a set of values, judgments, and expectations. For example, suppose we find that a two-parent family with three children is poor even though the father is working full time. What is the cause of the family's poverty? One could say that the father's wages are too low, that the mother is not willing to work, that the family cannot find affordable day care, that the couple was irresponsible to have children when they could not support them, or that the father did not get enough education or has not worked hard enough to get a "good" job. Even if we talked to the family, it is possible that we would not be able to agree on just one "true" reason.

But if we can decide what is reasonable to expect of two-parent families, we can do better at assigning a cause and finding a solution. For instance, if we were willing to say that we believe that any two-parent family with children ought to be able to escape poverty through the full-time efforts of one worker, then we can say that, at least for policy purposes, the problem is low wages. And then we might consider ways to raise the father's take-home pay.

The basis for poverty, then, is inevitably tied to our values and to our expectations of our society and its citizens. Once such values and expectations are determined, then it is possible to identify some direct and often correctable reasons for poverty. When the problem is low wages, then wage rates need to be raised. When the problem is a lack of work, then jobs are called for. When the problem is that one parent is trying to do the job of two, then support from the absent parent may be a start. Scientific methods can tell us a great deal about the nature of the problem, but the ultimate decisions will have to come from a deeper set of principles.

It may sound unrealistic or even arrogant to suggest that, in making policies to deal with poverty, we can and must make judgments about ourselves and our society. One appeal of welfare is that it seems to dispose of the need to determine what is the nature of poverty and what is expected of the poor. But any policy that ignores the causes of the problem cannot provide real solutions.

And, of course, welfare actually is loaded with implicit assumptions and expectations. The recent debate over welfare policy offers clear and convincing proof that deciding on a welfare-based strategy involves many value judgments. The body politic cannot decide whether welfare is for those who are not expected to work, those who are working but need an additional boost in income, those who are in temporary difficulty, or those who are healthy but who cannot or will not provide for themselves.

Given the clashes in values, it seems logical that welfare is a perpetual scapegoat. The public image of welfare recipients shifts from one stereotype to another. Benefits are raised and lowered, obligations are imposed and withdrawn, and eligibility conditions are expanded or restricted, depending on the current political winds. It is no wonder that all sides constantly want some alternative to welfare.

Reform Welfare or Replace It?

At this writing, the country is once again engaged in one of its occasional moves toward welfare reform. No one seriously expects the government to heed the conservative call to eliminate welfare. And few now suggest instituting a guaranteed annual income (the so-called negative income tax), as was recommended during the last major period of welfare reform. Instead, people talk of imposing new obligations and responsibilities on recipients. In exchange, the government will offer training or jobs.

Some of these steps are useful and important. They represent the beginning of a change from a system of support that is designed simply to provide assistance until a person is no longer poor to a more activist conception, in which the government's role is to help people make it on their own. Adding work and training moves the welfare system slightly closer to the general values we espouse. Imposing obligations is more ambiguous, since it seems to reinforce work but raises questions of dignity.

But the evidence from every careful experiment that has been done suggests that these steps alone will have only a modest effect on welfare caseloads and on the ability of the disadvantaged to provide for themselves. The reason is simple. Such modifications in the welfare system alone will not be sufficient to solve the real causes of poverty. They will not make single parents much more productive or eliminate their child care responsibilities. They will not raise wages. They will not reinforce and strengthen families. They will not give the poor real dignity or responsibility. They will not do much to integrate the poor into the economic mainstream. They cannot resolve the fundamental conflicts of the welfare system.

The tragedy of this new agenda is that, in recent years, the proclaimed goal of those at most points on the political spectrum has been the same: to make certain that people can make it on their own without the need, frustration, or stigma of welfare. In spite of this shared goal, all sides seem willing to settle for a system that falls far short of encouraging or reinforcing it.

I believe that we have too quickly accepted the view that we cannot achieve this dream of giving everyone a chance to make it without welfare. If we committed ourselves to that goal and designed our support systems around it, we could find a set of policies that would be more helpful to the poor and more in concert with our basic values. The aim must not be to make welfare function better. The objective should be to replace welfare with something that takes much better account of the problems faced by the poor—a system that ensures that everyone who exercises reasonable responsibility can make it without welfare.

In this book, I talk explicitly about values and argue that we can decide on reasonable expectations. Using such decisions as an anchor, we can try to understand why people are poor. I look separately at two-parent families, single-parent families, and the ghetto poor. In each case, I find that there are generally three groups among the poor.

The first, large, group consists of families in which the adults are already doing a great deal for themselves: both two-parent families with one or two full-time workers and single-parent families in which the parent works full or part time and tries to balance the dual roles of nurturer and provider. These people ought to be encouraged and rewarded. Instead, they often receive no medical protection or additional support. Or they are put into the welfare system that penalizes their work, imposes extra demands on them, and stigmatizes them. The treatment of these hard-working families is one of the most disturbing features of our current system.

The second group includes those who are suffering temporary difficulties because of a job loss, a change in their family's circumstances, or some personal problem. These people need help, but only until they get on their feet. But they are often left to fend for themselves. Or they are put into a public assistance system that provides little cash assistance; limited, if any, services and training; and no incentives or pressure to regain their independence.

The third group consists of the few who are healthy but who seem unable to find work on their own and need some form of long-term support. This support often comes in the form of welfare. Some people end up collecting benefits for many years, never gaining control over their lives, and always dependent on and belittled by a stingy and unpleasant welfare system. These long-term unemployed people need work more than welfare.

I contend that a far better system would have three different types of support that would reflect the needs of each of these groups:

- *Supplemental Support.* People who are willing to work as much as society deems reasonable ought to be able to support their families at or above the poverty level without relying on welfare or welfarelike supports. Instead of welfare, the government should use such tools as tax policy and child support to ensure that such people can make it without entering a welfare system. For a two-parent family, the reasonable standard of work should be one full-time worker or the equivalent. For a single-parent family, the expectation should be half-time work from the custodial parent and child support from the absent one.
- *Transitional Support.* People who are not working because of temporary difficulties, such as the loss of a job or a recent change in their family's circumstances, ought to be offered short-term transitional assistance that includes training and services that are designed to help them become self-supporting, coupled with short-term cash support.
- *Jobs as a Last Resort.* Long-term income support beyond the supplemental support measures designed to ensure that anyone can make it through work ought to come in the form of jobs—not in the form of cash welfare for an indefinite duration.

Our goal should be to increase both the security and the responsibility of poor families. Anyone who is meeting reasonable responsibilities ought to be guaranteed of "making it" without welfare through a system of supplemental supports that are designed to reward work and responsibility. People with short-run and transitional problems deserve to be treated generously and sympathetically. But, ultimately, there ought to be some expectation that people will provide for themselves through work. Such an expectation is fair if (and only if) sufficient supplemental assistance is in place so that people need not work more than is "reasonable" and if the government ensures that last-resort jobs are available for people who have used up their transitional assistance.

Organization of the Book

Chapter 2 begins the discussion of the most important values that influence policy. It points to the inevitable way in which welfare brings those values into conflict. It also shows how nonwelfare solutions have been used with great success in many situations to avoid the conflicts inherent in welfare. Chapter 3 focuses on what is often seen as the primary cause of increased poverty in families: changing family structure. That chapter seeks to explain those changes and explore what policies, if any, are likely to influence them. Chapters 4–6 are devoted to each of three groups among the poor: two-parent families, single-parent families, and the ghetto poor. In each case, I explore the causes of poverty for families in those settings and examine policies to deal with the problems. The last chapter—chapter 7—explores the hopes of changing the nature of welfare and poverty in the future.

One special note: this book is exclusively about the poverty of families with children. Originally, I had hoped to talk about all of the poor: families, the elderly, single individuals, and childless couples. But I found the diversity of these groups was too much to cover in one book. So the focus is on families with children—the group that seems to raise the greatest passions and concerns.

2

Values and the Helping Conundrums

Those who want more money spent on the poor often argue that it is in the public's self-interest to help. It is easy to do calculations that suggest that the ultimate cost to taxpayers of each teenage mother who is on welfare may exceed $100,000 over her lifetime. Others note that criminal and other antisocial activities often spring from poverty. Politicians argue that when able-bodied people fail to work, the waste of resources can be enormous.

These are powerful arguments, but they are not necessarily convincing. We could save most of the money spent on dependent mothers simply by refusing to provide benefits. Although crime has been linked to poverty, is it so clear that we ought to spend money on all the poor (most of whom certainly are not criminals), rather than on strengthened law enforcement and expanded prisons?

I think America's support for the poor comes not from our most selfish instincts or greatest fears, but from our highest virtues. Helping is motivated by a sense of compassion and a desire for fairness. People are troubled when they see or even think of hungry or homeless people. They find it difficult to reconcile ill-fed, ill-clothed, and ill-housed Americans with the image of America as the land of plenty. They sense that our economy does not always provide for everyone who is willing to participate and that accidents of birth and nature leave some people in a weak position to compete. They fear that the poor do not succeed partly because they have not been given the same opportunities as have other Americans.

The National Conference of Catholic Bishops expressed this idea well when they claimed that our willingness to aid others ought to flow directly from our common sense of community and dignity.[1] We help because we feel empathy for our fellow citizens, recognize that the troubles of one could have befallen another, and believe that poverty is not necessarily a reflection of bad character.

But our sense of community and the resultant desire for fairness is but one of our closely held values. Other attitudes, such as a belief in the importance of work, family, or self-reliance also color our thinking, and they do not always lead so clearly to charitable feelings. If the desire to help comes from one of these closely held values, then we ought to be conscious of this and other values when we consider and evaluate programs designed to help the poor. Programs that tap into and reinforce common values are likely to enjoy the support of the poor and the nonpoor alike. In contrast, programs that bring closely held values into conflict are sure to be politically volatile and controversial.

Four Value Tenets

I have yet to find a definitive and convincing statement of our fundamental American values. The work of philosophers is often esoteric and the results of surveys are difficult to distill. Yet, I see recurring themes in public and academic discussion of what it is Americans believe. Four basic tenets seem to underlie much of the philosophical and political rhetoric about poverty.

- *Autonomy of the Individual.* Americans believe that they have a significant degree of control over their destinies and, at a minimum, that people can provide for themselves if they are willing to make the necessary sacrifices. The rags-to-riches American dream pervades our culture. Rugged individualists win respect even if their behavior borders on the eccentric or even the criminal.
- *Virtue of Work.* The work ethic is fundamental to our conceptions of ourselves and our expectations of others. People ought to work hard not only to provide for their families, but because laziness and idleness are seen as indications of weak moral character. The idle rich command as much disdain as jealousy; the idle poor are scorned.
- *Primacy of the Family.* The nuclear family is still the primary social and economic unit, and, certainly, its foremost responsibility is to raise children. Families are expected to socialize children, to guard their safety, to provide for their education, to impose discipline and direction, and to ensure their material well-being while they are young. The husband and wife are also expected to support each other.
- *Desire for and Sense of Community.* The autonomy of the individual and primacy of the family tend to push people in individualistic and often isolating directions. But the desire for community remains strong in everything from religion to neighborhood. Compassion and sympathy for others can be seen as flowing from a sense of connection with and empathy for others.

Many of the basic maxims that reflect the popular notions about our values follow quite directly from these tenets. The idea that people ought to be held responsible for their actions follows directly from the tenet that people have individual control over their lives. The universal standard that a family should provide for itself is a reflection of the sense that people have considerable control over their financial destiny combined with a view that families bear the primary responsibility for support. Society's apparent preference for two-parent families probably stems, in part, from a belief that two parents can do a better job of providing financial security for and of carrying out the critical task of socializing and nurturing children. The view that people ought to be treated with compassion, dignity, and fairness arises from our common connection to others.

If our compassion comes largely from a sense of community, the preference for programs that integrate, rather than isolate, the needy is natural. So is the tendency for people to be more understanding of others who are like them. Yet the compassion is tempered by the tenets of autonomy and family, so that people whose current difficulty is obviously outside their immediate control are considered more worthy of help than are those who are seen as being responsible for their plight or at least in a position to improve it through individual or family actions.

These precepts also translate easily into goals for public policy. The ideal social policy system would encourage self-support and independence through work, make people responsible for their actions, strengthen families, and integrate the poor, while providing dignity and security. There is nothing novel or even controversial about these goals or the values behind them. If one looks at the goals espoused by those who would reform poverty policy, one often finds terms like *family stability incentives, work incentives,* and *independence.* [2]

It is not a coincidence, therefore, that recent works on poverty have emphasized these tenets. Indeed, four of the most visible recent works might be characterized as focusing primarily on a different one of these tenets even though they touched on the others. Charles Murray wrote about autonomy, motivation, and personal responsibility and the ways in which the social welfare system undermines it.[3] Lawrence M. Mead emphasized the importance of work and the legitimacy of imposing work obligations.[4] Daniel Patrick Moynihan's *Family and Nation* called for more explicit family policies.[5] And, as was noted, the Catholic bishops urged America to help the poor out of a sense of community.

In emphasizing one value over the others, the authors found it possible to prescribe coherent and plausible changes in policy. It certainly is true that if one selects just one or two of these values for emphasis, one's choices about policy are easier. If autonomy is key, then any policy of assistance seems dangerous because it will certainly reduce the responsibility of individuals. If work is essential, then individual obligations make sense. If the family is paramount, we need family policies. If community is primary, then the society is obliged to ensure the economic security and dignity of its citizens.

The nub of the issue, though, is that Americans would like to avoid compromising on any of these dimensions. After all, people who work to support themselves and their families can believe that their actions reflect all these values. Yet, a poverty policy seems to bring these tenets into conflict. The essential question is this, Can we design social policies that are consistent with all these values or that at least minimize the conflicts between them? The usual answer is that conflict is inevitable. It is inevitable because of the helping conundrums.

Three Helping Conundrums

The *American Heritage Dictionary* defines a conundrum as "a problem admitting to no satisfactory solution."[6] A conundrum is a damned-if-you-do and damned-if-you-don't situation. Both liberal and conservative academics agree that any poverty policy inevitably poses some difficult conundrums, largely because one is tempted to help those who could conceivably help themselves. These conundrums seem to suggest that poverty policy must always be an awkward compromise among competing values and perspectives. Let me pose and discuss three helping conundrums: the security-work conundrum, the assistance-family structure conundrum, and the targeting-isolation conundrum.

The Security-Work Conundrum

This conundrum reflects the oldest of the struggles over aid to the poor. When you give people money, food, or housing, you reduce the pressure on them to work and care for themselves. No one seriously disputes this proposition. Indeed, a very large part of the social science research on poverty in the past twenty years has been designed to answer the question of how much less people will work if they are given income support.

The conundrum is posed most starkly in a true welfare system—one that gives money to the poor solely on the basis of their income (the poorer you are, the more money you get). Welfare could discourage work for two conceptually different reasons: it reduces the pressure to work and it reduces the rewards of working.

Many liberals have argued that welfare can free people from exploitation and that this freedom is desirable. Others point out that welfare gives mothers the opportunity to stay home and raise their children rather than be forced to work to keep their family at a subsistence level. Nevertheless, when unemployed people get support, they clearly have less of a need to work. They find it is less urgent to take any job, regardless of how unpleasant or low paying it may be, or to have all able-bodied members of the household work. As a result, people are not as likely to work.

Moreover, if a poor person goes to work and increases his or her earnings, welfare benefits will be reduced, since he or she will be less poor and will qualify for less assistance. The rewards of working will be diminished because the increased earnings will be at least partially offset by the reduced welfare benefits.

Indeed, most welfare systems reduce welfare benefits at least fifty cents for each one dollar increase in earnings. The current system of Aid to Families with Dependent Children (AFDC) takes away nearly a dollar for each dollar increase in earnings. Thus, the poor who are on welfare face a tax on their earnings that often exceeds 50 percent and may even exceed 100 percent.

Whether the actual effects of welfare policies on labor supply are large or small is something of a matter of interpretation. Robert Moffitt's review of the literature suggests that single mothers on welfare would increase their current average hours of work from nine hours per week to perhaps fourteen hours if the major welfare program was abolished, implying that the program reduces work by 30 percent.[7] The 30 percent reduction in work looks big, though an absolute change of five hours per week seems less extreme. Similarly, Gary Burtless estimates that in the so-called negative income tax experiment (which will be discussed below), two-parent families reduced their earnings by $1,800 or 12 percent. But these families only received an average of $2,700 in government benefits during the experiment. Thus for every three dollars given in benefits, average earnings were reduced by two dollars.[8]

The exact numbers are not the issue. Whenever some security is provided, particularly cash security, the recipients feel less pressure to work. If that security is in the form of welfare and benefits are reduced as earnings increase, then the gain from working is reduced. Thus, the evidence shows that a pure welfare system has significant effects on work. The security-work conundrum, therefore, suggests a direct conflict between our desire to help those in need and our desire to encourage work and self-support.

The Assistance-Family Structure Conundrum

No issue in poverty policy engenders more controversy than does the charge that the welfare system may be inducing changes in the family. The recent changes in the American family have been dramatic. In 1960, one child in ten lived in a female-headed household. By 1985 the figure was roughly one child in four. The economic consequences for children can be severe, since the poverty rate for children in female-headed families was 54 percent in 1985, while the rate for those in all other families was 12 percent.[9] Conservatives charge that the social welfare system may have played a crucial role in weakening the family. Liberals claim that welfare was one of the few forces that protected children during this period of change. The conundrum is transparent: the economic insecurity of single-parent families leads to a natural desire to provide some level of support through welfare, yet such aid creates a potential incentive for the formation and perpetuation of single-parent families.

Our current welfare system gives virtually nothing to poor single individuals and childless couples. It provides only slightly more to poor two-parent families. It offers much more (though still far less than enough to avoid poverty) to single-parent families. Hence, it offers a greater subsidy to single-parent families than to any other healthy and nonelderly group.

There is logic in such a system. Single individuals and childless couples have fewer responsibilities and fewer constraints on working. Two parents in a family can share the responsibilities for childrearing and economic support. Single parents are in a much more difficult position. There is only one parent to perform both the nurturing and provider roles. The wages and earnings of women are usually considerably lower than those of men, so the potential earnings in households with no man are reduced. It really is no surprise that so many single-parent families are poor. It is also no surprise that the desire to help that group would be most strong.

But, of course, the problem with this logic is that it ignores the possibility that the higher benefits to single parents may encourage families to split up and young, unmarried women to have babies. The solution that is sometimes proposed is to establish a more uniform system that protects poor people, regardless of their family status.

Clearly, such a system could reduce somewhat the incentives to form single-parent families over the present system. But extending welfare to two-parent families would not resolve this conundrum. The mere existence of income supports for the poor—even income supports available to both two-parent and single-parent families—will inevitably increase the incentives to form single-parent families because it will reduce the costs of being in such families. Precisely because single-parent families are more insecure than are two-parent families, a welfare system will provide more help to single-parent families than two-parent ones. Welfare reduces the income differential between two-parent homes (which are not usually poor and therefore usually do not need welfare) and single-parent homes (which are usually poor and are likely to need welfare). Or, in the language of conservatives like George Gilder, welfare reduces the need to rely on a man for support.[10]

There are good reasons to wonder if such a situation is entirely bad. Surely a system that allows children and their mothers to escape an unhappy, destructive, or even dangerous family environment can be beneficial to the individuals and to society. And many feminist and liberal thinkers argue that it is precisely the reliance of women on men that has forced women into subservient and inferior roles. Yet few would be sanguine about a system that encourages unmarried women to have children and then become dependent on welfare for a long time.

Perhaps it is surprising, then, that virtually every careful social science study that has investigated this issue has found that the welfare system has had little effect on the structure of families. This issue will be discussed in the next chapter, so I will not explore the empirical findings here. It is enough to say here that most people simply do not believe these studies. Roughly half of all Americans say they believe poor women often have babies so they can collect welfare, and an even larger fraction of *poor* Americans say they believe it to be true.[11] Moreover, there is no question about the direction of the economic incentives. Single-parent families tend to be poor; welfare diminishes their poverty and thus reduces the cost of being in such a family.

The acknowledgment that welfare could increase the number of single-parent families certainly does not imply that such assistance should not be given. The poverty of such families is extreme and the options that are available to them are often limited. And certainly the wealth of statistical evidence indicating that the receipt of welfare does not have much of an impact on the structure of families is reassuring. But both the need for aid and the negative incentives of providing it are clear. That is why it can be such a vexing conundrum.

The Targeting-Isolation Conundrum

Although the other two conundrums get all the attention, this one may be the most important of all. A natural goal of policy is to target services to those who are most in need, but the more effectively you target, the more you tend to isolate the people who receive the services from the economic and political mainstream.

Because social policy costs money, there is a desire to focus that money on the "truly needy." In welfare policy, that means focusing resources on those who are the poorest. In employment and training policy, it often means spending the most on those who have the most serious deficiencies, even if it means turning others away. In education, it means providing special services for the educationally or physically impaired. The logic behind such targeting is obvious: put the dollars where they are needed most.

Yet targeting carries other costs that do not show up on the bottom line of the budget. Any time people receive special treatment, a clear signal is being sent that those people are somehow different. In the case of welfare, the message seems to be that people on welfare are deficient in some way. That signal, which is often received by both the recipients and the society at large, can have a host of unintended consequences. Targeting can label and stigmatize people. It tends to alter society's rules and rewards for those in need. And it heightens the differences between those who are in need and the rest of society, making for a weak political base of support.

People who are labeled "truly needy" can easily be viewed as "truly failing"—failing in their responsibilities to provide for themselves. Those who are told they are failures sometimes start to believe it. Even though the aid may be designed to improve their chances in life and to open up options, a carefully targeted program may worsen their self-image and self-esteem.

Moreover, others in society may interpret the aid to mean that people who receive it have little ability or motivation. One experimental program provided a group of disadvantaged persons with special vouchers which guaranteed that the government would pay a portion of wages paid by employers who hired them. Those in the program had *lower* levels of employment than did those in a randomly matched control group who had no vouchers. The apparent conclusion was that employers took the vouchers as a sign that the holders would be bad workers and so they were less inclined to hire them even though the cost of these workers to the employers would be less.[12]

Targeting can change the apparent rules and incentives for those who are in need. Normally, those who work the hardest and learn the most, get the greatest rewards. When money or services are targeted to those who are most in need, the rules seem to be reversed, and the basic incentives are inevitably dampened. To some degree, I am only restating the basis of the two previous conundrums: security may erode personal responsibility. But there is a more subtle point. The more attention paid to those who fail, the less seems to be the reward to those who succeed. The danger is that traditional routes to success lose both their status and their appeal.

When people see the most support and services going to those who are doing worst, it appears to the nonpoor and possibly to the poor that the needy live by different rules than does everyone else. Middle-class Americans who do not work face severe economic consequences. If there is a liberal system of support, the consequences will appear relatively less severe for those who are the poorest. And so the rewards for initiative and hard work will be smaller.

Targeting tends to isolate politically the "truly needy" from the rest of society. If our generosity and compassion come from our sense of community, a program that creates an us-versus-them mentality tends to break down the natural connections and empathy among people. The less the public perceives that "there but for the grace of God go I," the more the public will see the needy as a different class of people with different values and attitudes from the rest of society. The erosion of empathy by targeting often shows up in diminished political support as well as less sensitivity and understanding.

People who are not succeeding need help. Many have suffered enormous deprivation and hardship. Many long for a chance to succeed. Those who are doing better do not need the help nearly as badly as those who are not. So we tend to target. Yet when we target people, we often label them, change the rules, lower their incentives, and break down the political links that help maintain public support for aid. That is the conundrum.

Nowhere to Hide, Nowhere to Turn

The essence of the recent conservative critique of the welfare state is that these conundrums have overwhelmed us. Our attempts to help have generated such adverse effects on the work habits and family structure of the poor and have so isolated them that the government's policies have actually made things worse. The critics point to a dramatic decrease in poverty until the late 1960s, when the War on Poverty was mounted, followed by no real improvements in the lot of the poor (except for the elderly) since then. Our policies ended up being so perverse, they argue, that the War on Poverty itself was the worst enemy.

The liberals have not denied the conundrums, for their existence is readily accepted by most academics. Rather, they have asserted that the damage has been small in relation to the good that has been done. Liberals argue that the most important influence on the poor is economic conditions. Average wage rates are lower now than they were in 1973 (adjusting for inflation), and unemployment has risen. Therefore, it is not surprising that poverty has increased, and, in the absence of these programs, it surely would have been higher. The response, then, is essentially that the damage done has been modest and that the good has been significant. And some are bold enough to call for considerable expansion of the social welfare system to help those many needy people who are still so poorly protected.

For many observers, I suspect, the response that our social welfare system does more good than harm is both unappealing and unconvincing. Calling welfare a reasonable compromise in the face of frustrating conundrums does little to inspire or reassure. It seems as if we can neither abandon the poor nor avoid the quandaries. We can put a man on the moon, but we cannot solve the problem of poverty. It appears that social policy is inevitably doomed to swings and cycles and marginal reform as dissatisfaction with one aspect of the welfare system is replaced by another.

Is such conflict inevitable? Is there no way to sidestep the conundrums, to minimize their influence, or even to find social policies that reinforce all our values, rather than create tensions between them?

These conundrums are not new. Social policy has had to wrestle with them from the beginning. Yet only recently have they seemed so dangerous and so insurmountable. It seems natural to ask how we avoided them in the past and how we might overcome them in the future.

The History of Social Policy and the Conundrums

The history of social policy can be seen as a series of attempts to help people without interfering too seriously with the basic values of autonomy, work, family, and community. Until recently, social policy succeeded in avoiding the dilemmas to a remarkable degree. But it did so by eschewing pure welfare forms that would offer generous benefits to all needy applicants, choosing instead to rely chiefly on nonwelfare forms of support linked to specific problems. If we are to avoid the conundrums in the future, we must look more to other nonwelfare supports that reflect the diverse causes and effects of poverty.

I will briefly review how we have wrestled with the conundrums in the past by looking at three different periods: the foundation, the takeoff, and the retrenchment.

The Foundation: 1930–60

At the risk of oversimplification, I shall lump together the diverse period between the 1930s and 1960 and label it the "foundation" era.[13] During that time, the basic structure of our social welfare system was formed, and, by 1960, a clear and defensible system had developed. The conundrums had largely been avoided by helping essentially only those who clearly could not be expected to work and by relying heavily on universal "social insurance" benefits. The mission was clear: help only those who cannot work through no fault of their own. Protection was offered at three levels: Social Security, employment-related benefits, and means-tested benefits.

Social Security. Social Security was brilliant in its conception, for it managed to reinforce the values of autonomy, work, family, and community. By 1960, Social Security provided benefits to three principal groups: the elderly, the totally disabled, and families with children of deceased workers. Thus, benefits were generally limited to people who (1) had some problem or condition that was beyond their control and (2) were not expected to work. (One could argue that by 1960 widows could have been expected to work, but originally there was no such expectation. And few would suggest that they were worthy of no benefits.)

Social Security was designed as a universal system to cover

all working Americans and it remains in place today. No groups are targeted, so none is isolated. In Social Security, benefits are linked directly to past earnings: the more one earned in the past, the higher the benefits in the event of retirement, disability, or death. (The decision to avoid targeting and to tie the program to work had been a conscious one. In response to pressures to focus benefits on the poor President Franklin D. Roosevelt replied: "We put those payroll contributions there so as to give the contributors a legal, moral, and political right to collect their pensions.")[14]

And the system respects and reinforces the traditional conceptions of the family. A couple gets more in Social Security benefits than does an individual, even if their contributions were the same. Families of deceased workers receive help because they usually have lost their primary earner.

By being universal, by linking benefits to past work, by giving support only to those who demonstrably have work-inhibiting conditions, by being explicitly supportive of families, the Social Security system has seemed to avoid the conundrums. There are complaints that the elderly work less because of their benefits and that some people who could do some work get into the disability program. And the system probably has diminished the responsibility of extended families to care for each other and the need for workers to save for their retirement. But such complaints have never generated any real enthusiasm.

Few minded if the old wanted to retire. Indeed, such behavior was welcomed in the depression of the 1930s. Then, as now, workers did not object to contributing to a fund that they thought of as offering insurance and pension benefits. People believed they were getting back only what they had put in.

In fact, Social Security is much more than a pension-insurance plan, and contributions are not actually saved. Current workers pay for current retirees. When the system started up, retirees who contributed little got back a great deal. Even today, retirees receive far more in benefits than they ever contributed. And the system has a strong redistributive element;

the structure of the benefit formula actually means that low-income workers get considerably higher benefits per dollar contributed than do high-income workers. But the program has always been considered to be for middle Americans, and the overwhelming majority of resources have gone to the nonpoor.

Employment-related Benefits. The second tier of protection established during the foundation period was employment-related benefits. These benefits included unemployment insurance and workers' compensation, as well as some veterans' benefits. These also remain largely intact today. Workers' compensation provides medical and cash benefits to those who are injured on the job. It is somewhat like Social Security disability protection, except it is limited to job injuries and provides aid to those who are less-than-permanently disabled.

Unemployment insurance is different. Some people clearly lose their jobs through no fault of their own and they often have troubles finding new ones. The problem is that it is hard to determine whether unemployment is voluntary. Any system that gives benefits to the unemployed may discourage them from working, may isolate them, and may cause them to become dependent. Unemployment insurance is a clever way to provide help while avoiding the most serious worries. Benefits are given only to those who have had work experience and whose former employers certify that they neither quit nor were fired for misbehavior. Like Social Security, benefits are available to workers at all levels, and benefits are higher for upper-income workers. To ensure that the unemployed do not become dependent, unemployment insurance is limited in duration usually to twenty-six weeks or less. Additional benefits cannot be collected until the person has accumulated enough work experience to be eligible again.

The program covers workers at all income levels, so targeting is not an issue. There is a clear link to past work; because benefits are limited in duration and are offered mostly to those who have been laid off, the work-security conundrum has been largely avoided. Initially, there was some worry that people would not search for jobs while they were receiving benefits and that seasonal workers could abuse the system. The system tried to solve these problems by having job-search requirements and by charging seasonal employers more for the coverage of their workers. These concerns remain real even today, but they are modest in comparison to those inherent in a true welfare system. For the most part, unemployment insurance was, then as now, a short-term insurance system for those who lose their jobs.

The combination of Social Security and employment-related benefits would seem to cover most families whose easily verifiable external problems prevent them from working. The disabled and old get Social Security, as do widows and their children. The unemployed get unemployment insurance. There was no attempt or desire to help the "working poor." In a system born of the depression, those who had jobs were the lucky ones.

Means-tested Benefits. During this period, a third tier of support—*means-tested benefits*—was available mainly to the aged, the disabled, and single-parent families (or two-parent families in which the fathers were disabled). These families were protected by federally sponsored but state-administered programs which were available only to people of limited means. Virtually no welfare money was available for healthy two-parent families, single individuals, childless couples, or working families. The single-parent, elderly, and disabled households who received benefits typically got little money and they were subject to severe restrictions on their assets, on the presence of an able-bodied man in the house, and so forth. Caseworkers had considerable discretion over these benefits. They were allowed to make unannounced searches and sometimes could cut off benefits if the family had so much as a telephone!

When these programs were first designed, they were seen as temporary or transitional programs that would end once Social Security was phased in and expanded. The elderly and disabled were expected to be covered by Social Security, not welfare.

AFDC was viewed as a program to protect families in which the father was dead, incapacitated, or, in rare instances, had abandoned them. The consequences of either the death or the incapacity of a breadwinner were to be eased by Social Security. Abandonment was a small problem. "Welfare" programs were thus for the small group who were not expected to work but who got so little protection from Social Security and employment-related benefits that they were still destitute.

Figure 2.1 shows where the money was being spent in 1960. (All dollar figures are in 1984 dollars.) The figure and table show that Social Security was the big program, costing $55 billion and consuming over half of the social welfare dollars. Employment-related benefits added another $24 billion, although they would have been higher if 1960 had been a weaker year economically. Means-tested benefits were just 16 percent of the total, or $16 billion.

Table 2.1 reveals in even more detail where the money was going. The vast majority of social welfare dollars (75 percent) went to the aged and disabled. Means-tested benefits for people who were neither aged nor disabled—"welfare"—were under $8 billion and amounted to just ½ of 1 percent of the total

Figure 2.1
Expenditures in Major Social Welfare Programs (All in 1984 Dollars)

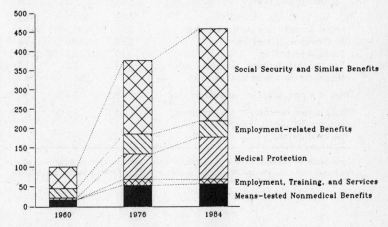

TABLE 2.1

Expenditures in Major Social Welfare Programs
Providing Direct Benefits
Detailed Breakdown
(Billions of 1984 Dollars)

	1960	1976	1984
BENEFITS FOR THE ELDERLY	54.7	199.9	284.2
Social Security and similar benefits	47.0	152.2	205.6
Employment-related benefits	—	—	—
Medical protection	0.7	38.7	68.0
Employment, training, and social services	0.0	2.6	2.0
Means-tested nonmedical benefits	7.0	6.4	8.6
BENEFITS FOR THE INJURED OR DISABLED	21.0	68.4	85.1
Social Security and similar benefits	4.2	24.5	26.1
Employment-related benefits	13.3	22.3	26.1
Medical protection	2.1	15.0	25.5
Employment, training, and social services	—	—	—
Means-tested nonmedical benefits	1.4	6.6	7.4
BENEFITS FOR ALL OTHERS	24.6	108.8	92.2
Social Security and similar benefits	3.9	13.5	11.1
Employment-related benefits	10.4	29.7	15.4
Medical protection	1.1	12.4	15.7
Employment, training, and social services	1.4	12.5	9.3
Means-tested nonmedical benefits	7.8	40.7	40.7
Public Assistance (primarily AFDC)	6.0	20.8	17.1
Food Assistance (Food Stamps/Child Nutrition)	1.4	14.4	16.2
Housing and Energy Assistance	0.4	5.5	7.4
TOTALS FOR ALL PERSONS	100.3	377.1	461.5
Social Security and similar benefits	55.1	190.3	242.8
Employment-related benefits	23.8	52.0	41.5
Medical protection	3.9	66.1	109.2
Employment, training, and social services	1.4	15.0	11.3
Means-tested nonmedical benefits	16.2	53.7	56.7
Total as a percentage of national income	6.9%	15.0%	15.2%
Means-tested benefits for the nonelderly and nondisabled as a percentage of national income	0.5%	1.6%	1.3%

NOTE: Since no breakdown was available for social services spending, 50 percent was attributed to the elderly and 50 percent was attributed to the nonelderly, nondisabled. SOURCES: See notes.[15]

national income in 1960. Just 3 percent of the American children were in families receiving AFDC. Welfare for families with healthy adults was a minor factor, indeed.

Thus, the policies of 1960 were generally compatible with the values of autonomy, work, family, and community. The vast majority of money was going to universal insurance-type programs. Welfare was only a tiny expenditure, and what little was spent went to single mothers, who still were not expected to work. The conundrums were hardly evident. They had been avoided by emphasizing universal programs that were targeted to specific and clearly recognizable impediments to work.

These policies had been controversial, to be sure. Many feared the intrusion of the government into the private and social realm. And even in 1960, there was talk that welfare mothers were abusing the system. Still the country seemed to be generally satisfied with its social policies. President John F. Kennedy was moved to proclaim in 1962 that "few nations do more than the United States to assist their least fortunate citizens."[16] As Peter Drucker proclaimed in 1960: "The Eisenhower Administration . . . leaves with the New Deal policies enshrined in comfortable respectability and anchored in the consensus of a broad moderate majority."[17]

Takeoff: 1960–76

The satisfaction would not last. America discovered its hungry. It discovered discrimination and prejudice. It fought an unpopular war that galvanized its young people. And it did all these things in one of the most remarkable periods of economic growth in the history of the United States. It was easy to see the poor as victims when they were so clearly hungry and when discrimination so blatantly held people back—especially at a time when the government was worrying about how it would spend all the surplus taxes that kept rolling in.

By the end of the 1960s, the debate about poverty had been dramatically transformed. A revolution in thinking had occurred—a revolution led by intellectuals. According to Lawrence Friedman, ". . . there was no 'demand' (in the interest group sense) for a war on poverty."[18] As Senator Daniel Patrick Moynihan noted, "it was from the first an affair of scholars and bureaucrats."[19] Potent and troubling books like Michael Harrington's *The Other America* and Kenneth Clark's *Dark Ghetto* stirred the hearts and minds of the increasingly professional policy analysts by describing the dehumanizing environment of the poor and the consequences of their isolation.[20] And the media began to portray images of hungry children living in shacks.

At first, most of the attention was focused on policies that sought to remove the barriers that prevented people from advancing. After its adoption in 1964, the Job Corps trained out-of-school youths by moving them to separate residential training centers. Head Start was adopted to help disadvantaged preschoolers in the same year. The Elementary and Secondary Education Act of 1965 provided money for the educationally disadvantaged who were already in school. Affirmative action and antidiscrimination efforts ballooned. Busing and the desegregation of housing were supposed to offer blacks a route out of their neighborhoods and give both races a chance to understand each other better. Urban development and community action organizations were designed to rebuild the cities.

Insurance and protection policies also expanded dramatically. Significant medical protection was added through Medicare for the elderly and through Medicaid for those who qualified for public assistance (impoverished aged and disabled persons and those in single-parent families). Social Security benefits were raised dramatically as the rapid growth in wages raised contributions far above the benefit payments. Unemployment insurance was extended to far more workers. Table 2.1 and figure 2.1 show that, by 1976, employment, training, and social services had grown by almost 1,000 percent, moving from $1.4 billion in 1960 to $15 billion in 1976. Medical protection, which had begun mostly in the late 1960s, was up to $66 billion by 1976.

Social Security benefit payments had more than tripled; employment-related benefits had almost doubled (although this increase was caused, in part, by the recession of 1975, which temporarily pushed up payments for unemployment insurance, rather than by a policy decision).

If the revolution had stopped there, the conundrums would have remained a minor concern. Training and education policies are "human investment" measures. Such policies are generally in keeping with mainstream attitudes, although, to be sure, affirmative action and integration are controversial. Helping people to help themselves has always been seen as reinforcing of autonomy, work, family, and community.

As I have already mentioned, the basic structure of Social Security and unemployment insurance is more reinforcing of values than destructive of them. Thus, the expansion of these programs caused little conflict. Medical protection would seem to fall in the same basic category as the other insurance programs. Medical protection that was focused on the poor had some potential for causing problems. Yet the logic of insuring people against medical catastrophe seems similar to the logic of protecting them against disability: the need for such insurance is created by events that are largely beyond the control of the individual. Investment and insurance sidestep the conundrums.

Unfortunately, it soon became clear that Social Security, employment-related benefits, medical protection, and human investment strategies would not be nearly enough to ensure the security of the employable and healthy poor. The early programs showed that these groups could not dramatically transform their lives with a modest bit of training or services. Academics and policy makers concluded that if the poor were really to be pushed out of poverty, cash transfers had to be expanded. According to Henry Aaron: "By making his objective 'total victory' while refusing to rely primarily on cash transfers, President Johnson made failure inevitable."[21]

During the takeoff period, welfare started to be viewed in a new light. Welfare rights advocates argued that the degrading and dehumanizing treatment of welfare recipients was part of the problem. Welfare robbed people of their self-esteem. It stigmatized and brutalized them. The distinctions in the welfare system between the "deserving poor" (who got public assistance) and the undeserving poor (who got nothing) seemed arbitrary, judgmental, and unfair. The "working poor" got little, while single parents were given benefits. Analysts and advocates pointed out that welfare need not be an alternative to work. It could be a supplement to earnings. If benefits were cut less than $1 for every $1 in earnings, those on welfare would have more incentive to work, since they could both work and be on welfare.

By the late 1960s, a new goal seemed to be emerging for social policy: the government should guarantee that everyone achieved a minimum standard of living. The goal translated into more than just investing in people and protecting them from old age or disability. It implied that government should also provide a guaranteed annual income. In policy circles, the guaranteed annual income was called the negative income tax, since policy makers hoped that it could be implemented through the tax system. The negative income tax seemed to be the logical extension of the view that the poor were victims of the social and economic system in which they lived. It represented a sort of noblesse oblige of the American government toward the poor.

This new policy goal was a radical departure from the previous goal of supporting those who could not work. Indeed, advocates of the negative income tax repeatedly emphasized that it was a way of supplementing the income of the working poor—a group who had, until then, been left out of the social welfare net. It got government off the backs of the people by removing all the stigmatizing rules; benefits were to be based solely on income. The negative income tax was considered to be pro-family, since two-parent families could now receive benefits. Soon it was endorsed by most social scientists, particularly economists, who were attracted to its simplicity and seeming equity. Two prominent supporters were Milton Friedman and James Tobin, eventual Nobel laureates who came from opposite ends of the political spectrum. An experiment was set up to test the idea in several cities. And, in late 1969, the Nixon administration proposed a highly modified version of it.

The public, however, was never much enamored with the idea of a guaranteed income. In 1969, the Gallup poll asked about the idea of guaranteeing every family of four an income of $3,200 per year (roughly the equivalent of $9,000 in 1984 dollars). Less than a third of the public supported the idea. President Richard M. Nixon tried to sell the plan as a way to get poor people to work (the plan had some modest work-registration requirements) and thereby garnered public support. But, according to Dennis Coyle and Aaron Wildavsky:

This was a somewhat misleading portrayal of the legislation actually submitted to Congress, which . . . would, in Moynihan's words, "place a floor under the income of every family. Whether the family is working or not. United or not. Deserving or not." Such a plan offended widely held public attitudes about who deserves what from government.[22]

The plan was never adopted. It was ultimately defeated by conservatives who wanted work to be a more central part of the aid and liberals who worried that the plan was still too punitive.

Thus, contrary to popular belief, the great social planners did not get the policy they really wanted for their War on Poverty. Those who believed that the government must be responsible for ensuring a modest standard of living had to settle for much less. In the end, modest reforms were enacted. Under the Supplemental Security Income (SSI) program, the federal government took over most of the administration and financing of welfare benefits for the aged and disabled starting in 1974. SSI raised benefits for many poor aged and disabled persons but did not extend eligibility to people outside of these categories.

AFDC was expanded, both by court cases and by social planners. Courts essentially forced many states to raise their benefits and eliminate the man-in-the-house rule. Legislation introduced "work incentives" so that single mothers who worked would not lose $1 in benefits for every $1 they earned. These new work incentives also made single-parent families who were somewhat less poor newly eligible for benefits.* And there was a changed attitude about welfare. Welfare now was seen as more of a right than an embarrassment. In some cases, a two-parent family with an unemployed adult could qualify for assistance, although the restrictions were tight. These changes led to a considerable expansion of AFDC.

Yet the basic premise and structure of AFDC remained intact. It was a program for single mothers, a group who were not expected to work. States were given complete discretion over benefit levels. Some states paid moderate benefits, while others were incredibly stingy. (In 1975, Michigan paid the 1986 equivalent of over $800 per month for a family of four, but Mississippi paid $120. The average state paid around $520.)[23] Recipients still faced a mountain of red tape, invasive questions, and considerable stigma.

The only really major change in the structure of assistance came in the form of the Food Stamp program, which became a kind of mini negative income tax. Any poor person could get at least some food stamps. But the benefits started low and were cut as income rose. To a family with no other income, they offered the 1986 equivalent of seventy-five cents per person per meal. For a family whose income was half the poverty line, benefits were about thirty-eight cents. Thus, there was a guaranteed income, but it was in the form of food stamps that were worth at most $3,300 per year (in 1986 dollars). To get any kind of serious income support, families usually still had to be aged, disabled, or headed by a single parent.

As table 2.1 shows, these changes pushed up means-tested

---

*Strictly speaking the "$30 and ⅓" work incentive rules do not apply to applicants; they go into effect only after a person has first gotten onto welfare without them. But the income of single parents is so dynamic that people who would have been pushed off could now stay on.

benefits from $16 billion in 1960 to almost $54 billion in 1976. The level and ease of collecting benefits had been expanded for the groups who had been getting them earlier (the aged, the disabled, and single mothers). In many states, some two-parent families with an unemployed worker could collect AFDC. Medicaid protection had been added for these same groups. And every poor person was at least eligible for food stamps.

Yet, by many measures, the welfare budget for the non-elderly and nondisabled was still small even after this expansion. Nonmedical benefits for the healthy were $41 billion (see table 2.1) or just 11 percent of the social welfare expenditures and roughly 1.6 percent of total national income. On the whole, social policy still meant nonwelfare policy.

Retrenchment: 1976–87

In the eyes of many, even the expansion of welfare to 1.6 percent of national income seemed to go too far. Also, by the mid-seventies, the world had changed. The strongest ally of the War on Poverty was probably the booming economy. A growing economy typically generates higher wages, lower unemployment, and increased opportunities—all good friends of the poor and of programs that attempt to improve their economic condition. A growing economy also generates greater tax revenues and a more generous public. But in the early 1970s, wages stopped growing. Adjusted for inflation, even as late as 1986, the median wage of full-year full-time workers was still well below the peak it reached in 1973.

Families coped by sending more workers into the labor market and by doing with less. In this more austere environment, it seemed increasingly hard to justify expanded aid to the poor. The means-tested programs seemed to gall those Americans who were trying hard just to break even. Why should some people live off the government's largess while others were struggling to survive?

Two additional trends further undermined the legitimacy of the welfare system even in 1976. The number of single-parent families was skyrocketing. No one quite knew why, but the welfare system was suspect. And the participation of mothers in the labor force was rising sharply. Welfare mothers no longer were poor widows desperately trying to raise their families on a small income. Single parenthood looked more like a matter of choice. Work by mothers also seemed a matter of choice. Many Americans seemed to think that welfare recipients made the wrong choices on both counts.

And the results of the negative income tax experiments were coming in. They suggested that the conundrums really might be serious. Work efforts clearly declined among the experimental groups, though whether the declines were "large" or "small" was a matter of debate.[24] What was even worse, perhaps, the vastly expanded means-tested benefits of the negative income tax seemed to decrease, rather than increase, the stability of families, as its advocates had suggested. Families seemed to be splitting up more often in the experimental groups. (These latter results have since been sharply criticized as inaccurate or misleading.)[25]

Figure 2.1 and table 2.1 show that there was no increase in means-tested programs after 1976. Indeed, AFDC benefits were not even adjusted for inflation, so in the next decade in most states, their real value per family fell by 30–50 percent. Eligibility rules were retightened, and workfare became more acceptable. Advocates tried mostly to protect means-tested programs, not expand them.

The administration of President Jimmy Carter expanded training and other types of human investment programs. It also presented a welfare reform proposal. But the proposal was far from the pure guaranteed income of the previous era; work rules and jobs and categories were in abundance. The proposal was defeated, in large part because it meant spending more on the poor. When Ronald Reagan entered the White House, he had a clear agenda to cut such spending. As a result, even though a weakened economy and the changing family structure had pushed the number of poor Americans from 25 million in 1976 to almost 34 million in 1984, figure 2.1 shows the total spending on means-tested programs was only slightly higher than it had been in 1976 after adjusting for inflation. Welfare expenditures per poor person had fallen dramatically—almost 30 percent per poor person on average.

The public harbored deep-seated fears that social policies, particularly welfare, were counterproductive. In one survey, 59 percent of the public believed that welfare made "poor people dependent and encourage[d] them to stay poor." Only 19 percent thought it gave people a chance to "stand on their own two feet and get started again," and almost two thirds believed that welfare encouraged irresponsibility by fathers.[26] A large majority believed that welfare often encouraged divorce and illegitimacy. For the public, welfare policies seemed to have trapped the poor in a quagmire. The poor, they thought, were different from other Americans. Thus, when America's ghettos became front-page news again in the mid-eighties, as they had been in the mid-sixties, Americans seemed far less willing to blame the environment, discrimination, or the economy.

Even though the true dream of social reformers—the guaranteed annual income—had never been realized, all three conundrums (work-security, assistance-family structure, and targeting-isolation) had come home to roost. Much of the public seemed to believe Charles Murray, George Gilder, and others who argued that social policies were now a big part of the problem.

The liberals protested that the conservatives' claims that welfare had caused enormous damage were highly exaggerated. The lion's share of the money was going to Social Security, employment-related benefits, and medical protection (and the vast majority of the medical care dollars were being spent on the elderly and disabled as is shown in table 2.1). Moreover, these policies had made a big difference. For example, poverty among the aged fell from 35.2 percent in 1959 to 12.4 percent in 1984. By several measures, the health of the poor improved during the seventies. Social policy can rightly claim considerable credit for this success.

In addition, expenditures for means-tested nonmedical benefits for the healthy and nonelderly—remained small in 1984, totaling less than $41 billion. This amount represented less than 4 percent of the government's expenditures, and it was just 1.3 percent of national income—down from 1.6 percent in 1976.

The various studies referred to earlier suggested that the greatest fear, that welfare was causing single-parent families to be formed, was wildly exaggerated. The *typical* child born in the United States in 1986 would spend some time in a single-parent home. Was it really plausible that programs that rose from 0.5 percent of national income in 1960 to 1.3 percent in 1984 had caused the massive changes in American society that people feared? Furthermore, the timing was all wrong. The problems of the poor worsened the most and family structures changed the most when the means-tested programs were being cut back during the retrenchment period. If rising benefits made things worse, why did not falling benefits make them better?

Yet, in a real sense, these counterarguments seem hollow and pointless. Saying that our social policies did not do too much damage is small solace. Traditional welfare programs must inevitably face the conundrums. Society may not have been gorged on the horns of these dilemmas, but the conundrums seem to have thwarted serious changes in policy for almost a decade. Furthermore, the negative income tax experiments did show that the conundrums would be serious in a generous and comprehensive system such as that envisioned by proponents of a guaranteed annual income.

So helping the poor increasingly has come to look like a no-win proposition. At least until recently, there has been no clear vision. Society could not accept the old goal that only those who were unable to work should be helped. It could not even agree on who was unable to work (surely the aged and disabled should not work, but what about single mothers?). Nor could it accept the view that the government should guarantee security for all. So, for over a decade, social policies for the poor have languished, seemingly trapped between Scylla and Charybdis, wanting to help the poor but skeptical that the government would only encourage dependence and aid the irresponsible. Thus, we are left with a set of social policies for the poor that everyone hates.

Searching for a New Direction

Looking over the history of social policy, I am struck by the fact that the further we move toward a system that makes judgments about the causes of poverty, that tries to link benefits to work, and that avoids excessive targeting, the less bothersome the conundrums seem to be. Conversely, the closer we move to time-unlimited, cashlike, income-tested assistance—that is, the closer we move to pure welfare programs—the more difficult the value dilemmas become. By turning to welfare, we are actually turning away from our values and ignoring the causes of poverty. In giving welfare to the healthy, the government and citizens can avoid making judgments about the expectations that society may have of its citizens. They can also avoid deciding what opportunities society ought to guarantee its citizens. Instead, they are retreating to a "neutral" world of income guarantees.

Welfare would be the perfect policy if poverty was caused only by the lack of money. But poverty is never simply a matter of limited income. Poverty is the result of other problems. When people are poor because they are too sick to work, it is their disability that prevents them from working. When people work but are still poor, they are poor because their wages are too low. When the unemployed are poor, the problem is that they cannot find work they are willing to take. When single mothers are poor, they may be poor because they are trying to balance two responsibilities—that of nurturing their children and providing for them—without outside support. When people are poor in the ghetto, they may lack the education, the opportunity, or the vision to make it.

The most practical and politically viable policies of the past have always reflected society's expectations and sought to link benefits and treatments to the causes of deprivation. Social Security goes to the disabled, the widowed, and the old. Unemployment insurance goes to those who had been working, and it is limited in duration because society believes people ought eventually to find work for themselves.

Conversely, welfare programs like AFDC cannot decide what their goals should be. Should programs be generous in recognition of the dignity of the recipients and the problems they face or punitive to discourage dependence and encourage people to make it on their own? Should welfare mothers be required to "work off" their checks, or do such policies only serve to damage further the self-esteem of a group who already feels powerless and inadequate? Should welfare be a source of embarrassment or seen as a right? Welfare represents a failure, but no one is quite sure whose failure it is. Either the recipients failed to do enough for themselves or society failed to provide enough opportunities.

These issues cannot easily be resolved in a program that is designed only to provide income to those who lack it. The answers can be found only by looking deeper at the causes of poverty and the responsibilities of both the society and its citizens. If we look at the *why* rather than the *who* of poverty, we ought to be able to come far closer to the American ideal—not of a guaranteed income, but of a guarantee that people who strive and who meet reasonable social responsibilities will be able to achieve at least a modest level of dignity and security. Ideally, social policy would be used to further the American dreams of opportunity, prosperity, and independence, rather than to pick up the pieces when the dreams are shattered.

3

The Transformation of America's Families

It is by now a familiar refrain: children are being raised by one parent rather than two. And with these changes in the family has come increased poverty. Poor families and single-parent families are being used as synonyms in many popular discussions. The "feminization of poverty" commands considerable press. It is, we are often told, the big issue of poverty in the eighties and nineties. Thus, the first and most obvious question for understanding the causes and nature of family poverty is, Why is the structure of the family changing?

The figures are dramatic. In 1960, just 7 percent of the families with children were female headed.[1] By 1985, the figure was roughly 20 percent.[2] But these figures understate the magnitude of the change. We have reached the point at which the majority of children born in the United States today will spend some part of their childhood living in a single-parent home.

There is no doubt that these changes put children at a far greater economic risk. The figures presented in chapter 4 show that the vast majority of children who are raised entirely in a two-parent home will never be poor during childhood. By contrast, the vast majority of children who spend time in a single-parent home will experience poverty.

There is a danger, of course, that in worrying so much about single parents, we will ignore other poverty issues. Half the poor children in America are still in two-parent families. And the debate continues over how much the changing structure of the family actually contributed to poverty.[3] Still, there can be little doubt, according to popular perceptions and in fact, that one of the most important influences on the level and nature of poverty in families and of children is family structure. The assistance–family structure conundrum described in chapter 2 suggests that we need to think hard about the ways in which policy may influence the structure of the family.

In this chapter, I will explore the reasons for the changing family structure. I will reserve discussion of why single-parent families are so often poor once they are formed to a later chapter. My major conclusion here is that the changes in the structure of the family are probably the result of some sizable and largely unstoppable changes in social and economic patterns. Because family structures are influenced mainly by forces that are outside the control of the government, I am pessimistic that any practical governmental policies are likely to alter them much, especially in the short run. Thus, governmental solutions to the poverty of families and children will have to involve something more direct and immediate than trying to influence the type of families that are formed.

A Changed Economic and Demographic Landscape

In popular discussions and in a considerable amount of scholarly work, one hears the increase in single-parent families discussed as though it were a startling anomaly in an otherwise unchanging or consistent world. When hypotheses are offered, welfare seems to get most of the blame. The twin notions that family structures changed independently and that welfare was the primary culprit reflect a naivete that is dangerous because it can distort policies toward single parents.

In fact, the changes in the family came in the midst of at least four major social, economic, and cultural developments: the entry of more women into the labor market, the diminishing earnings of men, more liberal welfare benefits, and changing attitudes about sex, marriage, and the family. In some respects, welfare seems the least likely culprit. I will begin by briefly illustrating these four key trends. Then I will explore how they may have influenced families.

Increased Participation by Women in the Labor Force

It is now so common for women to work outside the home that it is easy to forget how much the labor market behavior of women has changed in a short time. Figure 3.1 shows the percentage of women aged 20–24 and 25–34 who were in the labor force from 1948 to 1983. The proportion of women of both age groups changed little between 1950 and roughly 1964; less than half the younger group and just over one-third of the older were in the labor force. Then these figures began to rise rapidly, so that by 1983, roughly 70 percent of each group was working or looking for work. The changes were most dramatic for women with children, particularly young children. Figure 3.2 shows that the proportion of mothers with children under age 6 who were in the labor force rose from less than 20 percent in 1960 to over 50 percent in 1983.

Figure 3.1

Percentage of Women Aged 20–24 and 25–34 in the Labor Force

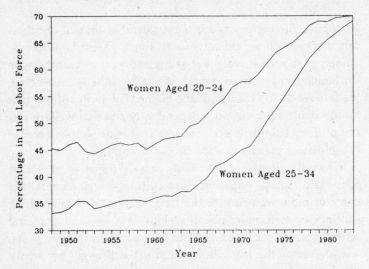

SOURCE: U.S. Department of Labor, *Handbook of Labor Statistics* (Washington, D.C.: U.S. Government Printing Office, 1985), table 5, p. 19.

The implications of this trend for families are profound. To begin with, the financial and social effects on two-parent families that remain intact may be significant. The entry of a mother into the labor force is likely to mean that the family has more income than it otherwise would have and more resources to draw on in times of crisis. It also means that the children will grow up seeing both parents working outside the home. The impact on a single-parent family may be a greater potential and expectation that the single mother will be able to support her family.

Just how well the children fare is still controversial. A family with more income and a mother who has a greater sense of independence and self-esteem may provide a far better environment for children to grow and learn. The children will have to be raised at least partly by others. Some argue that this

Figure 3.2

Percentage of Mothers in the Labor Force, by Age of Children

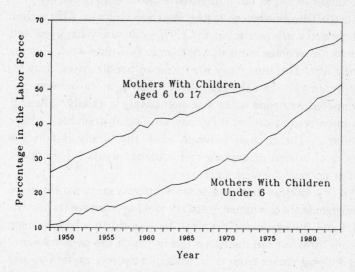

SOURCE: U.S. Department of Labor, *Handbook of Labor Statistics* (Washington, D.C.: U.S. Government Printing Office, 1985), table 54, p. 123.

outside exposure is beneficial, while others think that young children at least are best raised by their parents. The academic evidence to date shows relatively little difference in children who are raised in two-parent families in which the mother works and in which she does not.[4]

It is certainly plausible that increased participation of women in the labor force would have a significant influence on fertility, marriage, and divorce. Women who are interested in pursuing careers may have fewer children, have them later, or not have them at all. Victor Fuchs has forcefully argued that children often hamper women's careers.[5] He claimed that even after controlling for factors that ought to influence work performance, mothers have lower pay and their earnings rise more slowly than do those of nonmothers; the same is not true for fathers.

Fuchs's proposition has some critics, but it seems like simple common sense. In our still-sexist world, mothers usually bear most of the burden of caring for their children. Often they choose to work part time, and such work surely pays less and promotion comes more slowly than in full-time work. Even if they work full time, they need time to handle crises, doctors' appointments, and the like. Until recently, a "career woman" connoted someone who was not raising a family. Thus, if women want a career, they may not find it desirable to have children. The struggle between work and family is now the focus of dozens of popular and academic works.[6] There have been no easy answers so far.

It is also clear that outside work offers a greater measure of independence to women, possibly making marriage less essential and divorce more practical. In a world in which women work little outside the home and in which the preponderance of support comes from men, women must rely on fathers and husbands for economic support. Outside earnings can free women of this dependence.

The hypothesis that work outside the home offers greater opportunities for autonomy is shared by those on both ends of the political spectrum. To the religious fundamentalists, this development is a tragedy, for it weakens the traditional family. According to Rev. Jerry Falwell:

In a drastic departure from the home, more than half of the women in our country are currently employed. Our nation is in serious danger when motherhood is considered a task that is "unrewarding, unfulfilling, and boring."[7]

To many feminists and liberals, work offers the hope that women can gain a more equal status and greater self-esteem, as Betty Friedan noted:

American women's long movement for control and power, in and through the family, developed throughout the nineteenth century, then came into conflict with women's new needs—economic and psychological—to move and earn in man's world, in the twentieth century. The family, which in a certain sense was woman's power base . . . then became her Frankenstein monster.[8]

Virtually all those to the left of center argue that limited opportunities, a shortage of affordable day care, and low wages inhibit the earning power of women. The argument is that women need even greater opportunities for independence. Several studies, including the one by Sam Preston and Alan Richards, have suggested that when opportunities for women are greater, marriage rates are lower.[9]

Those on all sides seem to believe that work is linked to independence. It seems inevitable that it will have some influence on families. Women's dependence on men through marriage is diminished. And many hope that equal status for women will redefine familial roles and make for a stronger family unit. Still, careers other than child rearing open up. Marriage may be postponed or forsaken. The financial pressure to remain in an unhappy marriage is reduced.

As families adjust to the new roles of men and women, the employment of women outside the home may introduce a new source of stress. Several studies have suggested that husbands sometimes have lower self-esteem when their wives are working.[10] Catherine Ross, John Mirowsky, and John Huber reported that stress seems to be confined mostly to couples in which the woman is working for financial reasons and when the couples believe it would be better if the woman stayed home.[11] Heather Ross and Isabel Sawhill found that the odds of divorce rise as the earnings of the wife rise in relation to the man's.[12] Here, too, there is controversy, since the lack of money can also increase marital conflict. If a woman stays home and feels subservient or inadequate, tensions in the family may increase.

As of yet, there is no definitive evidence on the net effect of women's employment outside the home. But Eli Ginzberg, former head of the National Commission of Manpower Policy, once declared that effects of the changed work patterns of women are "bigger than the atomic bomb or nuclear power."[13]

Diminished Wages and Increased Unemployment of Men

During the first part of the period when women were entering the labor market in large numbers, the economy was strong and growing. But in 1973, there was the Arab oil embargo; partially for that reason and partially for others, the economy stalled, and it has never regained its momentum. Those who were working were facing the combination of a weak economy, a vast increase in the number of women and young people competing for jobs, increased foreign competition, and a changing mix of industries. As a result, since 1973, the median earnings of full-year full-time male or female workers (after adjusting for inflation) have not grown.

Figure 3.3 shows the astonishing pattern of men's income from 1955 to 1985 (expressed in 1985 dollars). Between 1955 and 1973, the median income of men grew steadily and substantially—from $17,000 in 1955, to over $19,700 in 1960, $22,500 in 1965, $25,400 in 1970, and to nearly $27,800 in 1973. Then suddenly, the growth stopped. Earnings, adjusted for inflation, started to fall. By 1980, earnings were down to $25,000, and they were still roughly $25,000 in 1985. Thus, in 1985 the income of the typical full-time male worker was below the level it had been in 1970.

Prior to 1973, a man and his family could count on a steady growth in wages as he moved up the job ladder and as the economy grew. They could count on their family's standard of living to rise even if the wife chose not to work. Suddenly, after 1973, there were no such guarantees. Even if a man had a full-time job, his wages often did not keep up with inflation. A man could no longer count on staying in the same place, much less advancing.

Figure 3.3
Median Income of Full-Year, Full-Time Male Workers (1985 Dollars)

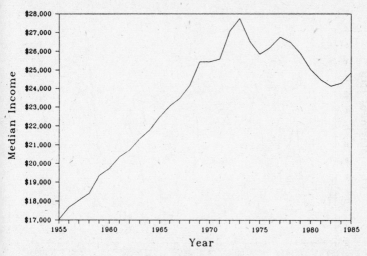

SOURCE: U.S. Bureau of the Census, *Money Income of Households, Families, and Persons in the United States: 1985, Current Population Reports,* Series P-60, No. 156 (Washington, D.C.: U.S. Government Printing Office, 1987), table 30, p. 101.

Effect on Young Men. Perhaps even worse was the fact that more and more young men were not working. Figure 3.4 shows the unemployment rate for young men aged 20–24. Unemployment rates fluctuate much more than do other indicators, but several patterns are apparent. The mid-1960s was a time of extraordinarily low unemployment. After hovering around 10 percent through much of the 1950s, the rate dipped to as low as 5 percent in the mid-1960s. Since then, though, there seems to have been a general trend toward higher unemployment, especially in the 1980s.

Few observers have realized the magnitude and potential significance of these changes. Frank Levy is an exception. In his book *Dollars and Dreams,* Levy presented figures to show just how dramatic the changes were. The earnings of the cohort of men aged 25–34 in 1949 grew an average of 57 percent in the next decade after adjusting for inflation. Similarly, the earnings of

53

Figure 3.4
Unemployment Rate for Men Aged 20–24

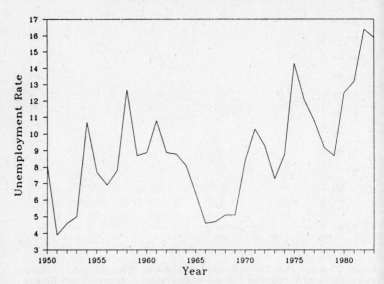

SOURCE: U.S. Department of Labor, *Handbook of Labor Statistics* (Washington, D.C.: U.S. Government Printing Office, 1985), table 27, p. 69.

men aged 25–34 in 1959 grew an average of 52 percent by 1969. By contrast, the earnings of men aged 25–34 in 1973 actually *fell* slightly over the next decade. Furthermore, at almost any time from the 1940s until 1973, men aged 35–44 could count on their real earnings to rise by roughly 30 percent over the next ten years of their lives. But the men who were aged 35–44 in 1973 saw their real earnings fall by 15 percent in the following ten years.

If men were expecting to follow in the footsteps of their fathers and older brothers, then they were expecting to earn much more than they actually were. As Levy noted, "A young man who left his parents' home in 1973 is now earning 25 percent less (rather than 15 percent more) than his father had earned in the early 1970s."[14] Therefore, after 1973, the typical family who wanted to increase its standard of living, as earlier families had done, needed more workers. Women filled that role. Whether impelled by financial considerations, pulled by the satisfaction and independence of working, or for other reasons, women, we have seen, went to work in increasing numbers. As a result, the family incomes of two-parent families did not suffer as much, on the average, as did the earnings of men. Even with the additional workers, however, there was little real growth in family income. For families with just one worker—single-parent families and those in which one parent stayed home with the children—the decade was much worse.

The poor were particularly hurt by these trends. In chapter 4, we shall see that families of the working poor are particularly sensitive to the condition of the economy. When wages rise and unemployment falls, such families are helped a great deal. Conversely, stagnant wages and increasing unemployment hurt them.

But the most serious effects of the economic slowdown may have been on the formation and stability of families. Men's earnings and employment were suffering. Although women's wages also were stagnant, the simultaneous enormous growth in the labor force participation of women led to increased earnings for women. So, precisely at the time when women began to achieve a measure of individual security and independence through outside work, men began falling behind all reasonable expectations.

It would seem inevitable that these simultaneous trends would weaken the economic incentives to form nuclear families. Dreams deferred must have been a new source of stress for the families that were formed. Unfortunately, no comprehensive studies have been conducted on how much these declining economic fortunes contributed to changing the marital, divorce, and women's work patterns for the country overall. Most of the research has looked only at the effect of unemployment on the structure of families, not at the impact of flat or falling wages or of unmet expectations.

Effect on Black and Other Minority Men. The economic problems of men have been particularly serious among minorities. The earnings of fully employed black and other minority men have followed much the same pattern as those of white men. But fewer and fewer minority men seem to be able to find work. Figure 3.5 shows that the unemployment rate for black and other minority men aged 20–24 rose steadily in the 1970s and 1980s, reaching almost 30 percent by 1983. Even these high rates understate the magnitude of the problem: people who have dropped out of the labor market—who are so discouraged that they stop looking for work—are not even counted as unemployed. In fact, in a typical month in 1983, only about half the civilian minority men aged 20–24 reported having any job at all!

In 1965, Daniel Patrick Moynihan was one of the first to suggest that the structure of families is likely to be closely

Figure 3.5
Unemployment Rates for Men Aged 20–24, by Race

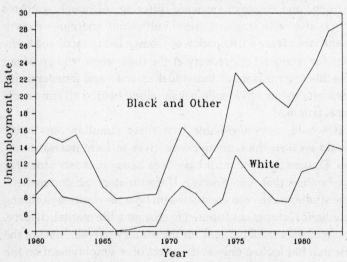

SOURCE: U.S. Department of Labor, *Handbook of Labor Statistics* (Washington, D.C.: U.S. Government Printing Office, 1985), table 4, p. 14, and table 26, p. 65.

related to the fortunes of men. His then maligned and now hailed "Moynihan Report" suggested that high unemployment among men leads to an increase in the number of female-headed families—especially in the black community.[15] Moynihan's thesis was dismissed as racist and sexist and received little attention until recently.

Now William Julius Wilson and Katherine M. Neckerman have suggested that the dramatic decrease in marriages among blacks can be directly traced to an equally dramatic fall in the number of "marriageable men"—that is, men who have jobs.[16] They note that along with the drop in employment, there has been a rise in mortality and in incarceration among black men, which has sharply diminished the number of men who look like reasonable marriage partners. Although this hypothesis requires further verification, Wilson and his colleagues have compiled an impressive array of evidence to support it.[17]

The question is not settled yet (and may never be). Nevertheless, it is obvious that flat or falling wage rates have to spell worse problems for families. Families seem likely to change when men are earning less than did their fathers, while women are earning more than did their mothers.

Increased Welfare Benefits

The most popular explanation for the change in the structure of families is that welfare caused the problems by giving benefits to single parents. A woman can now rely on the state rather than on a man. The hypothesis certainly seems to make sense. It is the essence of the assistance–family structure conundrum described in chapter 2. And it also has been the most carefully researched hypothesis. Therefore, it is ironic that no highly regarded study has indicated that welfare has played more than a minor role in the changing patterns of families overall.[18] Rather than getting bogged down in the technical and statistical issues, I will present a few simple facts that illustrate why it has been so hard to find much of a relationship between the changing family structure and welfare.

Welfare benefits expanded considerably during the period 1960 to 1973. Despite the wide variation in benefits from state to state, figure 3.6 shows that in 1960 a "typical" single-parent family of four with no income could get the 1984 equivalent of $6,700 in benefits for Aid to Families with Dependent Children (AFDC).[19] By 1972, AFDC plus food stamps (which did not exist in 1960) amounted to almost $9,000 (in 1984 dollars). Moreover, the eligibility requirements had been liberalized considerably, so that unannounced searches were a thing of the past and penalties were rarely imposed for having a man in the house. Medicaid also had been added. As a result, the caseload rose rapidly, much faster than the increase in single-parent families.

Charles Murray, among others, has used this period of growth to highlight the ways in which welfare may have influenced families.[20] By 1972, the combined benefits of AFDC and food stamps often paid as much as a full-time job at the minimum

Figure 3.6

State Average Combined Annual AFDC and Food Stamp Benefits for a Family of Four With No Income (1984 Dollars)

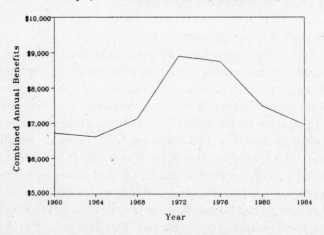

SOURCE: Committee on Ways and Means, U.S. House of Representatives, *Background Material and Data on Programs Under the Jurisdiction of the Committee on Ways and Means* (Washington, D.C.: U.S. Government Printing Office, 1987), table 28, pp. 660–662.

wage. And few minimum-wage jobs offer medical protection. It is easy to construct an argument that welfare looked much more attractive in 1972 than it did in 1960 and that people would be induced to split up or have a baby to collect it.

But the growth in benefits and the growth in recipients stopped in 1972. The retrenchment period set in; inflation rose while benefits were essentially frozen, eroding the real value of assistance. By 1984, a family of four could get an average of only $6,955 in AFDC plus food stamps—a decrease of over 20 percent since 1972, adjusting for inflation. Indeed, that total was just 3 percent higher than the benefits were in 1960! Along with the cuts in benefits were increasingly tight bureaucratic rules. Note that these changes were not primarily the result of Reagan administration policies. Most of the cuts were made before 1981.

Things were better than they had been in 1960, since all recipients got Medicaid and some had other forms of assistance. But there is no doubt that the disposable income available to welfare mothers fell considerably between 1972 and 1984.[21] As a result of these cutbacks, even though the number of children in female-headed families grew by 3 million between 1972 and 1984,[22] and even though the economy was much worse in 1984 (unemployment was higher and real wages were lower), the number of children on AFDC actually fell by over a half million during this period![23]

The temporal pattern can be clearly seen in figure 3.7, which shows the percentage of children in female-headed families and the percentage receiving AFDC. Between 1960 and 1972, the proportion of children on AFDC grew rapidly—more rapidly than that of children in female-headed families. But after that, the percentage of children on AFDC held constant or fell, even while the percentage of children in female-headed families continued to skyrocket.

Therein lies the problem with the welfare-as-villain argument. If increases in AFDC benefits caused the rise in single-parent families, why did the cuts not reverse the increase or at

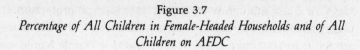

Figure 3.7
Percentage of All Children in Female-Headed Households and of All Children on AFDC

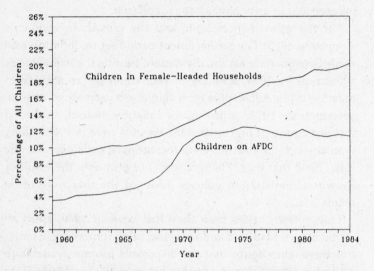

SOURCE: U.S. Bureau of the Census, *Characteristics of the Population Below the Poverty Level, 1984, Current Population Reports,* Series P-60 (Washington, D.C.: U.S. Government Printing Office, 1986), table 1, pp. 5, 6; *Social Security Bulletin, Annual Statistical Supplement,* 1986, table 204, p. 282.

least slow it? Thus, figure 3.7 is devastating for those who claim that AFDC played a large role in the increase of female-headed families. How on earth can AFDC be the cause of the growth in children in single-parent families when fewer and fewer children are getting benefits?

One cannot even claim that AFDC influenced behavior by offering support to those women who were becoming heads of families. If AFDC was allowing women to become single parents, the number of recipients would have grown along with the number of single parents. But the number did not increase; it fell. The pattern holds for black children as well as white children. The number of black children in female-headed families grew by over 25 percent between 1972 and 1984[24] while the number on AFDC fell by 15 percent.[25]

One could still contend that welfare played an important role before 1972 and that other forces were more important after 1972. Even then, it is startling to realize that when we brought benefits down almost to their 1960 level and when fewer and fewer children got on welfare, the structure of families continued to change. At least it is clear that sizable changes in welfare benefits have little obvious effect on trends in family structure.

One more bit of evidence is available. AFDC benefits vary widely across the nation. In 1980 the combined benefits for AFDC and food stamps ranged from $328 per month for a family of three in Mississippi to $637 in California. This variation created what social scientists call a natural experiment. If welfare was the cause of changes in the family structure, then there ought to be more single-parent families in the states where benefits were highest. But there were not. Figure 3.8 shows that the highest percentages of children living in female-headed families in 1980 are often in the states with the *lowest* benefits.

This pattern is partly a reflection of the demographic characteristics of different states. And some of it surely reflects variations in attitudes and expectations. Indeed, demographics and attitudes seem to have something to do with this pattern. But when the dust settles and researchers do everything they can to adjust for all these differences, they still find little relation between the level of benefits and the number of families headed by women.

When one thinks about the level of money involved, the welfare argument really does not make much sense. In chapter 3, we saw that all the means-tested programs for the nonelderly and nondisabled poor combined amounted to less than 1.5 percent of the gross national product (GNP) in 1984. If we look only at the cash and near-cash assistance that went to single-parent families, the figure is below 1 percent of the GNP. Is it really plausible that such expenditures have brought us to the point at which the typical child in America will spend some time in a single-parent home?

Figure 3.8

Percentage of All Children Not Living With Two Parents, by Benefit Levels for AFDC and Food Stamps, 1980

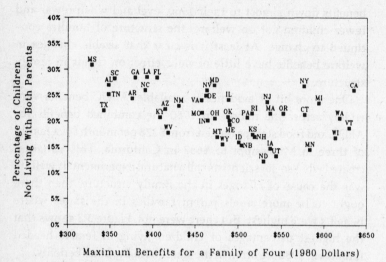

Maximum Benefits for a Family of Four (1980 Dollars)

SOURCE: U.S. Bureau of the Census, *General Social and Economic Characteristics,* individual state volumes (Washington, D.C.: U.S. Government Printing Office, 1984), table 100; Committee on Ways and Means, U.S. House of Representatives: *Background Material and Data on Programs within the Jurisdiction of the Committee on Ways and Means* (Washington, D.C.: U.S. Government Printing Office, 1987), table 28, pp. 660–662.

Changing Attitudes

The decade of the sixties was a watershed: a time of protest against the Vietnam War and for civil rights. It was the time of the sexual revolution and of the increased empowerment of women. There is considerable evidence that at least on a few critical issues, the cultural landscape underwent a massive upheaval in just a few years.

This period marked the beginning of the modern women's liberation movement. To hear the conservatives tell it, the movement reshaped the thinking of tens of millions of women, leaving them dissatisfied with themselves as housewives. Betty Friedan's *The Feminine Mystique* offered a clear and appealing message to women that their roles as housewives hurt both them and their husbands.[26] The liberation of women meant getting out of the house. There is considerable debate over just how deep or significant the early liberation and feminist movements were. However, there seems little doubt that the movement contributed to the view that women deserved better treatment and that better treatment meant getting outside the traditional family roles.

Changes in attitudes toward premarital sex were even more evident. Irwin Garfinkel and Sara McLanahan summarize some of the evidence on sexual mores:

Two surveys carried out by the National Opinion Research Center ... indicate that the proportion of adults who believed in total sexual abstinence before marriage dropped from 80% in 1963 to only 30% in 1975. The shift in attitudes was even greater among college students. The proportion of students who believed in total sexual abstinence for unmarried women dropped from 55% in 1967 to about 11% in the early 1970s.[27]

Sharp increases were reported in premarital sexual activity. Almost half (44 percent) of the first-time brides in the period 1960–64 claimed to be virgins, compared to only about one-quarter (26 percent) in 1970–74; now the figure appears to be below 20 percent.[28] (No figures are available for the percentage of male virgins.)

There are persistent claims in the press that attitudes toward giving birth to a child out of wedlock have softened over time. According to one survey in 1974, only 31 percent of the women who were questioned agreed with the statement, "There is no reason why single women shouldn't have children and raise them if they want to"; by 1985, 49 percent agreed.[29] Other surveys have shown less favorable reactions, but there is some evidence that attitudes toward single parenthood are more positive in ghetto areas.[30] And Americans clearly do not think that imposed marriage is the solution for a single woman who is about to have a baby. In 1985, only about 20 percent of Americans agreed that "a couple having a child out of wedlock should marry for the sake of the child even though they don't want to."[31]

Attitudes toward divorce have also changed. As Andrew Cherlin noted, surveys showed that in 1968, 60 percent of adults thought divorce should be made "more difficult to obtain"; but in 1978, even after the divorce laws had been liberalized considerably, only 42 percent thought divorce should be tougher.[32] By 1985, the large majority of Americans clearly viewed divorce as a legitimate option; in one survey, roughly 60 percent of adults said they favored divorce if "a marriage isn't working out" and another 20 percent said "it depends."[33]

In her provocative book, *The Hearts of Men,* Barbara Ehrenreich argued that another major change took place. She began her summary chapter as follows:

This book can be read as a story of mounting perfidity. We began in a moral climate that honored, in men, responsibility, self-discipline and a protective commitment to women and children. We moved, chapter by chapter, toward a moral climate that endorsed irresponsibility, self-indulgence, and an isolationist detachment from the claims of others.[34]

Ehrenreich claimed that a variety of events, from women's liberation to the narcissism of the 1970s and 1980s, left men with less interest in long-term commitments to women and children. The argument is controversial.[35] Still, it is significant, for it illustrates an increasing tendency of those on both the left and the right to point to the changing expectations and attitudes of men as well as women as an explanation of shifts in the structure of families.

It is always difficult to know if attitudes reflect cause or effect. Do American women work more because they no longer think work interferes with child rearing, or have they changed their attitudes because they work more? There is a perpetual and vociferous debate in the social psychological literature about whether attitudes mainly affect behavior, or vice versa. For our purposes, it probably is not important because behavior and attitudes were moving together. Sex outside marriage was more acceptable and more common, and marriage was less important.

What the Changes Have Wrought

Collectively, these trends imply insecurity for America's families. They spell economic insecurity because stagnant wages were only partially offset by the increase in the number of women who went to work. Single-earner families were particularly badly hurt. Welfare benefits rose for a period but have declined dramatically in recent years. Single-parent families and their children thus had to face both stagnant wages and falling welfare benefits. It should come as no surprise that poverty rates rose.

But what is even more important is that these forces all push toward altered family structures. The four changes pointed in the same direction. Each tended to increase the independence and economic position of women and decrease the economic status of men. They generally made marriage look less essential. A woman who has earnings from her own work (or access to welfare) has less need for a man's financial support. A man who earns less than his father did may not look or feel like a good provider; he may look less favorably on marriage and may be seen as a less desirable marital prospect. A married woman must enter the labor market if her family's consumption is to grow at the previously expected pace. Once she is in the labor market, both her attitudes and her husband's attitudes about their respective roles may start to change. Liberation may mean that women refuse to maintain their subservient roles. The sexual revolution means that "good" boys and girls do not have to marry to have sex. In such an environment, the obvious attractions of having children must be weighed against the impact of children on a woman's career, the fact that motherhood may pull one of the wage earners out of the labor market and cause a fall in the level of consumption, and the danger that the family will split up and the woman will be left to care for the children on her own.

I am not suggesting that the changes were undesirable, although the drop in the earnings and employment of men certainly was. Nor am I implying that women are even remotely close to economic parity with men. But women are closer; they have more independence, and the trade-offs involved in being married and having a family are greater than ever before for both men and women. Divorce seems less catastrophic for either party.

In light of these trends, it probably is not surprising that American society witnessed the most dramatic changes in family structure in its history. The marriage rate plummeted. Marriages per 1,000 single women aged 20–24 fell from 260 to only 100 between 1960 and 1983.[36] The birthrate fell just as sharply—from 260 births per 1,000 women aged 20–24 in 1960 to 110 in 1983.[37] Some of these figures reflect a postponement of marriage and childbearing, but even for older women, the marriage and birth rates fell. Divorce rates shot up as well, more than doubling from 1960 to 1980 before falling off slightly in the 1980s.[38]

What these changes meant for families is best understood by looking at three different groups: white families, nonwhite families, and teenage mothers. Teenage mothers are included in the first two groups, but they deserve extra attention. Roughly one-quarter of all single parents first became mothers as teenagers.

White Families

In white families, the increased divorce rate meant that more and more children were living with a divorced or separated parent. Meanwhile, younger women were not marrying as frequently and those who did marry had fewer children. Existing families were being split apart, and new ones were slow to form. As a result, the proportion of white children in female-headed families grew from 5 percent in 1960 to over 15 percent in 1984. However, at least 30 percent have lived in a single-parent family at some time, and several authors estimate that nearly half the children born today will do so in the future.[39]

It is impossible to know which of the factors just reviewed played the central role in this unfolding drama. It is obvious that no one factor can get all the credit or blame. The growth in single-parent families began in the 1960s, when attitudes, welfare, and women's behavior in the labor market were all changing. It continued into the 1970s, when the number of welfare recipients began to fall, changes in attitudes were slowing, men's earnings had stopped rising, and more and more women continued to enter the labor market.

Nonwhite Families

During the period when the proportion of white children in female-headed families rose from 5 percent to 15 percent, the proportion of nonwhite children in female-headed families also tripled. However, the rate started at 15 percent, so its tripling meant that nearly half the nonwhite children were living in a female-headed household. The vast majority of nonwhite children born today will spend some time in a single-parent home, and an important minority will never live in any other setting.[40]

The divorce rate shot up, the marriage rate plummeted, and the birthrate for married women dropped dramatically for minorities, just as it did for whites. Thus, nonwhite intact families (as well as white intact families) were coming apart more often and new ones were being formed less often than even before.

But the story for nonwhites was more complicated than was the story for whites. The rate of births to unmarried nonwhite women has always been higher than it has been for unmarried white women. In 1960, there were roughly 155 births per 1,000 nonwhite women aged 15–44; just under 35 of these births were to unmarried women and 120 were to married women. Between 1960 and 1985, the marriage rate dropped sharply, attitudes changed somewhat, sexual activity increased, and, for a period, welfare benefits rose. Under these circumstances, one would expect the number of out-of-wedlock births to nonwhite women to skyrocket. But it did not. It did not even reach 40 (per 1,000 nonwhite women of childbearing age) until the late 1970s, and it is only slightly higher today.[41]

The lack of growth in the out-of-wedlock births to nonwhite women is rather extraordinary, particularly in light of the fact that a much larger percentage of women were unmarried in the 1980s than in 1960. Hence, the many more unmarried nonwhite women were giving birth to only a few more babies. For that to happen, the birthrate *per unmarried nonwhite woman* had to drop considerably. And so it did: by more than 25 percent—in spite of welfare, attitudes, and increased sexual activity.[42]

Unfortunately, the story does not end there. With the marriage rate plummeting and the birthrate to married nonwhite women falling rapidly as well, the number of children born to married women declined very sharply. Where married nonwhite women had 120 births (per 1,000 women) in 1960, by the late 1970s there were only 45! Thus, even though the number of births to unmarried nonwhite women had hardly changed, births to married nonwhite women had collapsed. As a result, out-of-wedlock births as a percentage of all births to nonwhite women rose form 22 percent in 1960 to almost 50 percent in the 1980s.[43]

The trends can be seen easily in figure 3.9. (The same trends for whites are shown in figure 3.10.) The figure puts the changes in the structure of the nonwhite family in a whole new light. The reason for the changed proportion of nonwhite children born out of wedlock is not that more and more babies are being born to unmarried nonwhite women. The reason is that fewer and fewer babies are being born to married nonwhite women. Nonwhites are marrying much less often, and they are having fewer babies when they do. Thus, the *changes* in the family structure among nonwhites need not be seen as a reflection of

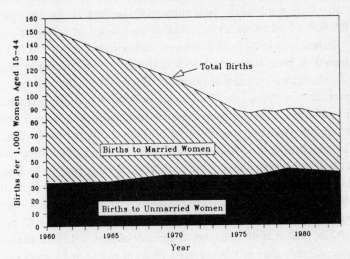

Figure 3.9
Births to Nonwhite Women (per 1,000 Women Aged 15–44)

Source: Inferred from U.S. Bureau of the Census, *Statistical Abstract of the United States, 1986* (Washington, D.C.: U.S. Government Printing Office, 1985), table 83, p. 57, and table 94, p. 62.

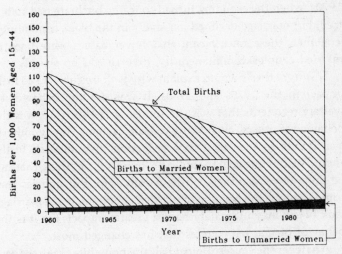

Figure 3.10
Births to White Women (per 1,000 Women Aged 15–44)

Source: Inferred from U.S. Bureau of the Census, *Statistical Abstract of the United States, 1986* (Washington, D.C.: U.S. Government Printing Office, 1985), table 83, p. 57, and table 94, p. 62.

"abandoned morality" or a turning to welfare. They are a reflection of marriage and childbirth postponed or foregone.

Foregone marriage and delayed and reduced childbirth happened in both the nonwhite and the white communities. But the changes were most dramatic for the former. Why? The most plausible story, at least for blacks, is Wilson and Neckerman's hypothesis. Whereas white men at least held their own in the stagnant period of the 1970s, black men did worse and worse. Those who worked full time kept pace with the white men, but fewer and fewer did so. The pattern of decline happened long before 1972, but it surely worsened then. According to Wilson and Neckerman, there were 70 employed civilian black men aged 20–24 for every 100 black women in 1960 but only 45 per 100 in 1980.[44] Both marriage and children look a lot less attractive when a man is not working or soon may not be working.

One might refine this hypothesis as follows: In the 1960s, when women's opportunities were improving and women were working more and more, the rate of marriage declined somewhat in the black community, and the birthrate fell a lot. In the 1970s, when the economy turned sour, the birthrate had stabilized, but marriage declined massively in the black community. Together, these rates meant that fewer babies were born to married couples. Simultaneously, divorce was up sharply.

This hypothesis would explain why welfare cuts had so little impact in the 1970s and 1980s. It was not the behavior of welfare recipients that was the source of the shifts. It was the behavior of others, outside the welfare system. The hypothesis also points to the fact that a reduction in unmarried births should be but one goal for policy. Obviously, anything that can be done to reduce these births would help. But policies that could improve the position of married couples or make marriage look better may ultimately have a greater impact. For it is the behavior of married couples that has changed most.

Whatever the causes, almost half the nonwhite children were living only with their mother in 1984. For slightly over half of these children, the mothers were divorced or separated and for 5 percent the mothers were widows. The remaining 43 percent were living with never-married mothers. Because of the dramatic declines in marriage and fertility among married women, the never-married proportion is growing fast. In contrast, for 79 percent of the white children living only with their mothers, the mothers were separated or divorced. For another 8 percent, the mothers were widows, and for the remaining 13 percent, the mothers were never married.[45]

Teenage Pregnancy

From the mass media, one might think that all single parents are teenage mothers. I estimate, however, that about one-quarter of all single parents in 1984 had their first child when they were teenagers.[46] And most of them were married at the time of the birth or got married shortly thereafter. Nonetheless, women who start as young mothers typically fare much worse in the labor market, stay on welfare longer, and may have more trouble in raising their children properly. Simple tabulations suggest that 40 percent of the welfare dollars go to women who were teenage mothers; others put the figure above 50 percent.[47] What is tragic is that teenage pregnancy seems both irrational and preventable.

There has been a substantial increase in sexual activity among teenagers. Just between 1971 and 1979, the proportion of girls aged 15–19 in metropolitan areas who said they had had intercourse jumped from 28 percent to 46 percent. By age 20, three-quarters of all girls and an even higher percentage of boys report that they have had sexual activity, and fewer than half these sexually active teenagers report using contraceptives all the time.[48]

Yet, amazingly, between 1960 and 1976, the birthrate of teenage women declined considerably and has been stable since then. Why? For one thing the use of contraceptives increased; from 1976 to 1982, the proportion of active teenagers who never used contraceptives fell from 36 percent to 15 percent (earlier figures are not readily available). Abortion probably played a crucial role as well. Pregnancies were actually higher in 1984 than they were in 1972, but abortions doubled and so the number of births diminished.

At the same time, however, women and men stopped feeling as compelled to get married when they expected a baby. Thus, even though there was a decrease in the overall teenage birthrate, there was actually an increase in the number of babies born out of wedlock. Whether the decline in marriage for this group is a good or bad thing is a matter of considerable debate. Remember that only 20 percent of Americans believe that a couple should get married for the sake of their unborn child if they do not want to.

Virtually all teenage mothers (80 percent) black or white, report that the pregnancy was not wanted. And the long-term costs to society and the mother can be extremely high. Teenage mothers are much more likely to become welfare recipients, less likely to finish high school, and less likely to marry than are other women. Their children will generally fare worse than other children. Unwanted and unnecessary births offend everyone. No one believes it is good for children to have children.

Can the Major Economic and Social Forces Be Altered?

To cope with poverty, we can move in several different directions. We can focus on specific problems of particular groups and individuals or we can try to change the larger economic and social environment. Policies on poverty have mainly emphasized help for individual families or occasionally communities. But if an important part of the well-being of families and children is the result of much larger forces, a natural place to begin our discussion on policy is the question of whether the government can or should change the broader trends in the economy and in the structure of families. Frankly I am not optimistic that anything the government might do, other than changing macro-economic policies, is likely to have much influence on these basic patterns.

It is hard to imagine how or why the trend in women's participation in the labor force would be reversed. And even if policies could be found that might reverse the trend, most Americans would probably not favor them. Attitudes toward work and family are changing rapidly. In the past ten years alone, the proportion of women who said they would prefer to have a job outside the home even if they were free to stay home has risen from 35 percent to over 50 percent; among women under age 30, the figure is 60 percent.[49] Even as late as 1977, over 60 percent of American women thought that a preschool child would probably suffer if his or her mother worked; today, less than half do.[50] Among working mothers of preschool children, 80 percent believe their children "are 'just as well off' as if the mother did not work."[51] There seems little that the government can or should do to slow this trend. Indeed, a large portion of the population favors increasing such supports as day care and paid leave to facilitate the work of parents. Women still face far more constraints on working and a lower return for their work then do men.

The government has more of an influence on the overall economy—on the rate of savings and economic growth and thus on wage rates and unemployment rates. Anything that restarts economic growth and gets real wages rising again will pay dividends on many different dimensions. I leave these broader concerns to others, but the importance of the performance of the macro-economy should not be minimized. Strong economic policy is good poverty policy. Indeed, as we shall see vividly in chapter 4, for a large segment of the poor, trickle-down really works.

Almost everyone is in favor of a strong and growing economy. The reasons for favoring economic expansion extend well beyond the condition of the poor. Generally, policies to improve the economy can be pursued simultaneously with policies to aid the poor more directly. Programs that are designed mainly to help the poor are likely to have only a modest impact on the overall health of the economy. After all, the welfarelike programs represent less than 2 percent of the GNP, and, in the view of most economists, their total effect is modest.[52]

However, it is clear that the government must improve the general economic position of some subgroups, notably black men. There is accumulating evidence that part of the problem for young black men has been both a lack of jobs and a lack of skills. The evidence also points strongly to the possibility that the structure of the black family is suffering because of the weak performance of young men in the labor market. The problems of black men are complex, and efforts to remediate them have had mixed results. But there are clear signs that a job shortage is a big part of the problem. The strong economy of Massachusetts is a case in point. In 1985, when the state's unemployment rate was 4 percent for whites, the rate was just 5 percent for blacks—far below the national average for whites.[53] (The special problems of the black ghetto community are covered in a later chapter.)

The government might try to change attitudes. There continues to be considerable debate over whether and how the government can influence the thinking of its citizens. Overall attitudes are probably influenced more by social forces and the mass media than by the government. One of the few factors that could have a profound impact on attitudes and behavior is the AIDS epidemic. With such a severe penalty possible for those who engage in extramarital sex, behavior could change rapidly. In some arenas, notably education, the government has some potential to help shape attitudes. Still, the total impact of government seems likely to be small.

In essence, then, governmental policies are not likely to have a significant enough effect on most of the economic and social forces to make much of a difference in the structure of families. However, the government obviously can change welfare policy.

This issue probably is better discussed in the larger context of whether a policy that is specifically directed toward influencing the number of single-parent families might make a difference.

Can Governmental Policies Directly Influence Family Structure?

It is important to realize that attempts to influence family decisions directly can be divisive and ethically ambiguous. Do we want to make it more difficult for a woman to leave an abusive man? Do we believe that everyone would be better off if an unhappy couple stayed together and took out their frustrations on each other and their children? Do we think that a single parent ought to be forced to marry just to support herself and her children? A minority of Americans favor tightening the divorce laws. Furthermore, most Americans seem to think that it is undesirable for a woman to have a child out of wedlock, but once she does so, few favor forcing her to marry or to put the baby up for adoption.

The notion that single-parent families are undesirable is clear only when the alternative is a happy, loving, and secure two-parent home. Because that is rarely the alternative, the danger is that policies designed to inhibit the formation of single-parent homes will encourage the maintenance of equally unsatisfactory alternatives. So as we think about such policies, we must avoid the illusion that any policy that inhibits the formation of single-parent homes is desirable. Rather, only policies that encourage better arrangements should be devised.

The government has only a few broad policy levers. First, it can *provide information, education, and even moral guidance*. Moral guidance is often treated as different from information, but it is abundantly clear in the current debates over the prevention of AIDS that one person's education is another's indoctrination. Information seems most likely to have some influence in the area of teenage sexuality and pregnancy. Fortunately, teenage pregnancy has been the subject of numerous studies and reports.[54] A number of policies look quite promising, particularly school clinics that offer contraceptives along with other health information and care.[55]

Anything that helps people make better, more informed, and more appropriate decisions about sexuality and childbirth certainly seems to be a critical element in any long-range strategy. Accidental and irrational pregnancies have no winners. Teenage pregnancy is one of the few aspects of single parenthood that is clearly undesirable. The overwhelming proportion of teenagers do not want children and those who do simply cannot realize what they are in for. It is not rational to get pregnant at 17, no matter what the alternatives appear to be. Teenage pregnancy is a matter of information, contraception, and sexual activity, all of which might plausibly be changed.

A second tack is to *strengthen the position of two-parent families.* If we can find ways to help two-parent families cope more effectively and be more independent and economically secure, marriage should become more viable. This seems a desirable alternative because we can institute policies that both signal and promote more effective and secure two-parent families. The ways in which this might be done are the subject of chapter 4.

A third approach is to *give less and expect more from single parents.* Strangely, it is this alternative that seems to get most of the attention when poverty is discussed. The call is to "cut these women off welfare." But consider briefly the logic of making things worse for single mothers now, in the hope of making things better for children in the long run. The moral dilemma in such a policy would be severe even if we believed it would work. Currently, over 50 percent of the children in single-parent homes are poor even though they receive cash aid from the government. Yet, some conservatives propose that we should eliminate welfare and all other forms of governmental support. They ask that we sacrifice the current generation of children in single-parent homes in the hope that the next generation will not be born.

Attacking the financial position of single-parent families may inhibit the flexibility of families to split up even when there are good reasons for doing so. It might reduce births to unmarried women somewhat, but it also might force single mothers to leave their children in unsafe surroundings, turn to unsafe or exploitive work, or to marry men they do not love.

Pragmatic politicians rarely suggest that welfare should be eliminated. Instead, they recommend cutting benefits or refusing to pay extra for second or third children. But we have already tried cutting welfare. We cut benefits by at least 30 percent since the early 1970s, and the number of single-parent families continued to grow. Remember, cash benefits are now roughly at the level they were in 1960! The forces influencing the formation of single-parent families are much stronger and broader than the 1 percent of the GNP we spend on cash assistance for single mothers. Even many conservatives concede that modest cuts in benefits will not noticeably affect the number of single-parent families. And no one denies that cuts in benefits hurt the economic position of single parents and their children.

Some argue that although it would be unreasonable to cut benefits further, obligations could be imposed in the form of work requirements. Such proposals can be appealing on some grounds, but not on the basis that they are likely to have a great influence on the number of single-parent families. Choices made about marriage, divorce, and childbearing seem far too momentous to be affected much by work requirements. There certainly is no evidence that family structure would be affected by work rules.

In making changes in the welfare system, one certainly ought to consider the incentives they create for the formation of single-parent families. That is the essence of the welfare–family structure conundrum. Such incentives are important, not only for their real effects, but for their effects on the perceptions of the public at large. This book recommends major changes in the welfare system that might even reduce the number of single-parent homes. But let us not be fooled into thinking that marginal changes in welfare are likely to have much effect on the powerful forces that are influencing the formation of single-parent families. And massive cuts in aid would surely cause considerable suffering.

Finally, we could *expect more from absent parents.* Almost every child has two living parents. But in this era of frustration over the welfare system, one rarely hears complaints about the absent parents who are doing little to support their children. All but 3 percent of Americans believe that absent fathers should contribute some child support even if the mother has custody of the children and can earn a reasonable living.[56] Yet two-thirds of all single mothers reported getting no child support in 1984. (These facts are discussed in chapter 5.)

We are sending a clear signal. Not only do absent parents generally not have any responsibilities, we offer financial rewards to fathers for avoiding their responsibilities in that they do much better away from their families than with them. This situation is morally reprehensible and economically foolhardy. Absent parents are an obvious source of nonwelfare, nongovernmental support. Moreover, if every man who fathered a child knew that as long as the child was under age 18, he would have to share a significant portion of his income with the child, his incentives would be sharply changed. There ought to be a financial disadvantage to divorce, not a financial gain, because the same incomes must be spread across two households. It seems likely that fewer babies would be born out of wedlock if men as well as women were held accountable for their conception. It seems so obvious that one wonders why we are not doing more about this issue. That question will be discussed in detail in chapter 5.

In sum, the least appealing way to discourage the formation of single-parent families is to make life worse for single parents. Such policies are of questionable effectiveness and they may harm some of the neediest families and children. Happily, the other three options have far fewer disadvantages. Information can help people avoid foolish choices. When the status of two-parent families is improved, the desirability of marrying, having children, and remaining together increases. Expecting more from absent parents makes both moral and economic sense.

Still, in the end we should be skeptical that the government can do much to change the basic family patterns in America. Just as there is little evidence that the government caused many of the trends, there is little to suggest that it can do much to alter them. Even if the government could do much, policies explicitly designed to change families might do more harm than good. In thinking about the problems associated with single-parent families, we must be conscious that our actions may alter family patterns. But we must avoid the illusion that policy is anything more than a modest element in a confusing puzzle of complex forces.

We are left with far-lower expectations about changing the world by sharply altering the trends in overall work, earnings, attitudes, or family structure. We must not ignore the larger trends or give up efforts to change them for the better. But if we care about helping poor families, we will have to find ways to help people help themselves within this larger context. Some will argue that working on poverty without changing the larger forces at work in society is ineffectual and even counterproductive. I disagree. A great deal can be done if we examine the poverty of different groups and seek solutions that adjust to and take account of the nature of the economic and social landscape.

In Search of Answers

The remainder of the book will focus on three groups: two-parent families, single-parent families, and the ghetto poor, with a chapter devoted to each one. The need for the separate treatment of single-parent and two-parent families is obvious. Single parents are in a more difficult and complex position than are husbands and wives in two-parent homes.

The need for a separate chapter on the ghetto poor arises from the perceptions of both the public and scholars that poverty in our nation's inner cities is far more complicated and confounding than is poverty in other areas. It is important to understand, though, that the overwhelming majority of poor Americans do not live in ghettos. By many recent estimates, no more than 10 percent of the poor live in big-city ghettos. And many of the problems of the ghetto poor are common to other poor persons. Thus even though the ghetto poor receive special consideration in chapter 6, they are implicitly included among the poor two-parent and single-parent families discussed in chapters 4 and 5.

Chapter 2 emphasized that poverty policy which is both effective and reinforcing of the values of autonomy, work, family, and community would be based on an understanding of why people are poor. Hence, the goal of examining the problems of each group is not simply to count or profile them. Rather, it is to understand the main reasons for their poverty and to find ways in which governmental policies can help people overcome it.

4

Poverty Among Two-Parent Families

The poverty of two-parent families is the poverty of the working poor. The fortunes of these families are closely linked to the performance of the economy. Good times help, but bad times may be devastating. By some measures, these two-parent families are the least secure members of society, for they get little in the way of income or medical supports despite their vulnerability to swings in the economy. If we are really serious about reinforcing the values of autonomy, work, family, and community, then we must find a way to improve the economic security of this group without putting them into a welfare system.

What Is Poverty?

In the mid-1960s, Molly Orshansky became famous by defining a poverty level. Essentially, the level was determined by figuring out how much a family needed to maintain a minimally adequate diet and then multiplying by three. The government adopted this standard, and, with minor revisions, it has been used since. Each year, the poverty line is adjusted only for inflation. In 1984, the poverty line for a family of three was roughly $8,277, and for a family of four $10,609. To put these figures in perspective, the median family income for a family of four in 1984 was $31,034.[1]

The adoption of a simple and widely accepted way to measure poverty did as much to focus attention on the poor as any march or movement. Suddenly, we could count the poor in any year using survey data on family incomes. Now when the poverty count is released each year, it commands at least one story in the evening news. And researchers now categorize poor people according to their education, race, family situation, age, sex, health status, living arrangements, geographic location, occupation, family size, and dozens of other classifications. Since we know who is poor and who is not, researchers have been able to see if the poor have adequate housing, health care, or food.

Defining a poverty line strictly on the basis of annual income is convenient and plausible to researchers, but it misses much of what stirs the heart and mind in any discussion of the poor. For the image of the poor often carries with it a much different time dimension. Although we are justifiably concerned about those who suffer short-term problems, it is the long-term group that generates the most passion, compassion, and disdain. The child of the ghetto—not the child of the construction worker—commands the most concern.

The poverty index makes no attempt to adjust for local differences in the cost of living; a $10,000-a-year income may mean something different in New York City than it does in rural Mississippi. And it is not adjusted when the overall standard of living rises. If everyone becomes better off, poverty will fall, even if the differences in income between the rich and the poor are as great or greater than ever.

Yet, for all its flaws, the poverty line has served the country reasonably well. It seems to provide a reasonable picture of economic deprivation. A family with a low income even in a single year clearly faces some problems and may be worthy of support. And there really are no better alternatives. No good regional cost-of-living indexes are available. And one cannot very well look only at ten-year intervals of income when determining a poverty count. The basic poverty line as an index of annual deprivation is what I will use here.

Official governmental statistics usually include governmental benefits when determining poverty. In this book, I generally classify as poor any family who is not able to support itself above the poverty line without help from the government. If we are to understand the underlying causes of poverty, then we need to look at the people whose private, nongovernmental family income falls below the poverty line. Logically, one wants to ask first who cannot provide for themselves and why, and then look to see what the government can do and is doing about it.

How Bad Is the Poverty of Two-Parent Families?

The poverty of single parents gets all the attention. It is easy to see why. If we exclude all governmental transfers from income, single-parent families with children had a "pretransfer" poverty rate of roughly 50 percent in 1984. (A pretransfer poor family is one whose income, *not counting any governmental transfers* such as welfare, Social Security and the like, is below the poverty line for its family size.) By contrast, the rate was 15 percent for two-parent families with children.

Moreover, poverty usually lasts a shorter time in two-parent families than in single-parent families. Figure 4.1 shows that if we look at the first ten years of life for children who grew up in the 1970s, those who lived entirely in two-parent families in the 1970s were far more likely to escape poverty, particularly long-term poverty, than those who spent at least some time in single-parent homes. According to this figure, some 80 percent

Figure 4.1

Years of Pretransfer Poverty from Birth to Age 10 for Children, by Living Arrangement

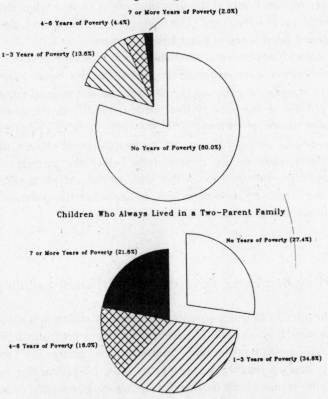

SOURCE: Author's tabulations of survey data from the Panel Study of Income Dynamics. See note 2.

of the children who were growing up in stable two-parent homes escaped poverty, and just 2 percent were long-term poor. By contrast, only 27 percent of those who spent at least some time in single-parent homes avoided poverty, and over 20 percent literally grew up poor.[2]

If poverty is relatively uncommon in stable two-parent homes and if it is often short lived, perhaps two-parent poverty deserves its uncelebrated status. Not so. Since so many more children live in two-parent families than in single-parent ones, half the poor children in America are living in two-parent homes—and they live in families that are suffering genuine economic hardship. Furthermore, the poverty rate for children in two-parent homes is not so low. It still exceeds the poverty rate among persons over age 65 (after governmental transfers).

Moreover, if we are really interested in supporting and promoting two-parent families, concentrating exclusively on single-parent families is not only uncaring but counterproductive. Most of the children shown in figure 4.1 who did not live entirely in two-parent families started out life in them, but the families split apart. Poverty may have been a contributing factor to the breakup of these families. In chapter 3, I made clear that one of the most appealing ways to try and influence the changing structure of families in America is to seek ways to strengthen two-parent families—ways that help poor families and reinforce our values.

Why Are Two-Parent Families Poor?

Unfortunately, there are few clear answers to the question of why a family is poor. Two people who observe the same family in the same situation can reach different conclusions. Suppose, for example, we observe a poor two-parent family in which the husband works full time all year and the mother stays at home with the children. What is the cause of the family's poverty?

One answer would be that low wages are to blame. The father is already working full time and the mother is taking care of the children. What more should it take to escape poverty? For some reason, the husband is not being paid enough to support himself and his family. This looks like a societal problem in the marketplace or in the educational system.

Another answer could be that the mother is not working outside the home to help support the family. After all, the majority of mothers now work at least part time. Surely, we can expect this mother to do so as well. A variation on this theme would be that the mother may not be able to work because affordable day care is not available.

Yet another answer could be that these people should not have become parents in the first place if they could not support their children. One might be particularly concerned if this was a large family that would be poor even with the earnings from a fairly good job.

If we could talk to the family in person, we might be able to decide which of these explanations seemed most fair. If it turned out that the wife had tried to work but quit when she found that her low earnings simply did not compensate enough for the high cost of day care combined with the stress that working placed on the family, then we would be less inclined to suggest that she was not doing enough. If she was alone at home while the children were in school, we might feel differently.

The case I just described is one of the easy ones. What about a family in which the husband and wife say they are unemployed? How could we tell if they really could not find work? What if one had lost a high-paying job but had recently turned down a low-paying one? What if one of the adults was not looking for work because of "child care responsibilities" even while the other was unemployed?

There is no way to look at every poor family and make a decision about the "true" cause of their low income. And we certainly could not expect the government to make such determinations on a case-by-case basis. It is precisely this ambiguity that leads academics and advocates alike to turn quickly to a welfare model of support. Welfare does not try to decide why people are poor; it only guarantees some minimal income.

But adopting a policy that recognizes no causes leads to no solutions. A great deal of the ambiguity comes from our unwillingness to decide what is reasonable to expect of families. If we are willing to decide on some minimal standards of responsibility for citizens and society, then we can go a long way toward determining the causes of poverty. From that determination, we can often find nonwelfare alternatives that support and reinforce people's efforts to support themselves.

Reasonable Responsibility

We might start by asking, "How much work should it take for a healthy two-parent family to achieve the *minimum* standard of living (as defined by the government's poverty standard)?" Whatever the answer, it simultaneously defines the expectations of citizens and of society. Society's responsibility is to ensure that everyone has the opportunity to fulfill the standard of work it sets and that wages are sufficient to achieve a minimum standard of living. If society meets that responsibility, then healthy citizens can reasonably be expected to provide for themselves by working at that level.

I believe that in a two-parent family, the earnings of one person working full year, full time (or the equivalent number of hours of combined work by a husband and wife) ought to be sufficient for a family to reach the poverty line. Consider the hypothetical couple already described in which the husband is working full time and the wife is at home taking care of the children. It is hard to expect more from the husband, although he could perhaps find a second job. We do not know whether the wife has tried to find work, but, without more information, it is hard to fault her chosen role of raising the children, especially since we cannot be sure that day care is available. This family already seems to be doing a lot to help themselves. The father is probably working at an unpleasant low-paying job to pay the bills. The mother is trying to run the household on too little money. They appear to be the "value rich" but "money poor" people described in a 1986 Reagan administration report on the family.[3]

If we accept this initial guidepost, we can break families into two obvious categories, those who are meeting the standard and those who are not. One reason why people may not be working fully is illness or disability. Such families ought to be considered in a different light. Thus, there seem to be three classifications with which we can start to examine the causes of poverty among two-parent families: full-time working families (defined as a case where one adult works fully or the combined effort of both adults is equivalent), families in which one adult is aged or disabled, and families in which the adults are partially employed or unemployed. Table 4.1 provides information on the distribution of people across these categories and shows the links to poverty.

It should surprise no one to learn that work and poverty are closely related. The poverty rate among fully working families before governmental transfers is just .06; for the others, it is ten times that level. Fortunately, the vast majority of two-parent families are full-time working families. Only 6 percent fall into the partially employed or unemployed category (and work is common even in that group). It turns out that only 1 percent of families have two healthy parents who both report no work at all during the year.

But, rather startlingly, even though the poverty rate among full-time working families is low, such families still make up 44 percent of the poor two-parent families. Thus, work does not always guarantee a route out of poverty. A full-time minimum-wage job (that pays $3.35 per hour) does not even come close to supporting a family of three at the poverty line. Even one full-time job and one half-time job at the minimum wage will not bring a family of four up to the poverty line. Therefore,

TABLE 4.1

Poverty, Work, Unemployment, and Disability in Two-Parent Families (1984)

Work, Unemployment, and Disability Status	Percentage Distribution of Poor and Nonpoor Families	Proportion Poor before Government Benefits[a]	Percentage Distribution of Poor Families before Government Benefits
Full-time Working Families[b]	90	.06	44
Partially Employed or Unemployed Families[c]	6	.61	35
Families with an ill, disabled, or retired adult[d]	4	.67	21
All Families	100	.11	100

[a]Proportion of families in each category whose income before governmental assistance is below the poverty line.
[b]Families with one full-year full-time worker or in which the combined hours of the husband and wife total 1,750 hours or more. (The standard definition of full-year full-time work is 35 hours per week for 50 weeks.)
[c]Families with no retired or disabled adults who work a total of fewer than 1,750 hours.
[d]Families in which the total work hours were fewer than 1,750 and in which at least one adult reported that he or she did not work because of illness, disability, or retirement.
SOURCE: Author's tabulations of data in U.S. Bureau of the Census, March 1985 Current Population Survey.

even though most full-time working families escape poverty, the ones who do not represent a large share of the poor.

Low Wages—The First Cause of Poverty

If we accept one full-time worker per family as the standard for escaping poverty, then it is easy to determine the cause of poverty for the 44 percent of two-parent families who are "working fully." These families are poor because their wages are too low. The statistical profile in table 4.2 shows that they are somewhat disadvantaged and are drawn from many parts of our society. Only in a small minority of cases is the husband under age 30. Many live in rural areas and are farmers, but roughly an

TABLE 4.2

Statistical Profile of Poor Two-Parent Families by Type of Situation
(1984)

	Full-time Working Poor	Partially Employed or Unemployed Poor	Disabled or Retired Poor	All Poor Two-Parent Families
RACE	100	100	100	100
White, non-Hispanic	67	64	69	66
Black, non-Hispanic	12	12	14	13
Hispanic	17	17	13	16
Other	4	7	4	5
FAMILY SIZE	100	100	100	100
Three	15	25	28	22
Four	34	34	29	33
Five	28	21	18	23
Six or more	23	20	25	22
RESIDENCE	100	100	100	100
Central city	23	31	24	26
Suburban	23	25	29	25
Small town and rural	46	37	38	42
Unknown	8	7	9	8

	Full-time Working Poor	Partially Employed or Unemployed Poor	Disabled or Retired Poor	All Poor Two-Parent Families
AGE OF HUSBAND	100	100	100	100
Under 20	1	1	0	1
20–29	26	36	8	26
30–39	43	34	24	36
40–49	22	19	19	20
50 and over	8	10	49	17
AGE OF WIFE	100	100	100	100
Under 20	3	3	1	3
20–29	34	44	16	33
30–39	43	36	30	38
40–49	17	13	25	17
50 and over	3	4	28	9
EDUCATION OF HUSBAND	100	100	100	100
Under 12 years	37	40	56	43
High school only	39	42	31	38
12–15 years	15	11	7	12
College or more	9	7	6	7
EDUCATION OF WIFE	100	100	100	100
Under 12 years	36	39	49	40
High school only	44	46	39	43
12–15 years	14	11	9	12
College or more	6	4	3	5

TABLE 4.2 (Continued)

	Full-time Working Poor	Partially Employed or Unemployed Poor	Disabled or Retired Poor	All Poor Two-Parent Families
WORK OF HUSBAND	100	100	100	100
Full-year full-time	67	0	0	30
Part-year or part-time	27	71	19	40
Did not work	6	29	81	30
WORK OF WIFE	100	100	100	100
Full-year full-time	15	0	0	7
Part-year or part-time	41	31	21	33
Did not work	44	69	79	60
WORK CLASS OF HUSBAND[a]	100	100	100	100
Private industry	57	77	82	66
Farm	15	2	2	9
Nonfarm self-employed	23	14	10	19
Government	5	7	6	6
WORK CLASS OF WIFE[a]	100	100	100	100
Private industry	56	81	81	65
Farm	24	3	2	16
Nonfarm self-employed	10	3	6	8
Government	10	13	11	11

[a]Work class is shown only for those who worked in the past year.
SOURCE: Author's tabulations of data in U.S. Bureau of the Census, March 1985 Current Population Survey.

equal number live in metropolitan areas. The large majority are white. Some two-thirds have a high school education.

In a majority of these families, the wives are working along with the husbands. When the wives do not work outside the home, they generally report that household and family responsibilities have prevented them from doing so. Two-thirds of these "housewives" have children under age 6. Nearly all (91 percent) have children under 12 years.

There is reason to suspect that at least some of these families may not be as poor as they appear. Some of the self-employed men may have small businesses with large deductions, leading them to report small incomes on the survey. On the other hand, some may be taxi drivers who work long hours for low pay. Around 9 percent of the men are college graduates; another 15 percent have training beyond high school. But the educational level is far below that of the nonpoor on average. Mostly, these appear to be families with adults who are working hard often at unpleasant and low-paying jobs, but they are not making it in America. They have traditional family structures and they have the work ethic—but they remain poor.

Unemployment—The Second Cause of Poverty

In roughly 35 percent of poor two-parent families, both parents are healthy, but no one is working fully (or the equivalent). This classification is more ambiguous, since the adults may not be working because there are too few jobs in the labor market or because they lack real motivation. Thus, the cause of poverty is much harder to determine for individual families, but in the aggregate, it should not be too difficult. If these families are genuinely interested in work, then the number of unemployed poor persons ought to be extremely sensitive to economic conditions.

And so it is. In 1983, when the overall unemployment rate was 9.5 percent, 1,017,000 husbands with children were poor and reported that their inability to find a job was the chief reason they had worked only part of the year or had not worked at all. In 1978, when the unemployment rate was 6 percent (still high by historical standards), just 341,000 of such husbands cited the lack of jobs as the cause.[4] So, there were three times as many unemployed poor persons when the unemployment rate went up 3.5 percentage points. The fact that poverty that is due to unemployment is so sensitive to economic conditions certainly argues for its largely involuntary nature.

Moreover, in most of these families, the adults worked at least part of the time. Roughly 75 percent of the husbands and 40 percent of the wives in these households worked part of the year. When asked why they did not work more, the husbands almost universally reported that they were unable to find more work. The wives who did not work usually pointed to household responsibilities, although a sizable minority said they wanted to work more but could not find work. Among the wives who cited household responsibilities as their reason for not working more, over 70 percent had a child under age 6, and 90 percent had a child under age 12.

Who are these unemployed poor adults? Some of them are moderately paid workers who lost a job and were slow to find another—displaced workers. But over half those who did work earned less than $5 an hour while they were working. In 1984, $5 an hour was not enough to push a family of four over the poverty line even if the person worked full time all year. Indeed, in many respects, a large part of this group looks like the fully working poor except that they were out of work for part of the year. Job insecurity is another side of low-paying jobs. Sheldon Danziger and Peter Gottschalk reported that low-wage workers who earn under $5.50 per hour and who head families are three times more likely to experience unemployment than are their higher-paid counterparts.[5]

Disability and Retirement—The Third Cause of Poverty

In the final quarter of poor families, no one is working fully, and one or both parents report they were unable to work more because they were ill, disabled, or retired. The cause of their poverty is obvious, provided they are telling the truth about their condition.

Their claims can be easily checked in many cases. Our social welfare system is comparatively generous with the disabled. There are several ways in which ill and disabled people can get some aid if their condition warrants it. Since all require some verification, we can get a sense of the veracity of their statements about retirement or disability by seeing if they report that they receive this form of aid. To get Social Security or Supplemental Security Income (SSI) people must be over age 62 or be certified as prospectively unable to work at all for at least a year. Some 60 percent of the families in this category report that they received one of these benefits. An additional 12 percent report that they got workers' compensation or veterans' benefits, which were presumably paid for injuries sustained on the job. So, roughly three-quarters of the people in this category are getting aid under programs that require evidence of their injury or retirement. (And these percentages are unquestionably underestimates of the proportion who actually receive benefits, since there is some underreporting.)

What about the remainder? Virtually no governmental programs offer protection for people who suffer a short-term injury or disability that was not sustained on the job (someone who is out of work for six months because of an automobile accident would not qualify for coverage). Others may have only recently sustained a long-term injury. It takes an average of three months and sometimes much longer to process new claims for Social Security Disability.[6] Some of those who are not receiving benefits will qualify for them eventually. One bit of evidence that short-term or recent disability may be an important factor is that 40 percent of the group that is not receiving benefits reported that they worked part of the year and that their injury prevented them from working during the rest of the year. In sum, although there may be a few people in this category who could be working, the overwhelming majority seem to be suffering from legitimate problems that limit their ability to work.

The Working Poor and Trickle-Down

The image that emerges of poor two-parent families is surprising. It is largely a picture of families who are struggling to provide for themselves and who are sharply affected by the availability of jobs and the wages being paid. This image is different from the one portrayed in recent conservative books on poverty that have emphasized the ghetto underclass and the television specials and newscasts that show the poor being isolated economically, socially, geographically, and culturally from the rest of society. Some of these isolated people may be found among poor two-parent families, but they are outnumbered by others who are not isolated. Remember that ghetto poverty probably represents less than 10 percent of the poverty in America. It is an even smaller part of the poverty of two-parent families.

Aside from the group that is disabled or retired, poor two-parent families really are the working poor. Perhaps the best proof of this lies in a test of an old conservative proposition: trickle-down. I have argued that there are three basic causes of poverty for these families: low wages, unemployment, and disability. Disability should be roughly constant from year to year. But wages and unemployment rates vary considerably over time. If those were the driving forces affecting the poverty of two-parent families, then we ought to be able to predict fluctuations in poverty for two-parent families by using only a measure of aggregate wages in the economy and a measure of unemployment. In short, the poverty of two-parent families ought to mimic economic conditions.

So I looked to see if I could predict poverty rates strictly on the basis of overall wage rates and unemployment. I plotted the actual poverty rate and the one I would have predicted on the basis of just two measures of economic conditions: median income of full-year full-time workers (a measure of wages for full-time workers) and unemployment.[7] Figure 4.2 shows the startling results—a perfect match. In the 1960s, when real wages were rising fast and unemployment dropped, poverty fell precipitously. In the 1970s, when earnings were largely unchanged (after adjusting for inflation), poverty changed little. And in the 1980s, when the economy turned sour, the poverty rate jumped up.

Contrary to the claims of Charles Murray and others, there is nothing mysterious or suggestive about the lack of progress in eliminating poverty among two-parent families in the 1970s and 1980s.[8] This is the group for whom trickle-down works well. When the economy booms and wages grow while unemployment falls, this group is carried with the tide. That is just

Figure 4.2
Actual and Expected Poverty Rates for Children in Two-Parent Families

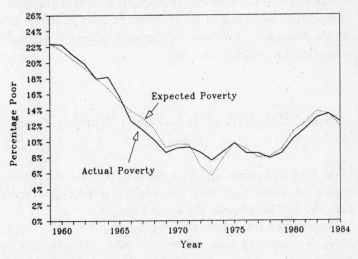

NOTE: Expected poverty based solely on the median earnings of full-year, full-time male workers and the unemployment rate.

what happened in the 1960s. If economic growth was strong over an extended period, the number of poor two-parent families would rapidly diminish and eventually those who were still poor would be the disabled and a much smaller pool of families with an unemployed adult who had just lost a job, who was just starting out, or who was living in an area where the local economy was weak.

The poverty line is not changed by growth, but the incomes of most two-parent families are. Growth may not reduce the difference in the incomes of the highest and lowest families (it may not narrow the distribution of income), but it will push more and more low-income families over the fixed poverty line.[9] Indeed, in Massachusetts in 1984, when the unemployment rate was under 4 percent and growth had been strong for several years, the pretransfer poverty rate for two-parent families with children was under 6 percent—less than half the national figure of 12 percent.[10]

So a couple of decades of strong growth would be just what the doctor ordered for most poor two-parent families. But no one knows how to recapture the dramatic growth of the 1960s. Instead, we seem locked in a period of slow growth. And trickle-down has its obverse side as well: when the economy stumbles, the working poor fall.

Social Policies and Two-Parent Working Poor Families

How does our social welfare system treat these two-parent working families? Generally very badly. Table 4.3 gives some indication of how poorly the system works.

The disabled and elderly are the only groups that do reasonably well. Starting with an income deficit—the amount of money they need to reach the poverty line—averaging $8,417, they receive an average of $8,237 in governmental benefits, and

TABLE 4.3

Effect of the Social Welfare System on Poor Two-Parent Families (1984)

Type of Two-Parent Family	Average Deficit in Income before Benefits[a]	Average Governmental Benefits[b]	Percentage Who Were Removed from Poverty	Average Remaining Deficit in Income for Those Who Were Still Poor[c]	Percentage with No Medical Protection
Full-time working poor	$4,451	$1,301	18	$4,443	36
Partially employed or unemployed poor	$6,961	$3,936	19	$4,343	38
Disabled or retired	$8,417	$8,237	42	$3,873	16
All poor two-parent families	$6,146	$3,656	23	$4,317	33

[a]Difference between the poverty line and nongovernmental income.
[b]Includes all nonmedical benefits. Housing assistance valued according to Bureau of the Census' market value methodology.
[c]Figure is larger than the difference between the first and second columns because only those who remain poor are included in the calculation.
Source: Author's tabulations of data from U.S. Bureau of the Census, March 1985 Current Population Survey; excludes medical benefits.

many are pulled out of poverty. But even some people in this group seem to get left out. The short-term disabled get little aid since they do not qualify for any of the major disability programs.

The partially employed and unemployed families start out with a somewhat smaller deficit, but they get much less aid. So few are pulled out of poverty. Most remain poor, and many have no medical protection. Worst of all is the treatment of the full-time working poor. Even though these families start out less poor than those in other categories, they get so little aid that they are actually the poorest group after transfers. Over a third have no medical protection, and those who have some protection often have to purchase it with their already limited income.

These results should come as no surprise to anyone who understands the current social welfare system. As shown in table 4.4, the long-term disabled and the elderly are covered by several programs, notably Social Security and SSI. The unemployed are supposedly covered by unemployment insurance and some welfare programs, but the coverage is imperfect.[11] Two-parent families with a full-time worker (and no other unemployed or disabled person), however, are eligible for almost nothing except food stamps, and few seem to find food stamp benefits worth the hassle and stigma of using them.[12] The majority of the working poor report getting no governmental benefits. But, then, the system is designed to help people who cannot work, not those who are already working.

The only surprise in these findings is the low level of protection for the unemployed. Unemployment insurance is supposed to be available to experienced workers who become unemployed through no fault of their own (they neither quit nor were fired for misbehavior). Yet in my tabulations, only 29 percent of these families report that they get unemployment insurance. No one quite understands why so few receive these benefits. The topic has been the basis of several papers and considerable speculation, yet the puzzle remains. Some poor

TABLE 4.4
Percentage of Poor Two-Parent Families Who Received Selected Types of Benefits (1984)[a]

Types of Families	Percentage of Each Type of Family Reporting Receipt of:			
	Social Security Benefits	Employment-Related Benefits	Means-Tested Benefits	No Benefits
Full-time working poor	6	19	35	54
Partially employed or unemployed poor	6	29	66	21
Disabled or retired poor	52	31	58	7
All poor two-parent families	15	25	50	33

[a] The rows total more than 100 percent because some families collected more than one type of benefit.
SOURCE: Author's tabulations of data from U.S. Bureau of the Census, March 1985 Current Population Survey; excludes medical benefits.

unemployed adults may not have worked in covered employ-ment.[13] Others may not qualify for benefits because they worked too few hours or they quit or were fired. Some may have used up benefits to which they once were entitled.[14] And a few may not realize that they qualify for benefits.[15]

Whatever the reason, national figures show that low-wage workers are far less likely to qualify for unemployment benefits than are those who earn more. Danziger and Gottschalk found that only 28 percent of unemployed heads of households who had previously earned below $5.50 per hour received unem-ployment insurance in 1984, while 54 percent of those with higher wages got such benefits.[16] What is perhaps even more troubling are the clear indications that the unemployment in-surance system is providing less and less support over time. Overall, the proportion of unemployed workers covered by this insurance has fallen from a high of 75 percent during the reces-sion of 1975 to a low of 34 percent today.[17] Danziger and Gottschalk stated that low-wage workers have been hurt the worst. The safety net of unemployment insurance clearly has large holes through which the unemployed poor fall, and these holes seem to be getting larger.

Still it is the treatment of the full-time working poor that is the most disturbing. The social welfare system creates an aston-ishing inverse relationship between work and poverty. After governmental aid, the disabled and elderly who do no work are the least poor. Those who are unemployed and partially em-ployed are the next worse off. The full-time working poor end up the least secure of all. One must worry about the signals that this system is sending to the working poor.

Moreover, table 4.3 actually understates the problems of the full-time working poor. The figures take no account of the fact that working families had to pay Social Security and income taxes in 1984, and the numbers are not adjusted for any day care, transportation, or other work expenses.[18] In recent years, the tax code has been reformed in such a way as to minimize the taxes that poor people have to pay, but many families who are near the poverty line still have to pay some taxes.[19]

In the end, full-time working-poor families are actually the poorest of the poor after transfers. On average, they are as far below the poverty line as are single-parent families on welfare in which no one is working. It is easy to see why welfare is such a divisive issue among the working poor. Many of them are working hard and yet have less income or medical protection than those who are on welfare. It is not that welfare benefits are so high; most welfare recipients remain well below the poverty line. Rather, it is that the wages and benefits of full-time working-poor families are so low. But no matter what the reasons, the system seems to mock the efforts of the working poor. It also does not present an appealing alternative toward which those on welfare can look.

In some ways, the biggest outrage is the level of medical protection. Any single parent who receives Aid to Families with Dependent Children (AFDC) gets Medicaid—a comprehensive medical insurance program. The full-time working poor must rely on medical protection provided by their employers (which, in a low-paying job, is likely to be inadequate), use their already limited income to buy protection (which is expensive because commissions on individual health insurance policies are high), or go without it. Governmental benefits and employer-provided benefits cover only half this group. Roughly 40 percent report that they have no medical protection at all.[20]

No doubt, most critically ill people get medical help even if they cannot pay. Despite the occasional horror stories of dreadfully sick people being turned away from hospitals, most people can get critical emergency care somewhere. But even a minor episode of hospitalization leaves the working poor with large medical debts that they can never repay. Many hospitals end up writing off these debts and charging higher rates to the rest of us, and the operating deficits of city and county hospitals are often paid by state and local governments. So the public ends up paying most of the bills. But whatever savings these families had are depleted and their credit rating is ruined. Families who were already in a fragile economic situation before the illness now have yet more strikes against them.

The facts presented here offer a devastating critique of the way in which the present system treats poor two-parent families—families with full-time workers and families with people who are looking to work more. These families ride the roller coaster of the broad economic trends, they pray that illness will miss them, and they hope for a better paying job. Eventually, economic growth could pull most of these families out of poverty. But while we wait for the Godot of economic growth, these families remain among the country's least secure people.

If we want to have a society of which it truly can be said that anyone who works can make it, if we want to help two-parent poor families, if we want to let all our people feel they are part of mainstream America, then, surely, we must find better rewards for the efforts of the working poor.

Support Without Welfare

We could provide welfare to working families, as was the intent of the negative income tax. Earnings could be supplemented with welfare payments to ensure economic security. But the reasons to avoid welfare can be found in the conundrums described in chapter 2. If we provide welfare, we will reduce work effort; the negative income tax experiments showed that for every three dollars given in benefits, earnings were reduced up to two dollars.[21] And we will reduce the rewards for working because when people work, their benefits will fall (since their outside income is higher), so their effective wage will fall. Finally, and perhaps most important, welfare is invasive, inadequate, restrictive, and isolating. The full-time working poor take little advantage of the one form of welfare they are offered—food stamps.

The last thing we want to do is create a system that discourages and penalizes work and that isolates and stigmatizes the very people who are struggling hard to become part of the economic mainstream. Instead, we want to find ways to reinforce their efforts, to integrate them, and to indicate that their work is valued and that work will pay off.

There are straightforward and appealing ways to help without resorting to long-term welfare support. I believe that policy ought to help low-income two-parent families on four different fronts:

- Ensure that everyone has medical protection.
- Make work pay.
- Replace welfare and food stamps with transitional assistance of a limited duration.
- Provide a limited number of jobs for those who have exhausted their transitional assistance.

Medical Care

I doubt that most Americans realize just how many people have no medical protection. They certainly are not aware that the working poor have the least medical protection of all. I have never heard any reasonable justification for this state of medical insecurity.

The helping conundrums need not apply to the provision of medical insurance. If everyone was somehow covered for most medical costs, it is hard to believe that anyone would work much less—except for the parents of critically ill children who work three jobs trying to pay the bills. Families do not break up because they have medical protection, although they might break up to get it if it was available only to single parents. And medical protection is certainly not isolating. Indeed, at a Ford Foundation conference on "Social Welfare Policy and the American Future" in November 1985, which heard papers that were prepared by the major think tanks from the far right to the far left, one of the few proposals that nearly everyone could agree on was that medical protection ought to be provided for all poor people. The other major industrialized countries have found ways to ensure that citizens are protected against medical costs, and so can we.

Medicaid is the primary federally sponsored health program for the poor, and it is usually available only to those who are on AFDC or SSI or who would qualify for them if medical expenses were deducted from their income. Thus, Medicaid is available mainly to those in single-parent families and to those who are aged or disabled. Medicaid is often attacked for being expensive. But the vast majority of Medicaid dollars—and virtually all the recent growth in Medicaid expenditures—have been for benefits to the elderly and disabled (especially nursing home care, which is not covered by Medicare).[22]

During the Reagan years, most social programs have been constricted. One of the few exceptions is Medicaid, whose eligibility categories have been expanded. Proposals have already emerged from the Department of Health and Human Services and the Congress to guarantee "catastrophic protection" for all elderly Americans so that no family would be forced to spend more than $2,500 on medical care. But it is hard to see why only the elderly are worthy of such protection. The elderly at least have Medicare (and Medicaid protection if they are poor). Many younger families have nothing.

National health insurance would be one way to ensure that everyone got medical care. But fears of the cost and disruption and the government's deeper involvement in such a system seem to have doomed the adoption of any such plan in the foreseeable future. Unfortunately, the fight for national health insurance may have also prevented more modest reforms that could protect the unprotected.

We do not need to go all the way to a national health insurance plan to ensure that everyone gets medical protection. One common proposal is to extend Medicaid protection to everyone whose income is below some designated level, not just to those who qualify for welfare. In a sense, this proposal would be a kind of medical welfare. People below the cutoff would get medical protection while those above it would have to "spend down" all their "excess" income on medical care to get any benefits. But like welfare such a plan would create a serious disincentive to work. Moreover, eligibility would still involve the answering of invasive questions and the myriad of red tape. Anyone whose income was slightly above the poverty line would have to become poor again to get protection. Public medical assistance that is administered like the current welfare system is not an appealing solution, although it would be better than the current situation.

Another proposal would require all employers to provide medical protection. Thus, any employer who hired someone for as much as twenty hours a week might have to provide medical protection for the employee and possibly even the employee's family if the employee wanted it. This plan would dramatically increase the cost and complexity of doing business for many employers. Most economists believe that such a plan would lead to reductions in wages (at least for those above the minimum wage) and possibly cutbacks in employment. Reductions in wages are the last thing the working poor need. Employers would have an incentive to hire workers who were not expected to use medical insurance, such as youths, single individuals, or secondary workers. And such a plan would still have to struggle with the issue of how to protect people when they become unemployed.

The simplest and most effective proposal may be a government-sponsored residual insurance plan.[23] According to such a plan, people might be required to list their insurance plan on their tax form. The government would stipulate which benefits must be in a private plan and would certify plans that met the minimum standards. Those who did not receive this certified insurance from an employer or purchase it individually would be required to buy into the governmental plan or plans. The price of this insurance would vary, depending on the income that people reported on their tax forms. People might be expected to contribute, say, 10 percent of their income to get benefits.[24] Or employers who did not provide their own insurance might be required to pay part of the costs of the government's plan for their employees, although that could create some of the same problems for wages and employment cited earlier.

Much of the money required to fund such a plan is already being paid in the form of free or uncompensated care or bad debts to hospitals. Since these costs would now be paid by the residual plan, private insurance costs should be lower. Thus, one could finance at least part of the cost of the government's residual plan from new taxes on existing insurance. Moreover, this plan would not be just for the poor; anyone could buy into it. There would be minimal work disincentives, since the premium would rise just ten cents for each dollar earned. There would be no sudden cutoff—no need to become impoverished to get medical protection. Private protection could largely be left in place, but everyone would be guaranteed medical protection without having a welfare-type plan.

There are problems with this or any other proposal, but, ultimately, it is a matter of will. Helping the poor sometimes involves difficult trade-offs among competing values. Not so for medical protection. Medical coverage primarily involves money—money that we generally are providing already. Medical protection outside a welfare system reinforces autonomy, work, and family and helps integrate people into at least one part of the mainstream. Failing to provide care or providing it only to nonworking and single-parent families puts us at odds with our values.

Making Work Pay

When someone works fully and his or her family is still poor, the most obvious problem is the person's low wages. So the equally obvious answer is to raise wages.[25] If we could magically raise wages among low-paid workers without diminishing the number of jobs, we would increase the reward to work and the autonomy of low-income working families; we also would probably strengthen families and help integrate people into the economic mainstream. There would be no conundrums to face. Those who are now the working poor would feel economically secure without the need for welfare.

Growth and Productivity. I have already noted the one surefire way to raise wages without diminishing employment: strong economic growth. Unfortunately, we do not know how to recapture the growth of the 1960s. The U.S. economy, battered by increases in oil prices, struggling with the changing demography of the work force, burdened with dangerous fiscal policies, and tripped up by some bad luck, has shown lackluster growth for 1½ decades. What little growth there was went to employing the vastly expanding labor force, not to higher wages.

There are mixed signs ahead. On the positive side, OPEC has weakened. Inflation seems under control. The labor force is growing far more slowly. Many analysts are predicting labor shortages for the future. These forces ought to help low-wage workers. On the negative side, the budget deficit continues to be enormous; it is drawing money out of investment and pulling in foreign capital, thereby worsening our trade position. And the manufacturing jobs that paid well and offered high benefits are being replaced by less lucrative ones in service industries. We simply cannot expect growth to conquer the problems of the full-time working poor for quite some time. Meanwhile, we need to find ways to make work pay better for the working poor.

An alternative approach is to train and educate workers so they can achieve a higher standard of living. Obviously, training and education must be a critical element in any long-term antipoverty strategy. Training helps people help themselves. It also avoids the conundrums and is politically popular.

The best place to start, of course, is by creating first-rate public schools. People who have had twelve or more years of excellent classroom work should be in a far better position to compete in the labor market and should help the country compete against foreign traders. When it comes to specific proposals for improving our public education system, I must defer to others. But the long-run health of the poor and of the nation depends on its educational system.

While we await a strong economy and a first-rate educational system, we still have families with working adults who are poor. My concern is to help them. Unfortunately, the history of training programs for adults has not shown much promise of eliminating poverty among the working poor. Most of the recent reports have found that the long-run impact of employment and training programs for men has been modest. Although the results for women have been somewhat more promising, annual increases in earnings have rarely exceeded $1,000.[26] There is little evidence that training is more valuable than the equivalent amount of work experience. Thus, I would encourage people who have found a job to stay with it and build up their experience. Training could thus be given primarily to those who are out of work. How, then, are we to raise wages for the working poor?

Raising the Minimum Wage. One approach would be to raise the minimum wage. Adjusted for inflation, the minimum wage has fallen dramatically in recent years. Figure 4.3 shows that, adjusted for inflation, the current minimum wage is roughly where it was in 1956. Just since 1981, the real value of the minimum wage has fallen from almost $4.50 per hour to $3.35. Between 1970 and 1979, a full-year full-time minimum-wage job provided about enough money to support a family of three at the poverty line: $4.25 per hour (in 1986 dollars). By 1986, it fell short by 20 percent.

Robert Reischauer has pointed out that between 1962 and 1981, the minimum wage averaged "48.2% of the average gross hourly earnings for production and non-supervisory workers in private non-agricultural industries."[27] If that ratio held true today, the minimum wage would be roughly $4.30 per hour.

Figure 4.3
Level of the Minimum Wage between 1956 and 1986 (1986 Dollars)

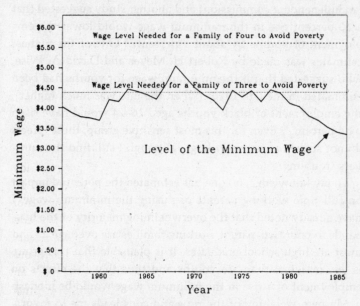

NOTE: Wage level needed to avoid poverty assumes 2,000 hours of work yearly.
SOURCE: U.S. Bureau of the Census, *Statistical Abstract of the U.S., 1987* (Washington, D.C.: U.S. Government Printing Office, 1986), table 684, p. 404.

Thus, by several different standards, it might be argued that the minimum wage ought to be $4.30 per hour today.

Unfortunately, raising the minimum wage is a blunt way of reaching the working poor. A study by the Congressional Budget Office estimated that only one-quarter of the workers who were paid below $4.35 per hour lived in poor or near-poor homes.[28] Consequently, most of the workers who would benefit from an increase would be in nonpoor homes.

Probably the biggest concern about raising the minimum wage is that it will hurt the employment prospects of workers who are near the minimum. Empirical evidence and economic theory both indicate that raising the minimum wage will reduce employment somewhat. But just how much remains the subject of considerable debate. The group that is most likely to be affected are youths. The Minimum Wage Study Commission (an independent commission) and another study suggested that a 10 percent rise in the minimum wage would lower the employment of youths by about 1 percent.[29] One of the highest estimates was made by Robert H. Meyer and David A. Wise, who suggested that if the minimum wage for youths had been eliminated in the late 1970s (when the rate was much higher), the employment of black youths aged 16–24 would have risen by 6 percent.[30] Even for this most sensitive group, these effects do not strike me as overly large, although I still find the numbers troubling.

To my knowledge, no one has estimated the potential impact on full-time working parents of raising the minimum wage. I have already noted that the overwhelming majority of the husbands in poor two-parent working families are over age 25 and most are high school graduates. It is plausible that this group is less marginal than are youths and thus that the effects on employment of a rise in the minimum wage would be modest.

My own weighing of the pros and cons leads me to favor a rise in the minimum wage in spite of its possible effects on employment. I favor raising it back to the level of the 1970s and adjusting it to the rate of inflation or the growth in other wages. Without such a change, it is virtually impossible to guarantee that work will pay enough to keep families out of poverty, even with the additional tax policies that I shall discuss momentarily. I also accept the argument of proponents that the lowest wage we pay workers, particularly those with families, sends an important signal about how valuable and important we think their efforts are. I think a subminimum wage for youths is worth considering because this group is rarely supporting poor families, and the potential effects on this group of a higher minimum wage are of greater concern.

A higher minimum wage alone will not guarantee the security of all or even most working families. If the minimum is raised to $4.30 or $4.40, families of four with one full-time minimum-wage worker will still be poor. Thus, whether or not the minimum is raised, other ways of making work pay better need to be explored.

Wage Subsidies. To many economists, one of the most appealing ways to raise wages is through wage subsidies, and wage subsidy proposals have a long history.[31] Most recently, Robert Lerman proposed that heads of low-wage families should get a governmental pay subsidy that would be equal to half the difference between their wage and six dollars per hour.[32] Hence, someone who was earning four dollars per hour might get a wage subsidy of one dollar per hour. In principle, a wage subsidy could be an ideal tool. It could be carefully targeted to just those persons in families who need their wages boosted. It would increase the rewards of work and, if anything, it would increase employment, rather than diminish it, as raising the minimum wage could do.

But administrative difficulties complicate such proposals considerably. Employers would have to report both hours and earnings. Both employers and employees would have an incentive to lie and claim that the wage rate was lower and that the hours worked were higher than they actually were. Moreover, many employers might be reluctant to hire people who received such a subsidy. In chapter 2, I mentioned the pay voucher experiment that showed that employers hired fewer workers who had a government-promised wage subsidy than those in a matched control group. This experiment looks like it was a case of targeting isolated people rather than integrating them. Either the employers thought the subsidized workers must be poor workers, or the employers were reluctant to go through the red tape of hiring such persons and getting the subsidy. Either way, the impact of the project was lessened. Another system that is now in place, the Targeted Jobs Tax Credit (this helps pay the wages of selected workers), has had modest effects at best.[33]

And there are more difficulties as well. What about families with two earners? Would both workers get a wage subsidy?

Lerman suggests that the family would designate one worker to receive the subsidy. But what if that family member lost his or her job? Would the other worker be designated? And would designating one worker as the "primary" wage earner (the one to be subsidized) inevitably raise the issue of sexism? Another concern is that the public would consider that employers were being given a free ride. Instead of paying workers what they were worth, employers would be letting the government pay a part of their employees' wages.[34]

Thus, wage subsidies, although theoretically appealing, remain unproven at best and may well be impossible to administer. We need to mount many more experiments before we can engage in a large-scale system of wage subsidies. Therefore, until these subsidies show more promise, we need to look elsewhere.

The Earned Income Tax Credit.　There is a simpler way to make work pay better: the earned income tax credit (EITC). The EITC is similar to a wage subsidy in many ways, but it largely avoids the administrative and targeting complications. And a modest EITC is already in place in the current tax system, so expanding it would be simple. The basic idea is simple: families with low earnings gain tax credits for each dollar that they earn. Under the current law, families with earnings below $6,200 per year now get tax credits of 14 cents for each dollar they are paid. Someone who earns $5,000 gets an additional $700 in tax credits. Since the tax credits are refundable, the worker's effective earnings are $5,700.[35] When earnings reach $6,200, the worker gets the maximum credit of $868. Those with incomes between $6,200 and $9,840 get a flat credit of $868. For those with incomes over $9,840, the credit is reduced by 10 cents for each dollar earned.

For low-wage workers, the EITC is similar to a wage subsidy. For those with earnings below $6,200, each new dollar earned brings an extra 14 cents in tax breaks; thus, it is like a 14 percent wage increase for low earners. Only those who work get the credit. And, up to the maximum, the more they work, the *more* they get (the opposite of the negative income tax and guaranteed annual income schemes).

Currently the EITC is low enough that it roughly offsets only the taxes a working person will pay into the Social Security system. Indeed, many of its supporters justify it strictly on that basis. But there is no reason why it could not be expanded to do far more. Suppose, for example, we doubled the current EITC to 30 percent and raised the maximum earnings credited up to $8,000. Someone who worked full time at a $4.00-per-hour job would get $8,000 in earnings plus a $2,400 tax credit. In effect, his or her wage would have been raised by 30 percent to $5.20 per hour. With the EITC, benefits come in the form of tax refunds, not some sort of special wage subsidy for employers or a welfare check. There is no reason why the tax refund could not be spread out over the year with some of it returned in each paycheck, so people could receive more take-home pay—a true negative tax. Indeed, such a negative tax is allowed under the current rules, though few families request it because the benefits have been small until recently.[36]

Thus, in every sense, for a low-wage worker, the EITC would seem like a pay raise—the exact opposite of welfare. The EITC helps the working poor while mainly avoiding the conundrums. The rewards of work are increased, not diminished. Benefits go only to those with an earned income. People are helped without any need of a stigmatizing, invasive, and often degrading welfare system, and their autonomy is increased, not decreased. Since it truly would be part of the tax system (unlike the badly named negative income tax, which really was welfare all over again), people would not be isolated. The negative impact on the work effort of the poor is likely to be small if it exists at all, but the benefits to the working poor may be large.[37] And employers would have no reason to change their hiring practices. Their cost of doing business would essentially be unchanged except for slight additional administrative costs for employers who provided negative withholding.

Since the working poor are usually two-parent families, an

expanded EITC would especially help two-parent families. Moreover, the EITC could be adjusted to vary according to the size of a family so that the biggest raise in pay would go to families with the most children and the greatest need.

The only real incentive or value problem with the EITC as a way of helping full-time working-poor families is that the subsidy must be phased out at some level of income. Thus, under the current system, families with earnings of $10,000 get a credit of $850, and families with earnings of $11,000 get $750. That is, in this middle part of the income distribution, an additional $1,000 in earnings brings in only $900 in net income because of the loss of $100 in tax credits.[38] Still even though tax benefits are reduced for earnings above a certain level, families who are entitled to the EITC are better off with the credit than without it. I find this a small and not particularly worrisome price to pay for subsidizing the work of the poor.

Other Steps.   Still other things can be done to help the working poor and to reinforce work. Any way in which the government can help to provide *child care* for working families makes work more attractive and practical, especially for mothers who still provide most of the child care. There are strong equity and access arguments in favor of such support. Many believe that the cost of day care is a significant deterrent to work for some mothers, particularly low-income mothers. Child care can be particularly important for single mothers (who will be discussed in chapter 5), but the costs and quality are likely to have an influence on the work of married mothers as well.

A modest child care tax credit is already available for families with second earners and for single parents, but it is of little benefit to the poor. Of the $3.4 billion projected cost of the credit for 1988, only $20 million, or less than 1 percent, is expected to go to families with incomes of less than $10,000. There are several possible explanations for the low benefits to the poor. Unlike the EITC, the dependent care credit is not refundable. The credit is applied only to reduce taxes that are owed. Most low-income families owe little taxes, so they get no benefit even if they have day care expenses. A report from the Ways and Means Committee of the U.S. House of Representatives mentioned several other factors that may be important.[39] In two-parent homes, both parents must work for the family to qualify for benefits, and many low-income families have only one worker. (But participation is low in single-parent families as well in which only one person must work.) The report also noted that for the large majority of low-income working mothers with a child under age 5, a relative provided child care.

Surely the child care credit ought to be refundable. A work subsidy that discriminates against the poor certainly seems counterproductive, to say nothing of ethically troubling. But whether the credit should be expanded in addition to making it refundable ought to be debated in the much larger context of women's rights and the overall needs of children. The dramatic increase in the number of mothers who are working outside the home obviously makes day care a critical issue for families and children in the 1980s and 1990s. Still, a policy on day care is not primarily a policy on poverty—at least not for most two-parent families. The majority of benefits would go to the nonpoor (which would make the policy expensive). In the broader debate, it should be remembered, however, that expanded child care arrangements have the appealing features of encouraging work and autonomy and helping people become integrated into the society. And low-income families are likely to be in the least favorable position to afford the cost of day care.[40]

Another alternative is a *children's allowance.* Most industrialized countries have some sort of payment for all families with children as a way of supporting, protecting, and often promoting children. The benefits are often small. Alfred Kahn and Sheila B. Kamerman reported that the subsidy per child is typically between 3 percent and 6 percent of the average production worker's earnings (in France it is over 10 percent).[41] In the United States, such percentages would translate into roughly $500–$1,000 per child. The appeal of a children's allowance is its universality and simplicity. Since allowances are usually provided for all children regardless of income, no stigma or isolation is associated with receiving it. Nor are any welfarelike administrative arrangements necessary. So a modest children's allowance can serve as a kind of low guaranteed income that a family can build on.

A children's allowance could be implemented in a variety of ways. It could be sent out as a monthly check to all families or it could show up as tax credit used in calculating income taxes. Our tax code has a standard deduction for each child, which means that taxable income is reduced for each child (the deduction is currently $2,000 per child). With $2,000 less in taxable income, taxes paid are reduced by $2,000 times the tax rate. The deduction is thus worth $200 in reduced taxes for someone with a 10 percent tax rate and $600 to someone with a 30 percent tax rate. Since the wealthy have higher tax rates it is more valuable to them. An alternative treatment would be to give a refundable tax credit rather than a deduction. Such a credit is like a children's allowance—the money is simply subtracted from taxes owed, and credit in excess of taxes owed is refunded. The deduction could be converted at no net cost to a roughly $500 refundable tax credit or children's allowance that would give all families the same dollar benefit.[42] (Of course, low-income families would be better off while high-income families would be worse off.)

A children's allowance is appealing when it is used as a low-level supplement of income. Such a benefit can be a foundation for a family to build on. But if the allowance is set at a high level, it becomes simply a guaranteed annual income for families. The higher the benefit, the more the program must wrestle with the helping conundrums. By offering a reasonable level of security, it may discourage work. It will appear to reward people for becoming parents and thus seem to be subsidizing births. If it is not heavily targeted, it will be expensive. It should come as no surprise that most countries have only modest allowances.

I would favor the conversion and possible expansion of the tax deduction for children into a tax credit. The additional money would help the poor without acting like a guaranteed annual income. But we should rely most heavily on programs that address the causes of poverty, rather than just provide unrestricted money.

Making Work Pay—A Simple Plan. Suppose that two simple changes had been implemented in 1986: the minimum wage was raised to $4.40 per hour and the EITC, which was already expanded in the tax reform bill of 1986, was roughly doubled and adjusted for the size of families. Suppose that a family of four would get a 30 percent credit for earnings up to $9,000 and a family of two might get an 18 percent credit up to $6,200 (the exact numbers are not important). The idea is that we could easily make work pay and thereby help the working poor without having to confront the conundrums. Table 4.5 illustrates what the impact of this plan would have been in 1986 on a family of four with a full-year full-time worker earning the minimum wage.

In 1986, the poverty line for a family of four was just over $11,000. Thus, under the proposed plan, a family that received some form of medical protection, either through an employer or from the government, would effectively be over the poverty

TABLE 4.5

The Earnings, Income, and Wages of a Minimum-Wage Worker under the Current Situation and under the Proposal to Make Work Pay

Earnings, Income, and Wages	Current Situation	Make-Work-Pay Proposal
Earnings[a]	$ 6,700	$ 8,800
Less Social Security taxes[b]	−$479	−$629
Plus EITC[c]	+$868	+$2,640
Total income	$ 7,089	$ 10,811
Minimum wage	$ 3.35	$ 4.40
Effective wage[a]	$ 3.54	$ 5.41

[a]Assumes 2,000 hours of work.
[b]Social Security taxes were 7.15 percent in 1986.
[c]Under the current law, the EITC is 14 percent up to $6,200. Under my proposal, it is 30 percent up to $9,000 for a family of four.

line. Hence, the plan would virtually eliminate poverty for families in which one person could find work at the minimum wage. If additional family members went to work or the original worker found a higher-paying job, the family would improve its position still further.[43] In effect, the pay for the lone working adult in this family would be increased to $5.41. We would have taken a large step toward eliminating poverty among the working poor without making major changes in current programs, without a new bureaucracy, and without giving these families a cent of welfare. The reward for working would be higher and the families would have more control over their lives, be stronger, and be even more a part of the economic mainstream.

How much would it cost? I cannot estimate exactly, since the plan involves changing wage rates that would affect the costs of the EITC. The current EITC is projected to cost roughly $6 billion in fiscal year 1988.[44] My guess is that we would at least have to double that expenditure to spend an additional $6 billion.[45] This increase would amount to one-fifth of 1 percent of the gross national product (GNP) and two-thirds of 1 percent of the federal budget. In exchange, we would make work pay and send a clear signal to our most poorly paid workers that their efforts are really valued. Even if the price tag was $20 billion, would we not be willing to pay one-half of 1 percent of our GNP to make work pay for the poor?

I have not worked out every detail of the plan. I am only offering a simple insight. A sizable proportion of poor two-parent families have someone who is working all year long. A large majority have someone who is working at least part of the year. It is not hard to find a way to help these families and to reinforce our values if we are willing to spend a modest amount of money. None of this money will go to people who do no work. It will all go to the working poor—the plan does not encourage dependence. It rewards work and responsibility. It is not an alternative to work. It provides a better level of pay for those who are willing to work.

And this program would actually cost less each year as the economy grows and real wages rise. If the economy grows and the benefits trickle down in the form of higher pay, the amount spent on the EITC will fall because the EITC automatically phases itself out when fewer and fewer people have the low earnings needed to qualify for benefits. Thus, the program would offer support while we were waiting for benefits to trickle down.

This proposal has a few weaknesses. It does not target perfectly. Some may argue that it would create some disincentives to earn over the income level at which the EITC would be phased out. Raising the minimum wage would reduce employment somewhat. And the proposal does not help the poor with day care. For this latter problem, I would add a third provision to the plan: a refundable tax credit for child care. Still, as one who is used to looking for ways to improve welfare and has found myself struggling with the helping conundrums time and again, it amazes me how much a relatively simple set of policies can accomplish without getting caught in any of the conundrums.

Transitional Support

If we did nothing more than ensure that everyone had medical protection and make work pay, we would go a long way toward solving the poverty of two-parent families. But there will still be people who are unemployed and not receiving unemployment insurance and people who are disabled for a short time and not receiving Social Security or workers' compensation. For the most part, these people will have worked in low-paying and insecure jobs but are now out of work. A higher rate of pay will not help those who are not working. What can we do to help them without greatly expanding our welfare system?

Unemployment insurance could be liberalized and expanded.

Minimum-hour requirements could be substituted for minimum earnings to avoid discriminating against low-income workers. The duration of benefits could be extended. A higher minimum benefit could be established. All these steps would help the poor, and they might help reverse the troubling trend of unemployment insurance providing help to fewer and fewer of the unemployed.

Still one must proceed with caution. The links to past work are one reason why unemployment insurance is popular, and limited duration prevents real dependence. Moreover, the vast majority of unemployment benefits do not go to poor families; they protect the middle class. Wholesale expansion will aid the poor only modestly.

Social Security could be changed to include temporary coverage for short-term disability. I think there is merit in this proposal, but the time necessary for certification may mean that people would not get help until after they no longer needed it. And one would have to wrestle with defining a legitimate short-term disability.

So one is left with the temptation to offer support to the unemployed and short-term disabled through a welfare system. But then our well-laid plans would begin to crumble. For if the welfare system is generous, we would still have to fight the conundrums. Even with the proposed increase in the reward for working, some people might choose to receive welfare rather than work. People would be isolated and "on welfare." And the public would object.

Think about the nature of the problem for these people. We have already seen that the poverty of most two-parent families is short-term poverty. Usually, the parent or parents have lost a job and are looking for work. In some cases, they are disabled for a short time. What these people usually need is help to get over a temporary period of hardship and to find a job or overcome some other problem.

I submit that the best way to treat this problem is to offer true transitional assistance, with a heavy emphasis on employment and training and supportive services. When people come on hard times, they could apply for transitional aid. They would be offered a wide choice of services and could get a cash stipend while they were not working. The services could range from job matching to vocational training to social services to child care. But the program would be strictly transitional; after some period, at least the cash assistance would come to an end. That period might be 12, 24, or even 36 months. Once people had used up the transitional aid, they would not be eligible for any more until they had worked some minimum number of weeks (like 50 or even 100 weeks), and then only a limited extension might be granted.

To some, this form of aid may look like another type of welfare, but I think it would be more like a combination of unemployment insurance and training than welfare. Unemployment insurance provides benefits for a limited time, but welfare benefits last forever. Welfare is an alternative to work. During the period when someone was collecting transitional assistance, such aid could be an alternative to work, but there would be a strong incentive to go back to work quickly so as to save as much of your transitional assistance as possible for other periods of hardship.[46]

It would be clear to administrators, beneficiaries, and the public that what was being offered was a chance to move into a more secure position—a chance to find some meaningful work. The goal would be to help people support themselves. People would be offered training, counseling, services, and temporary income support. The rest would be up to them. The goals of a welfare system are far more ambiguous and conflicting. To some, the goal is to guarantee a decent standard of living. To others, it is to help people become self-supporting. With mixed goals, nothing is done well. In the end, there is little support, little dignity, little work, and little training. Transitional support is an attempt to reverse that pattern.

Last-Resort Jobs

A transitional support system would provide most of the support needed by people who were not working for a short time. However, a few people would exhaust their transitional support and still be without work. Certainly, some people would not be able to find jobs even though they were willing to work. Are we to leave these people to fend for themselves? We often do that now in states that offer no welfare to families with two healthy adults. A far more humane approach would be to offer a limited number of minimum-wage jobs to those who had exhausted their transitional assistance. Thus, no one would be left in a position in which he or she could not be self-supporting. Working two-parent families need never be poor. They would always have something to fall back on even in the worst of times, but that something would be a low-paying governmental job—not welfare.

I would anticipate that the jobs program would be small, since, as I noted previously, only a tiny percentage of two-parent families experience long-term poverty. If the program turned out to be large, even though it paid nothing more than the minimum wage and was available only to those in families with children who had exhausted their transitional aid, then there clearly would be a shortage of private jobs and it would be inappropriate and irresponsible for society to expect people to support themselves without offering them work.

What about people who refuse to work or claim they cannot? Such people ought to be evaluated on a case-by-case basis. But if society has guaranteed that people who find jobs can achieve a modest level of security, if it has offered transitional assistance for those who are struggling through temporary hard times, and if it has offered jobs as a last resort, then I would argue that the society has met its obligations to the healthy.

Any proposal for a last-resort job program is highly controversial. Liberals would worry that it would pay poorly. In this case, the jobs would pay only the minimum wage, but with the EITC, it would be a "living wage." Union members worry that last-resort workers would be used to perform jobs that otherwise would be done by higher paid regular workers and that last-resort workers would weaken the power of the unions. These seem to be legitimate concerns. But workfare suffers the same problems. And these jobs would surely be temporary in nature. Few people are going to find a minimum-wage job attractive if they can find a higher paying job. And, in the past, unions have found ways to protect their position when job programs were offered.

Conversely, conservatives would worry about the expense and administration of a major program of last-resort jobs. Again, I doubt this program would be anything but small. Moreover, if conservatives really believed their rhetoric—that anyone can get a job who wants one—they would also think that few, if any, people would be attracted to the low-paying governmental jobs that would be offered.

Help for the Working Poor

Today, the stereotypical poor person seems to be a child in a single-parent family in the ghetto, who is locked in a hostile world and learning antisocial behavior that will lead to continued poverty in the next generation. Many commentators tell us that people in the ghetto have lost their morality and their work ethic and that it is time to get tough with them so they will learn to behave according to society's values and rules. This chapter has described a different kind of poverty. Half the poor children in America are in two-parent families. In most of these families, someone is working or trying to work. These families *are* playing by the rules. Unfortunately, they are losing the game. Indeed, after transfers, poor two-parent families who are working are often the poorest and most insecure of the poor! If the country is serious about supporting the traditional values of family, work, autonomy, and community, then it must find a way to help these people.

More welfare is not the answer because money per se is not the problem. The main problems are low wages and short-term difficulties such as unemployment—coupled with a general level of medical insecurity. And so the most logical policies are ones that will address those needs. I recommend a combination of medical security, measures to make jobs pay, transitional assistance, and last-resort jobs.

Americans do not believe that society ought to guarantee that every healthy person has a minimum income. What they do believe is that everyone who is willing to work ought to be able to make it in America and achieve some real measure of independence. That is what these suggestions are all about. My proposals mean that any family with two healthy adults will not be poor if at least one person works. Private work plus tax supplements will ensure that work pays enough to support most families. Transitional assistance will guarantee that those with a temporary hardship will get the support and training they deserve. And the last-resort jobs will be there for the small number who need longer term support. Anyone who is willing to work will not be poor.

Contrast this view with the extreme conservative or liberal visions. Conservatives are content to proclaim that everyone can make it in America. But, somewhat paradoxically, they say trickle-down is the best way to help low-income families. We have seen working families who are not making it. This plan is designed mostly to help the people who the conservatives say do not exist: poor people who are willing and able to help themselves. Under this plan, these poor people will not be granted a guaranteed income; instead, they will be guaranteed a chance to achieve security and independence through work.

Liberals talk about training and jobs, but when these efforts do not solve the problem by themselves, they ultimately rely on welfare. They say that welfare will help the working poor, the transitional poor, and the long-term unemployed. Welfare does a poor job of helping any of these groups. Welfare conflicts with work; it does not reinforce it. A program that offers long-term aid has a hard time emphasizing transitional help. It makes far more sense to solve different problems in different ways. Raise the wages of the working poor. Offer transitional assistance to help people through a period of temporary hardship and unemployment. Provide jobs for the long-term unemployed. And take medical protection out of the welfare system.

If we want to reinforce our values, if we want to support motivated two-parent families who are working, or who wish they were, then neither the conservative "do nothing" nor the liberal "welfare" approach will work. We need to help the the working poor by offering support that helps them help themselves.

5

Poverty Among Single-Parent Families

Single-parent families need help. Roughly one-quarter of America's children live in single-parent families. Even after transfers, the poverty rate for children in single-parent families exceeds 50 percent. And I reported previously that poverty in single-parent families lasts much longer than it does in two-parent families.

In chapter 4, I suggested that the poverty of two-parent families is relatively easy to understand. Aside from disability, it is the poverty of the working poor—indigence arising from low wages and unemployment. The poverty of single-parent families is more complex. At least three different factors are directly involved in combination. Part of the problem is the same set of labor market difficulties faced by the working poor in two-parent families: low wages and unemployment.

But, in addition, single parents typically must balance the dual roles of nurturer and provider. Doing both well can seem almost impossible. Finally, single parents are often supported by a welfare system that humiliates, stigmatizes, and isolates them while offering limited support or incentives to become independent.

The combined effect of these three factors—job market problems, the dual nurturer/provider role, and an isolating and often counterproductive welfare system—is to trap many single mothers and their children in poverty and dependence. If we are serious about helping people move toward independence, we will have to correct all three problems. Ameliorating any one alone will have only a modest effect, but improving all three could have a profound impact.

One note of definition: I will be focusing on female-headed families with children in this chapter—that is, independent family households headed by a woman. I will use the terms female-headed families and single-parent families as synonyms. There are a small number of single-parent families headed by men. There are also some very young single parents living with their two parents and therefore not counted among "female-headed families" (they are living in husband-wife families according to census definitions). The situation facing these other types of nonintact families, while obviously distinct, is similar in many respects to that facing the female-headed families discussed here.

Understanding Poverty in Female-Headed Families

I have emphasized the unstartling proposition that poverty is not "caused" by a lack of money but by more fundamental problems. If we are to develop nonwelfare alternatives that really eliminate poverty, we need to understand and treat the true causes. Previously I noted that the causes of poverty in two-parent families are sometimes a matter of interpretation. This is even truer for single-parent families.

Consider, for example, the case of a 25-year-old divorced woman with two young children who stays home to take care of the children. The woman's middle-class ex-husband owes child support, but his contributions are irregular at best. The woman relies chiefly on welfare and food stamps for support, although she works from time to time. When she does work, she often finds she is no better off financially than when she does not. Either way she is poor. And the strain on her and her children from work and child care is considerable.

What is the reason for her poverty? One interpretation might be that the mother is not working enough to support her family. Some would say that she is not accepting her responsibility to provide for her children. Instead of ensuring the economic independence of the household by work, she seems content to live on the government's largess. According to this interpretation, part of the problem may be that welfare benefits are too high and thus reduce the need for the woman to work.

A diametrically opposite view would be that the mother has quite reasonably decided that the protection and rearing of her children are more important than working outside the home at this stage in her children's lives. In this case, welfare benefits are too low because they leave her family poor and insecure.

Yet another possibility is that the woman would like to work, but no jobs are available—at least no decent jobs. Or it could be that high-quality day care is too expensive. In this case, it is the lack of well-paying jobs or the limited availability of day care that are the problems.

Still another view could be that the absent father is failing in his responsibility to provide support for the children. With no outside support and young children, the woman has little choice but to rely on welfare. And what about the decision to split up in the first place? Maybe the father bears most of the responsibility because he abandoned the family. But maybe the wife left and will not let him see the children. Maybe she left because she loved another man or because her husband was abusing her.

And what if the woman was not divorced? Suppose she had never been married, and the two children were born out of wedlock. To the already long list of causes, we would have to add another possibility: irresponsible parenting decisions. Perhaps the conception of the first child was an accident because she was ignorant of birth control devices, but what about the second child? However, what if the father of her children had no job and he did not look like he'd be a good provider? Perhaps the economic position of men is to blame.

In the case of two parents, simply deciding what was a reasonable set of expectations allowed us to choose easily from among the various explanations. But the poverty of single parents does not allow such straightforward isolation of a single cause for a given family. However, the three interrelated factors just mentioned collectively explain a large part of the poverty problems of single mothers.

Labor Market Problems

I devoted most of chapter 4 to discussing the labor market problems of two-parent families. Poor two-parent families often suffer from low wages, unemployment, and medical insecurity. I will not repeat that discussion here except to state the obvious. Whatever pay and unemployment problems two-parent families face, single-parent families face them far more severely.

Women's wages are unquestionably lower than men's, so a single mother is likely to have an even tougher time pushing her family over the poverty line through her own earnings. Women often enter the labor market late and thus have little seniority to help protect them from layoffs or to qualify them for unemployment compensation. And there is no second adult who can go to work to compensate for their low earnings. Finally, there are the children. A working single mother, especially a full-time working mother, faces some difficult obstacles, from finding and paying for day care to establishing a system of supports for handling emergencies.

Poor single mothers who work full time get almost the same callous treatment by the social welfare system as do their two-parent counterparts. They usually qualify only for food stamps. Whatever logic there is in helping working poor two-parent families obviously applies here as well. Those who are unemployed have the option of going on welfare, but we shall see shortly that welfare offers its own hazards, frustrations, and insecurity.

Dual Nurturing/Provider Role

One of the most common complaints about single mothers generally and welfare mothers in particular is that they are not working enough. After all, most married mothers now work. Surely, we can expect the same from single mothers. But what is a reasonable expectation? How much work should we expect single mothers to do?

Since the analogy is made so often, a natural place to start is to look at the work of adults in two-parent families. All families must fulfill two roles: a nurturing/child-rearing role and a provider role. In two-parent families, these roles are shared in a variety of ways. However, when we look at the levels of work, it is obvious that, on the average, the roles of men and women are different. Table 5.1 shows the work levels of husbands and wives in all families with children (poor and nonpoor) and the reasons they give for not working more when they are less than fully employed.

Husbands usually work fully if they are not disabled. If they do not work fully, they usually work part of the year and report that they were looking for work during the remainder of the time. Wives sometimes work fully but, more commonly, they work part time or not at all. They usually cite family responsibilities as the reason they do not work more. It is true that most married mothers work—almost two-thirds of wives report

TABLE 5.1

Work, Unemployment, and Disability Among Husbands and Wives in Families with Children (1984)

Level of Work	Percentage Distribution of Husbands	Percentage Distribution of Wives
Worked full year full time	77	27
Healthy, worked only part time or part year because		
Unable to find more work	12	7
Household/family responsibilities or other	4	31
Healthy, did not work at all because		
Unable to find work	1	1
Household/family responsibilities or other	1	31
Ill, disabled, or retired[a]	5	3
Total	100	100

[a]Includes a small number of persons who worked part year and reported that illness, disability, or retirement prevented them from working further.

Source: Author's tabulations of data from U.S. Bureau of the Census, March 1985 Current Population Survey for persons in families of all incomes.

working at some point during the year. But only 27 percent work full year, full time. Part-time work is the norm. And even fewer mothers with very young children work fully.

A provocative question is, Do we want single mothers to behave like husbands or like wives? Those who argue that single mothers ought to support their families through their own efforts are implicitly asking that they behave like husbands. If a woman is to have any real hope of supporting herself and her family, she will have to work all the time. We have already seen that a minimum-wage job will not support a family of three at the poverty level. Thus, a woman with two children and no other form of support will have to work full time, all year, at a job that pays more than the current minimum wage to keep her family out of poverty.

Conversely, those who say that single mothers ought to have choices about how much to work outside the home are saying that single mothers ought to have the flexibility of wives. Some wives choose full-time work, some chose part-time work, and some do no market work at all. Many argue that single mothers should be able to make the same decisions.

Either of these positions has troublesome implications. Asking single mothers to behave like husbands is asking a lot indeed. Only a small minority of married mothers work fully. Those who work part time apparently believe that the rewards they now get from working do not compensate for the time they would have to spend away from their children and home, for the cost of day care, and for the headaches associated with the full-time jobs they may be able to get. And work is even more difficult for single mothers than for wives. There is no one to help when the child is sick, no one to take the child to the dentist, and no one to help with the day-to-day crises. And surely the problems of day care and economic opportunity are at least as serious for single mothers as for married ones.

Moreover, most single-parent families are formed when a family splits apart. The period following a split is usually a time of stress for the parents and children alike. When a married mother goes to work, she may do so in a period when her family has achieved some stability. If a single mother is forced to go to work when she has just become the head of a family, work may increase the stress and tension she is feeling during an already difficult period.

Even more important is the question of what is best for the children. Voluntary full-time work by married mothers with young children is still controversial in both professional and popular circles. And there seems little doubt that a concern for the children must be an important part of the typical married mother's decision to work part time. Do we really believe that most children being raised by their mothers alone would be better off if that parent were forced by economic necessity to work all the time when so few married mothers are doing so? Do we really think that a family that is undergoing great stress is best served by adding to the pressures on it?

So perhaps the logical thing to do is to give single mothers the same options as wives. After all, their lives are generally much more difficult than are those of their married counterparts. But if we are to give single mothers the same choices as married mothers, we will have to provide some additional sources of financial support for them. Wives can rely on their husbands for support. Single mothers rarely can rely on enough child support to support their families. Thus, if we are to give single mothers the choice about whether to work, welfare seems almost inevitable.

If we provide sufficient welfare support to give single mothers a full choice, we have to recognize that some single mothers will choose not to work at all, just as many wives do. They will go into the welfare system. But then the attendant conundrums will be inevitable: work disincentives, the seeming financial encouragement to form single-parent families, isolation, and stigma. Some children will, no doubt, grow up in homes in which their single mothers rarely work at all, just as many children grow up in homes in which their married mothers rarely work.

Some feminists argue that being dependent on the government for support is no different from being dependent on a husband. I suspect that most people find this argument unconvincing. Income provided by a spouse looks and feels different, in terms of power, autonomy, initiative, and social stigma. In a two-parent home, when one parent works and the other raises the children, the *family* can still be independent, and the children still have working role models. In a single-parent home in which the mother does not work, the children grow up in an environment in which no one is working, in which the family is dependent on outside sources of support, and in which the family has little sense of control or power over its destiny. If we are worried about children, it is far from clear that a welfare system that allows some children to grow up in a welfare home is a good one. The longer a woman is out of the labor force, the harder it is for her to reenter it and earn a decent wage. Employers are more skeptical of her abilities, her job skills are likely to be lost, and her connections probably are eroded.

Finally, there remains the danger that the public will come to see the welfare system as promoting the formation of single-parent homes. Welfare will be perceived as being an alternative to having a husband, and, in some sense, it will be. The public has never seen welfare as a right—something that people ought to be able to count on indefinitely if their private means of support are inadequate.

So neither alternative—full work or full flexibility—looks attractive in today's world. When the welfare system was designed in the 1930s, it was not so hard. Most single mothers were widows who clearly were not responsible for their condition. And few married mothers worked. But now with single parenthood reflecting decisions about divorce and childbirth, there is a greater sense that single mothers bear some responsibility for their position and thus ought to bear some responsibility for the support of their family. And their long-term dependence on welfare is a genuine worry.

Single mothers are not the same as either husbands or wives. They typically are asked to fill the dual roles of provider and nurturer. They are sometimes in a period of stress and transition. It strikes me as unrealistic and undesirable to expect single parents to concentrate primarily on one role or the other over the long term. A more sensible idea is to look for ways to allow them to fulfill both roles simultaneously and effectively. Immediately after a single-parent family is formed, it may be uncaring, unrealistic, and even counterproductive to expect the mother to work. But, over the longer term, part-time work seems the obvious solution as long as it can be made practical. If a woman could get out of the welfare system and gain some control of her life by working part-time, she could balance her roles. Part-time work would give her the flexibility to handle crises. It would give her the chance to be with her children. Yet it also would ensure that she was providing some support for the household and maintaining contact with the labor market. It could be a stepping stone to full-time work.

By expecting single mothers to work part time, we would not be expecting them to behave like either husbands or wives. Since many nonworking wives achieve some measure of economic independence because of their husbands' earnings, we are expecting more work of single mothers than of some wives. But we stop short of insisting on the full-time work expected of most husbands. There will no doubt be special cases—mothers with very young children or nearly grown children, for example—who might be viewed differently, but, as a starting point, half-time work seems reasonable. However, in the current marketplace and in the welfare system, part-time work for single mothers makes little sense. Indeed, full-time work often makes little sense. This situation brings us to the third problem.

The Nature of the Welfare System

Our welfare/income support system sometimes seems to be the worst of all worlds. It antagonizes, stigmatizes, isolates, and humilitates. It discourages work rather than reinforcing and supporting it. It gives few aids or signals to point people toward self-support. It offers only two real options: work all the time or be on welfare. Part-time work usually does not make sense under the current system. In combination with the labor-market problems and the dual-role dilemma, it often leaves women who have few skills with only one sensible choice: be on welfare and remain poor.

Consider the situation of a healthy woman with two children, one a toddler, the other in elementary school. Such a woman now has three potential sources of support: her own earnings, welfare, and the absent father. Unfortunately, only one-third of all single parents receive any child support. Never-married mothers virtually never get child support. Even among divorced mothers, child support payments are received only half the time. And those who do receive child support often get so little and receive it so irregularly that it is not a reliable or practical means of support for the family. This situation will command a great deal of our attention shortly.

But for now, assume that the woman is typical and receives no child support payments. Thus, she is left with just two sources of support: welfare and earnings. Let us say that she lives in a state that pays Aid to Families with Dependent Children (AFDC) benefits to a family of three of $400 per month, or $4,800 per year.[1] If she does not work at all, she will get $4,800 per year in AFDC and $1,484 in food stamps, for a total of $6,284, which is well below the poverty line of $8,700 for a family of three (in 1986).

What if she goes to work? Suppose she can find inexpensive day care for which she pays just $1 per hour for her toddler's care and another $1 per hour for after-school care for her other child if she works more than half time. Then child care will cost her $1,000 annually if she works half time and $3,000 if she works full time.[2] Consider how much she would keep if she went to work and collected all the welfare and food-stamp benefits for which she was eligible. Table 5.2 summarizes her position.

This woman would essentially be no better off financially if she was working unless she worked full time at $5 an hour or more. Furthermore, if she worked, she would lose her Medicaid benefits (after four or nine months, assuming she did not qualify for a "medically needy" program). It seems unlikely that a $5-per-hour job would have good medical protection. Her net income from work, after paying for day care, would not bring her above the poverty line until she earned almost $6 per hour. Even at that rate of pay, her income would be only $2,700 higher than it would be if she did not work. From her $6-per-hour job, she would effectively keep $1.35 per hour.

This woman's case is not extreme. I have assumed modest

TABLE 5.2

Earnings, Taxes, Benefits, and Total Income for a Single Parent and Two Children (1986)[a]

Level of Work and Wages	Earnings	Day Care	Taxes and Earned Income Tax Credit	AFDC and Food Stamps	Disposable Income[a][b]	Receipt of Medicaid
No work	$0	$0	$0	$6,284	$6,284	Yes
Half time at the minimum wage[c]	$3,350	−$1,000	+$229	$4,577	$7,156	Yes
Full time at the minimum wage[c]	$6,700	−$3,000	+$373	$2,744	$6,816	Yes
Full time at $4.00 per hour	$8,000	−$3,000	+$171	$1,624	$6,795	No
Full time at $5.00 per hour	$10,000	−$3,000	−$172	$970	$7,798	No
Full time at $6.00 per hour	$12,000	−$3,000	−$515	$538	$9,023	No

[a]The figures in the table were derived using the regulations of the new tax law as of January 1987.

[b]Earnings plus AFDC and food stamps less taxes and day care.

[c]The minimum wage rate is $3.35 per hour.

SOURCE: Author's calculations. Modeled after an unnumbered table from Committee on Ways and Means, U.S. House of Representatives, *Background Material and Data on Programs within the Jurisdiction of the Committee on Ways and Means* (Washington, D.C.: U.S. Government Printing Office, 1987), p. 404.

day care costs and counted *no* additional work expenses like transportation or clothing. Nor have I chosen a state that pays particularly high benefits or counted any possible housing subsidies. Often it makes even less sense to work than in this example. If the woman had no day care expenses, she could do somewhat better than in this example. But not as much better as it might appear because welfare benefits are adjusted for day care costs. Thus, her welfare benefits would be cut back faster when her earnings rose.

Of course, financial rewards are not the only issue. Work carries with it more control and pride than does welfare. But a mother must still raise, feed, clothe, and protect her children. If she cannot do that realistically through work, welfare is the only real alternative.

Unfortunately, welfare implies far more than receiving a check. It requires stepping into an administrative apparatus that seems designed to frustrate, antagonize, and discourage those who are seeking help. Someone who is enmeshed in the public assistance system may have to deal with an intake worker, an emergency assistance worker, an eligibility worker, a caseworker, an employment and training worker, a food stamps eligibility worker, and others. If she wants other help, such as social services or housing or energy assistance, she must often deal with additional welfare personnel.

A potential recipient must satisfy the rules of each program for information, verification, and validation. She will often have long waits, she may have to make several different appointments, and she may even have to visit several different offices. If, as is almost certain, she has not brought the proper documentation with her, she will need to make several trips to the welfare office, often with her children in tow. She will have to tell her life story several times to workers who are supposed to be alert to catching applicants who are committing fraud. If the woman should go to work and still try to collect welfare, things get even worse. The system will likely identify her as an error-prone case (one that makes the welfare department look bad) because it is so easy for earnings to be misreported and, therefore, the caseworker will require even more information and validation.

In most states, a woman with no child under age 6 must participate in the work incentive program (WIN).[3] Usually, little training or other services are available and those that exist often go to the most job ready—those who need it the least and thus are the cheapest to serve. If the woman has children under age 6, her chances of getting services are even more remote because the "mandatory WIN" clients must be served first. Clients frequently have little choice about which program to enroll in; they are told where to go and when.

So imagine what happens to a woman who has just split up with her husband or who has recently had a child. The woman may never have worked, and she usually has small children. She often feels desperate. When she applies for welfare, she expects help and understanding. Although some of the welfare workers may be sympathetic, she finds that she has entered a maze of bureaucratic rules and regulations that she hardly understands and that there are many hurdles to overcome. Some welfare offices in some states treat people better than do others. But welfare inevitably requires that income, assets, and living situations be checked and verified, for there are people who abuse the system. Errors and fraud undermine the credibility and raise the cost of the system. To reduce fraud, the welfare system demands considerable verification. To limit errors, the system has people who specialize in one or another type of service. To target programs, the system offers several different programs under several different administrations. The result is a morass for the single mother.

Almost any AFDC recipient can tell stories of ludicrous and even inhumane treatment with seemingly endless requirements that must be satisfied. One activist recipient told me that the welfare system committed genocide by exhaustion. Another said she had eighteen different "bosses." Even in the best states, recipients seem to detest the system. It is not surprising, therefore, that those who work for welfare departments report that recipients are often cynical and apathetic, seem ungrateful for the system's generosity, and are resentful when asked to provide necessary information. Some of these workers are bitter because they are often paid only slightly more than the recipients receive.

It is easy to see why everyone hates the welfare system. The public sees a system that discourages work, allows dependence, and supports single parents. The recipients see a maze of rules and regulations that isolate, stigmatize, and, some say, brutalize them. Benefits are very low. Yet a woman who works full time at a minimum-wage job often does no better than her counterparts who do nothing and collect AFDC and food stamps. And part-time work is the cruelest joke of all. A woman is crazy to try and work part of the time and stay home with her children part of the time. She gets into even more hassles with the welfare system (because she must constantly report her earnings); she must arrange for day care; and she must cope with work, children, and sometimes several forms of welfare. Her reward for all this is a tiny amount of extra income and often less medical protection.

The 'Causes' of Poverty in Single-Parent Homes

So single mothers are often in a difficult job market with low wages, limited fringe benefits, and poor job security. They are trying to balance two roles—provider and nurturer. And they face a welfare system that isolates and dehumanizes, that offers little help, and that discourages work. What we see in terms of work and poverty is not difficult to understand in light of these problems.

There are four obvious groups of single mothers: those who work all the time, those who are healthy and work part of the time, those who are healthy and do no outside work, and those who are ill or disabled. The disabled face problems similar to the disabled in two-parent families, so I shall concentrate on the other three groups. Table 5.3 shows what percentage of women

TABLE 5.3

Work, Unemployment, and Disability Among Female Heads of Families (1984)

Level of Work	Distribution of All Female Heads with Children (%)	Pretransfer Poor[a] (%)	Distribution of Poor Female Heads with Children (%)
Worked full year full time	41	10	9
Healthy, worked only part time or part year because			
Unable to find more work	12	61	14
Household/ family responsibilities or other	13	64	16
Healthy, did not work at all because			
Unable to find work	4	94	8
Household/ family responsibilities or other	20	94	38
Ill, disabled, or retired[b]	10	70	15
Total	100	49	100

[a]Nongovernmental income below the poverty line. No adjustment is made for day care or work expenses.
[b]Includes a small number of persons who worked part year and reported that illness, disability, or retirement prevented them from working further.
SOURCE: Author's tabulations of data from U.S. Bureau of the Census, March 1985 Current Population Survey.

are in each situation and the reasons they give for not working more.

Just over 40 percent of single parents are working all the time. We have seen that the full-time work option seems to make sense only if women can command a reasonably high wage and have modest day care costs. Thus, it is not surprising that this is exactly the group that works fully. Special tabulations in table 5.4 show that over 80 percent of all single mothers who work full time are high school graduates. Indeed 40 percent have had some college or other additional education. Just 12 percent work at jobs that pay under four dollars per hour. More than half earn over seven dollars per hour.[4] Less than one-quarter have a child under age 6, and only 13 percent have more than two children. The ones who work full time are usually able to avoid poverty (because they can command a decent wage).

TABLE 5.4

Comparison of Selected Characteristics of All Healthy Female Family Heads by Level of Work (1984)

	Worked Full time, Full year (%)	Healthy, Worked Part time or Part year (%)	Healthy, Did Not Work (%)
Education of Head	100	100	100
Under 12 years	17	28	51
High school only	43	42	35
Over 12 years	40	30	14
Wage Rate	100	100	—
Under $4.00 per hour	12	37	—
$4.00–$4.99 per hour	12	16	—
$5.00–$5.99 per hour	13	14	—
$6.00–$6.99 per hour	12	9	—
$7.00 per hour and over	51	24	—
Number of Children	100	100	100
One or two	87	78	65
Three or more	13	22	35
Age of Youngest Child	100	100	100
Under 6	24	41	54
6–12	35	32	25
Over 12	41	27	21

NOTE: This table is for *all* single parents, poor and nonpoor. For completeness a statistical profile of *poor* female heads is included as an appendix to this chapter.
SOURCE: Author's tabulations of data from U.S. Bureau of the Census, March 1985 Current Population Survey.

Note, however, that the poverty line does not take account of work expenses like day care or transportation. Thus, some women who are not officially poor undoubtedly have disposable incomes below the poverty line. Still, this generally appears to be a group that is making it on their own.

At the other end of the spectrum are women who do not work at all. These women are often poorly educated and have more family responsibilities than do women in the other groups. The majority are high school dropouts; only 14 percent have had a post-high school education. Over half have children under age 6, and over one-third have more than two children. Virtually all are poor before transfers.

In the middle is the third group of women—those who work part time. These women seem to be trying to make it on their own but are not succeeding. It is not surprising that their characteristics fall in between those who work fully and those who do no work at all. Roughly 28 percent are high school dropouts, but less than a quarter were paid over seven dollars per hour for the period they worked. Some 41 percent have young children. These women seem to be trying to balance work, family, and welfare. Some are able to escape poverty either because they work almost full time at a reasonably high wage or because they receive reasonably generous child support.[5] But 60 percent remain poor before transfers.

If we compare table 5.3 with table 5.1, we see that single mothers work much more than do wives, but less than husbands. Whereas only 27 percent of wives work fully, 41 percent of single mothers do. And while one-third of wives say they are healthy but not working, only one-quarter of single mothers are in that position. Still, separate tabulations show that only 1 percent of the two-parent homes with two healthy adults had no parent working during the year, compared to 24 percent of single-parent homes. And, of course, when single mothers work anything less than full time, their families will almost certainly be poor.

It is obvious that single mothers would be poor indeed if they did not receive governmental supplements. Those who are poor often collect considerable benefits from many different programs. Still the money is rarely enough to push them out of poverty. Table 5.5 shows the percentage of single parents who receive certain types of benefits, and table 5.6 indicates what the money from these benefits does for them.

The pattern of benefits is predictable. The income of the disabled starts farthest below the poverty line, but they get the most money, and the vast majority have medical protection. Healthy women who are not working are even poorer before transfers. They get substantial benefits, but most are still left far short of the poverty line, and they also usually have medical protection. Part-time workers have less need (measured as the difference between their income and the poverty line) and they get far less support. Thus, they, too, remain far below the pov-

TABLE 5.5

Percentage of Poor Female-Headed Single-Parent Families Receiving Selected Types of Benefits (1984)[a]

Type of Family	Percentage of Each Type Family Reporting Receipt of:			
	Social Security Benefits	Employment-related Benefits	Means-tested Benefits	No Benefits
Full-time working poor	14	5	52	37
Partially employed poor	10	20	70	19
Nonworking poor	14	4	89	6
Disabled or retired poor	48	17	78	6
All Poor Female-headed families	18	11	78	13

[a]The rows total to more than 100 percent because some families collected more than one type of benefit.
SOURCE: Author's tabulations of data from U.S. Bureau of the Census, March 1985 Current Population Survey; excludes medical benefits.

TABLE 5.6

Effect of the Social Welfare System on Poor Female-Headed Families (1984)

Type of Family	Average Income Deficit before Benefits[a]	Average Governmental Benefits[b]	Percentage Removed From Poverty	Average Remaining Income Deficit for Those Still Poor[c]	Percentage with No Medical Protection
Full-time working poor	$2,679	$1,929	31	$2,244	31
Partially employed poor	$5,222	$3,520	26	$3,192	29
Nonworking poor	$8,999	$6,400	15	$3,549	12
Disabled or retired poor	$7,956	$6,843	33	$3,504	15
All poor single female-headed parent families	$7,136	$5,192	23	$3,338	19

[a]Difference between poverty line and nongovernmental income.
[b]Includes all nonmedical benefits. Housing assistance is valued according to Bureau of the Census' market value methodology.
[c]The figure is larger than the difference between the first and second columns because only those who remain poor are included in the calculation.
SOURCE: Author's tabulations of data from U.S. Bureau of the Census, March 1985 Current Population Survey; excludes medical benefits.

erty line after transfers. Full-time workers start with the least need and get even less in transfers. Both poor full-time and part-time workers often have no medical protection.

The refrain for single mothers is much the same as it is for two parents. Working people often do only slightly better than those who do not work. Full-time workers get little help. And the way in which part-time or part-year workers are treated is really disturbing. These women apparently are trying to balance their roles of nurturer and provider, yet they do only slightly better than those who are not working. Therefore, they remain stuck in the welfare system.[6]

So far we have talked only about how poverty looks in a single year. Even more dramatic patterns can be seen when we follow women over time after they form single-parent families. After a woman becomes a single parent, she often goes into the welfare system. Many women will use welfare only for transitional support. These women are typically the best educated, the ones with previous work experience, and those who came on the welfare rolls after a divorce and when they did not have very young children. But an important minority, at least one-quarter, will collect AFDC for ten or more years. These women are usually high school dropouts, never-married mothers, and those with little previous exposure to work, but not all are so disadvantaged. These long-term recipients also use a highly disproportionate share (almost two-thirds) of the funds spent on AFDC.[7]

Thus, although welfare often serves a transitional function, long-term dependence on welfare is a fact of life for a sizable minority of single mothers (and their children). And these figures overstate the extent to which women are able to use AFDC to get on their feet and then enter the labor force and be self-supporting. In fact, the most common way of leaving AFDC is through marriage. Only about 20 percent of the exits from AFDC are directly attributable to the increased earnings of women who remain single parents.[8] This percentage really should come as no surprise. Welfare typically offers no incentive, aid, or pressure to get off public assistance other than the unpleasant way in which recipients are treated.

This picture of single mothers and the way in which they are treated in our social welfare system is disturbing. Single mothers work much more than do wives, but many remain poor and dependent on welfare. The system offers only two real choices: work all the time or get welfare. And even some of the 40 percent who do work fully remain poor. The ones who make it out of poverty through their own earnings are usually the most advantaged. We are far away from a time when it will seem reasonable to expect all single mothers to support themselves.

And so we are left with a group of mothers who are not working, who collect welfare, and who see little prospect of working and getting off welfare. They are isolated and distrusted. They are seen as abusers of the government's largess in spite of their extreme poverty. They are accused of being lazy. But what can we expect from women with young children who cannot earn much more than the minimum wage under the current economic and social policy system? Full-time work appears to be difficult, both because of child care problems and the women's feeling that they should be with their children. Work is not likely to increase their income much and may leave them without medical protection. Part-time work is the worst of all worlds. Women get the hassles of work at a bad job yet suffer all the indignities of welfare anyway.

Not surprisingly, trickle-down does not work nearly so well for single-parent families as it does for two-parent families. In chapter 4, I showed that the poverty of two-parent families is incredibly sensitive to wages and unemployment. However, as figure 5.1 shows, despite some cyclical sensitivity, the poverty of single parents remains high in good times and in bad. The strong economy of Massachusetts again provides a good example. As I noted in chapter 4, the pretransfer poverty rate of two-parent families was less than 6 percent in Massachusetts, compared to 12 percent nationally in 1984. In contrast, the

Figure 5.1

Actual and Expected Poverty Rates for Children in Female-Headed Households

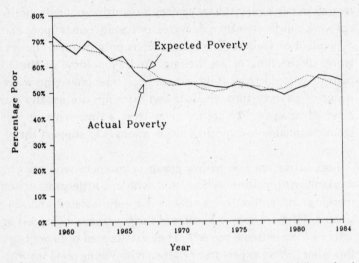

NOTE: Expected poverty based solely on the median earnings of full-year, full-time female workers and the unemployment rate.

pretransfer poverty rate for single parents in 1984 was 45 percent in Massachusetts and 49 percent nationally.[9] Thus, it is obvious that single parents have severe problems even during an economic boom.

It is not one factor, but all three in interaction—labor market difficulties, the dual role of single mothers, and the nature of the welfare system—that create the often impossible situation of many single mothers. Consider, then, the prospects for the nation's children over the next several decades. The majority of our children will spend some time in single-parent homes. Virtually all their mothers will be forced to choose: work all the time or go on welfare. We have seen that it is difficult for single mothers to make it on their own, given the current economic and policy structure. Therefore, most of our children are at risk of entering the welfare system and being economically insecure and dependent. When single parenthood is part of mainstream America but only a minority of single mothers can make it on their own, then something needs to be changed. It seems wrong that it should require heroic efforts for women to make it without welfare.

Welfare Reform—Big Promises, Modest Payoffs

The troubles of single parents and the problems in the welfare system have not gone unnoticed. There has recently been a plethora of proposals to reform welfare. Most of these proposals represent a sensible beginning of an effort to convert welfare into a more transitional system of support. Unfortunately, few of the proposed changes by themselves go far toward solving the poverty and welfare struggles faced by single mothers. They only begin to address the three main problems I have identified.

The current crop of welfare reform proposals usually involves mixing employment and training services with welfare. Sometimes they provide a voluntary job-search program and some training to help recipients find jobs and make the transition to self-support. Sometimes they include mandatory work programs for mothers with older children who have not found work. When work-welfare programs have been tried, both recipients and administrators are said to be pleased with them. Recipients, it seems, appreciate the opportunity to find work. Several evaluations have reported that clients who are put into mandatory work programs react favorably and are grateful for the opportunity to do something productive, although they think that the employers are getting the better end of the deal.[10]

A significant number of the experimental programs have been carefully and systematically evaluated. The results almost universally suggest that the benefits of the programs (including the increased earnings of recipients and the value of the work they perform in workfare plans) exceed the costs.[11] Many of the experiments have seemed to save taxpayers money; the reduced welfare payments received and the taxes paid by those served exceeded the cost of serving them. These programs clearly are the first attempts to change the nature of welfare by increasing the expectations of recipients to do something for themselves and increasing the government's efforts to help people get off welfare.

Unfortunately, even though the experimental programs have often been cost effective and the move toward a more transitional system is appealing, the overall reductions in the recipients' dependence on welfare and in the costs have been modest. For example, in San Diego county's job-search and workfare program, welfare recipients with no children under age 6 were required to participate in job-search workshops designed to help them find work. If they were unable to find work, they were required to work for their welfare check for three months. The benefits of this program exceeded the costs in a carefully controlled experiment.[12] The findings received widespread attention nationwide. The results of the program were so positive that the program became part of the framework of a major new welfare initiative in California called Greater Avenues for Independence (GAIN), which was implemented throughout the state.

Yet the results show that the total impact was modest. Over the course of a year, 60 percent of those who had been in the program were employed in the private sector at some point in the year, compared to 55 percent of the randomly selected control group which was not put through the program—hardly a massive change. The treatment group earned only a little more—an average of $3,800 compared to $3,100 for the controls over a year, or an increase of less than $14 per week—and used less welfare:—$3,400 versus $3,700 annually, or a decrease of 10 percent. Thus, on average, this program saved $300 in the welfare benefits of each participating recipient per year and raised the recipients' earnings by $700. Although these are helpful steps they do not move us far toward self-support or the elimination of welfare. Furthermore, these figures overstate the results in some respects. Many women were exempted from participating because they had young children or some other barrier to work. In fact, the overall reduction in welfare benefits from this program would be less than 5 percent even if the gains lasted forever.

Experiments all across the country have generated similar findings. Annual earnings are raised $200 to $750 and welfare savings are more modest.[13] Moreover, the programs typically serve only a minority of the caseload, so the overall average reductions are even smaller. But, in most cases, the cost has not been large either, so the programs pay off. Most work-welfare programs look like decent investments, but no carefully evaluated work-welfare programs have done more than put a tiny dent in the welfare caseloads, even though they have been received with enthusiasm.

So these work-welfare programs alone are not likely to solve the welfare "problem," in spite of the grand claims by some proponents. Some conservative critics argue that the programs are not tough enough on recipients; they say that virtually all recipients should be required to work off their checks.[14] "Hard workfare" might make welfare less attractive, although welfare is not particularly attractive now. It would prevent single parents from remaining on welfare for many years without doing work. But it is unlikely to do much to help mothers make the transition to self-support. It does not provide a woman with serious assistance to get over the time of initial stress and then gain control of her life. It does not replace welfare; it merely imposes more rules for those in the system. It mostly ensures that people do not avoid working.

On the opposite end, liberals claim that the programs would work better if we invested more in them. The current set of proposals usually involve little real training and education. But other, more intensive, approaches have been tried in the past. For example, the Supported Work program invested close to $10,000 in each long-term and poorly educated recipient.[15]

Over the long term, the benefits still exceeded the costs. But even this program did not affect the welfare rolls much, especially in the short run. Benefits exceeded costs, not because of a sudden and dramatic rise in earnings or a fall in welfare but, rather, because the program had a modest impact that lasted a long time. Initially, it raised weekly earnings by $40, but, after several years, the difference between those aided and those not helped was less than $10 per week, and governmental benefits fell by only about 10 percent. Thus, investment alone is not the answer either.

The problem with almost all schemes that focus exclusively on work-welfare programs is that they do not solve the three fundamental problems just discussed. They do not improve the job market much. The modest training does not substantially improve wages or lead to more secure jobs. Intensive training helps, but it still can improve prospects only somewhat. Minimum-wage jobs still pay too little to allow single parents to support themselves.

Moreover, the programs do not take account of the dual role of single parents in a useful way. Most proposals simply exclude mothers with young children from participating and then offer some temporary child care payments when the mothers go to market work. These efforts mainly sidestep the difficult problems associated with parenting. None makes it possible for people who are working part time to escape welfare.

Finally, few proposals deal with the problem that there is no real reward for working unless people can earn a great deal. Most do not change the fundamental role of welfare as a cash-support system, much as they try. None really changes the way welfare recipients are treated.

Programs involving minor modifications of the traditional welfare system still trip over the helping conundrums. Welfare discourages work. It inevitably is seen by the public as support for women who "marry" welfare rather than men. It inevitably isolates, stigmatizes, and scrutinizes. More training and support services, as well as increased responsibilities, seem like steps in the right direction, but these alone will not take us far toward a system that offers real support and real responsibility.

I think the goal should be to *replace* welfare with something that gives people real options, a real chance to be independent, and a real reason to work. Mixing work and welfare is not the answer. Welfare inevitably creates conflicts and contradictions among values. We need a new direction.

Child Support—An Obvious Starting Point

Most discussions of the poverty of single-parent families focus almost exclusively on the mothers. In the chorus of recent criticism about long-term dependence or the demands that mothers be put to work, it would be easy to get the impression that every child has but one parent. If one looks at the level of child support in the United States, that impression is reinforced. Only a small minority of single mothers get any child support payments.

The notion that mothers ought to bear the full responsibility for nurturing and providing for the children is ludicrous. A recent survey asked Americans the following question: "If a mother has custody of the children, and has or can earn a reasonable income, do you think the father should be required to provide full financial support for the children, partial support or what?"[16] Only 2 percent said no support; 67 percent said partial support; 29 percent said full support; and the other 2 percent were not sure. Everyone believes that fathers ought to contribute; the only question is how much.

The reason wives have options and single mothers do not is that wives can rely on their husbands for at least some financial support (and emotional and child-rearing support as well). Even wives with unemployed husbands are usually in a better position; their husbands often qualify for unemployment compensation, and they can expect additional support in the future. If they go to work when their husbands are not working, they have someone to help with the child care.

Reasonable Expectations of Absent Parents

What is it fair to expect of absent parents? The issues are complex, but we can at least consider some general principles:

- Except in rare circumstances, if an absent parent has income, he or she ought to share some of that income with the children. Obviously, if the absent parent has no income, there is nothing to share.
- The contribution should be adjusted for inflation and changes in the income of the absent parent. If inflation is high and wages and prices are moving up, child support payments ought to keep pace.
- The payments ought to be provided in a timely and reliable manner. They should not be the basis of power, fighting, or control by either party. They should represent support for children.
- The amount paid ought to be reasonable.

I regard the first three propositions as uncontroversial. Obviously, there may be certain extreme instances when they are not appropriate, but they seem to be simple common sense. The fourth proposition—how much should be paid—is more difficult. A large part of our judicial system specializes in divorce and paternity cases, and there is a large body of literature on these issues as well.[17] I will not presume to decide what is the right number. But I do believe that the following simple example can give some insight into what might be the appropriate range of support that is awarded.

Suppose that a married couple with two children were both working full time at a minimum-wage job in 1984 and together earned $13,500. These earnings put them 25 percent above the poverty line. They then decided to divorce and agreed that the wife would have custody of the children. What would be the husband's reasonable contribution for child support? The poverty line for a single-person family is $5,300 and for a three-person family is $8,300. If the father gives up roughly 25 percent of his income for child support and the wife continues to work at her minimum-wage job, then both families will be almost at the poverty line. The standard of living of both parents has fallen. It had to. Two individual households are more expensive to maintain than is one. But both have been hurt equally in the divorce, at least as measured by the poverty standard.

Suppose, instead, that the husband had been earning $13,500 and the wife had been earning nothing. If the husband contributed 25 percent of his income, then his income would be over $10,000. As a family man, he lived only 25 percent above the poverty line. As a single adult, his income would be almost twice the $5,300 level for a single person. The mother, however, would be in much worse shape. She would have only $3,375 in child support. If she went to work full time at the minimum wage, she could then almost achieve the same standard of living her family had before the divorce. So the husband's standard of living would rise, while the mother would have to scramble even to come close to the old one. Even if the father married and had another child and his new wife did not work, his new family would be about as well off as his old one in which his ex-wife would be forced to work full time at a minimum-wage job.

The point of this example is simple. Expecting a 25 percent contribution from an absent parent with two children seems modest. If both parents have equal earnings, this contribution will ensure that they end up with equal standards of living. If the incomes are unequal, as is usually the case, such a standard will often mean that the husband is financially better off after the divorce than before it. The example is somewhat misleading in that child support is taxable to the father rather than to the mother. But, still, a 25–30 percent contribution from the father seems more than fair. Many argue for much more. It seems hard to justify less.

There is nothing magical about the 25–30 percent range. Individual circumstances would certainly argue for more or less. Obviously, absent fathers with more children should pay more, and those with only one child should pay less. Wisconsin has already adopted a 25 percent child support standard for absent fathers with two children, and Massachusetts recently proposed roughly a 30 percent standard.[18]

The current child support system is a disgrace. Table 5.7 shows that, as of 1985, half the single parents had been awarded child support, and only slightly over one-third had actually received any payments. Divorced women got the most payments but, even in that group, only about half received any. The most unfortunate mothers were those who never married. Only 18 percent had awards and only 11 percent got payments.

Child support payments are incredibly small. The average annual payment for those who do pay is only $2,300. If we assume that payments ought to average at least 25 percent of income, then to justify this level of payments, the one-third of the absent fathers who actually pay child support (presumably the richest third of all absent fathers) would have to have incomes of $9,200. In fact, the median income for all *married* men was $24,251 in 1985.[19] Only 14 percent of married men had

TABLE 5.7

Percentage of All Single Mothers Who Reported Receiving Child Support, by Marital Status (1985)[a]

Marital Status of Mother	Child Support Award in Place (%)	Award in Place and Received Some Payment (%)	Average Payment Received by Those with Some Payment
Divorced	82	54	$2,538
Separated	43	28	$2,082
Never married	18	11	$1,147
Total	54	35	$2,318

[a]This data is for women who were living with their own children under age 21 from an absent father, as of spring 1986 (for the year 1985).
SOURCE: U.S. Bureau of the Census, *Current Population Reports,* Series P-23, No. 152. *Child Support and Alimony: 1985* (Washington, D.C.: U.S. Government Printing Office, 1987).

incomes below $10,000. Even if absent fathers are much worse off, on the average, than are married men, the notion that the mean income of the top third or even the top two-thirds would be $9,200 is absurd. Several studies have suggested that if a reasonable level of collection and payments were achieved, absent fathers would contribute over $25 billion more than they do now.[20]

The Current System—A Predictable Failure

How have we arrived at such an astonishingly low level of support and responsibility? Consider a common analogy (the origin of which I cannot place). Suppose the federal income tax system worked in the following way: Because of a concern for fairness, the government decided that decisions about the amount of taxes to be paid by each taxpayer would be determined in a court of law. The courts would take into account individual circumstances, including work history and expected future earnings, citizenship and contributions to the community, the extent to which the prospective taxpayer used or abused governmental services, and even some sense of whether both the citizen and the court agreed with the purposes to which the money would be put.

On the basis of these proceedings, the judge would assign each taxpayer a fixed dollar amount that would be his or her contribution to government for the foreseeable future. The tax would not change unless the taxpayer or the government went to court and had it changed.

If people did not pay their taxes, they would be warned repeatedly if they were still in the state and could be found. If, after multiple warnings, they still did not pay, they would be served with a summons. Some months later, they would be required to appear in court. If they failed to appear, they would be held in contempt of court and another court date would be set. If they could provide reasonable evidence at the next hearing that their or the government's circumstances had changed, their taxes could be adjusted. If the court determined that the taxpayers had been unreasonably and deliberately delinquent, it could attach a portion of their wages (if any) to capture the payments. The court would rarely use other sanctions.

How much money would be paid under such a system, and would the public perceive it as fair? The system would be a disaster. The government would not even try to get money from people with modest incomes, for the legal costs would probably outweigh the benefits. Furthermore, it is likely that the taxes assigned would differ astronomically. In spite of their best efforts, judges would inevitably let their feelings about a particular person and the government affect their decisions. The same person might be assigned a different tax in two different courts. Then the fixed dollar amount would not be adjusted for changing circumstances. If inflation were running at 10 percent per year, the real value of payments would fall by 10 percent per year. For the government to maintain its tax collections, every taxpayer would have to be brought back to court every year. But the cost of doing so might exceed the gain for quite a few years, so citizens would probably be brought to court infrequently. In the interim, even the most honest taxpayer would pay a smaller and smaller share of his or her salary in taxes.

With such a lax enforcement procedure, people who were determined to pay little or nothing could do so. They could move away or try to avoid detection. When confronted, they could offer evidence of their changed circumstance or some other problem. At the worst, they would be forced to pay through their paychecks.

Bad as this system sounds, it would be much better than our current system of child support. In addition to the features just described, child support must usually be sought and policed by the mother.[21] The mother may wish to maintain decent relations with the father, both to preserve a role for him with the children and to discourage him from making her life miserable by fighting over custody or withholding payments. Conversely, she may be bitter and wish to use child support to punish the man.

Child support inevitably creates a source of tension between people whose relationship is already strained. On many occasions, one or both parties are bitter, and they will go to extraordinary lengths to spite, discredit, or inconvenience each other both in and out of court. The father's threats to withhold payment give him power. Nonpayment puts the mother in an awkward position. She can bring the man to court, but only at financial and personal costs. And the court may do little if the father is having financial difficulties. Or a woman can use the court as a vehicle for her bitterness.

In the case of a husband and wife who are separated, one or both parties may be reluctant to go to court for fear that such an action will jeopardize the chances for a reconciliation. Only 40 percent of separated couples have court-ordered child support plans. Unmarried couples face these problems and more. The mother may be reluctant to identify the father, or he may be difficult to find. Once found, he may deny paternity, and elaborate procedures will be necessary to establish his responsibility. If he is young or he has little current income, there is little point in trying to get child support from him even if he can be found, since awards are based primarily on the father's current circumstances. So only 18 percent of never-married mothers have awards.

As Lenore Weitzman noted, "In the end the current legal system places the economic responsibility for children on their mothers and allows fathers the 'freedom' to choose not to support their children."[22] In many ways, it is a credit to the responsibility and compassion of both the absent and the custodial parents that any child support gets paid at all.

Recently, a "major reform" was unanimously passed by Congress. Now it is possible to impose mandatory withholding of wages after just one missed payment. And states are required to experiment with some uniform income-based guidelines for child support. The law may have some effect. It should be obvious from this discussion, though, that an easier system of withholding wages is likely to have only a modest effect on child support. It does not create more awards,[23] it does not adjust them for inflation or changing economic circumstances, and it still requires the woman to go after a man she may not want to antagonize. We are a long way from a time when all or even most absent fathers will pay.

It is easy to decry fathers as irresponsible and unreasonable. But the sad truth is that the child support system itself is impossible to work with. Many fathers pay because they care and because it is right. Many others do not because they feel they have been wronged or denied access to their children or because they are supporting a new family. Until we move to a vastly different system, massive inequities and ridiculously low levels of payments will be a fact of life.

It is hard to imagine a worse outcome. This discussion implies that few fathers need to worry about paying child support if they do not want to. A young man who fathers a child out of wedlock will rarely be expected to contribute to the child's support. So we send absent fathers a clear signal that they have no real responsibilities. It should come as no surprise that fathering a child out of marriage is often seen as a badge of manhood rather than a troubling set of new responsibilities.

As long as we have a system where judges set fixed dollar awards on the basis of their evaluations of men's and women's current circumstances, where mothers are responsible for bringing all actions against fathers, and where sanctions are minimal, we shall have the abomination that we now call child support. Awards will vary widely. Fathers who have no current income will not be brought to court. Mothers will often be reluctant to antagonize the fathers by demanding payments in court. Inflation will inevitably erode the value of awards. Some fathers will continue to pay, while others will default. Most mothers will get almost no help from the fathers. Each parent may use child support as a club to attack, antagonize, and humiliate the other. Our children will be left to suffer.

The message is clear: absent fathers do not necessarily have financial responsibility for their children. If we come to accept that proposition, then children in single-parent families will be at an insurmountable economic disadvantage. They will often be left with only one potential earner, who must do both nurturing and providing. And single mothers will likely be left in a work-welfare environment that offers little real help toward independence. What mothers desperately need is some nonwelfare supports they can count on and supplement with their own earnings. Child support seems an obvious place to look for that help.

Reforming Child Support

Ideally, both parents should do as much nurturing and providing as possible even if the family is separated. At a minimum we must ensure that both parents have some financial responsibilities.[24] When half the children in America will spend some time in a single-parent family, it is time to recognize that we cannot continue to subject our children to such an arbitrary and uncertain system. We ought to take a page from the tax system and create a far more uniform and straightforward method of child support. Three major steps toward reform would be these:

- Society would commit itself to identifying every child's father and mother. In the future, the Social Security numbers of both parents would appear on a child's birth certificate. Most experts claim that getting the father's name is not difficult and proving paternity is feasible as well. What can be more difficult is finding the father years later if one does not have his Social Security number.
- All absent parents would be expected to contribute a portion of their income (earnings), and the portion would vary with the number of children they fathered or bore. There would be a roughly uniform formula for child support. For example, Wisconsin uses a plan that calls for 17 percent of the absent parent's income for one child; 25 percent for two children; and up to 34 percent for five or more children. Courts could deviate from the standard if the circumstances justified it.
- In all cases, payments would be collected by employers just like Social Security taxes. Indeed, the payments could be part of the

Social Security system. Employers would deduct the appropriate percentage of earnings just as they now do for taxes. The government would then send this money to the custodial parent. All absent parents would be included in the system, not just those who had been delinquent. The failure to pay would be an offense comparable to tax evasion.

If we did these three things—identify both parents at the birth of a child, move to a uniform system of payments based on the income of the absent parent, and have employers collect all payments automatically—we would go a long way toward improving the situation of children in single-parent homes. This system would be far easier to administer than is the current one. A line for child support could simply be added to the form that taxpayers already fill out telling employers what percentage to withhold (according to the number of dependents). There would be no need to adjust payments for inflation, since payments would go up (or down) along with wages. Best of all, the new system would get parents out of court and get child support outside their relationship because the government would collect child support in a standard and uniform matter.

We would also dramatically change the signals sent to those who parent children. Anyone who parents a child would be required to share a portion of his or her income with the child, either directly, because the parent is living with and raising the child, or indirectly through automatic child support payments.

Unfortunately, a better system for awarding and collecting child support will not, by itself, necessarily reduce the welfare caseloads much, although it is likely to save considerable welfare costs.[25] The 25 percent or 30 percent collected even from fathers with moderate incomes will not be larger than the current welfare payments in most states. So welfare costs will be reduced, but women will remain on welfare. And the collections from absent fathers with low salaries will not be of much help to their children. Furthermore, when fathers become unemployed, their earnings (and, therefore, child support) could fall to nothing. Therefore, many low-income mothers could not count on child support payments in making decisions about their lives. But if we add one more element, we get a system that can provide a reliable level of nonwelfare support to all single mothers.

Child Support Assurance: Social Insurance for Children

Irwin Garfinkel has suggested a simple but effective way to make child support far more helpful. Suppose we added a fourth element to the child support system:

- When the collections from the earnings of the absent parent were insufficient to provide some minimum level of child support, say $1,500 to $2,000 per child per year, the government would provide that minimum. In effect, when the father failed in his obligation to provide sufficient income for child support, the government would ensure that his children would get at least some minimum amount.

The idea of a minimum level of child support can be justified on several grounds. The first and most obvious one is that it is a kind of unemployment insurance for children in homes in which one parent is absent. When a working parent loses a job in a two-parent home, unemployment insurance is supposed to provide help and protection. Child support assurance offers the same sort of protection for children of absent parents. When absent parents fail to provide a reasonable level of child support, the children and the custodial parents need some sort of protection: social insurance for children.

The second justification is that the minimum can become a *stable* foundation on which single mothers can build. Suppose a woman with two children could count on $3,500 a year in child support payments no matter what. Then she would need $5,100 in earnings to reach the poverty line. A woman would know that if she worked three-quarters time at the current minimum wage or part time at $5 per hour, she would be able to escape poverty. If she worked more than that she'd move well above the poverty line.

If child support assurance was combined with the measures suggested in chapter 4—medical protection, a higher minimum wage, an expanded earned income tax credit (EITC), and a refundable child care credit—the options available to single mothers would be changed dramatically. Table 5.8 shows how different a woman's position would look with these policies, if each child got $1,750 annually in child support.

A single mother working half time at the minimum wage would be above the official poverty line of roughly $8,700, since day care costs are not counted in determining poverty. If she actually paid $1,000 for day care (as in this example), her disposable income would still be close to the poverty line. Anything more than half-time work or a wage rate even slightly above the minimum would virtually guarantee that she would be out of poverty. With these measures in place, mothers could work half time and yet be completely outside the welfare system. And full-time work would give them a real measure of independence even if they had to pay modest day care costs.

An expanded child support system with a minimum benefit would significantly alter the situations of single mothers and absent fathers. Mothers could count on at least some modest support outside the welfare system. They could work part time and still support their families (along with the support collected from the fathers). Thus, it would be feasible for them to balance work and family. Women who were willing to work at least part time would not be poor. Child support alone would not keep a single-parent family out of poverty, but by combining it with a modest level of work, a woman would be able to make it on her own *without welfare*—in dramatic contrast to the present system.

A man would know that when he fathered a child, he would be fiscally responsible for providing some support for the next eighteen years, regardless of whether he married or lived with the child's mother. Indeed, the only way he could avoid paying formal child support would be for him to live with the child or not have a child at all.

TABLE 5.8

Earnings, Taxes, Benefits, and Total Income for a Single Parent and Two Children (1986)

Level of Work and Wages	Earnings	Day Care	Taxes and EITC[a]	Child Support[b]	Disposable Income
Half time at the minimum wage	$4,400	−$1,000	+$1,085	$3,500	$7,985
Full time at the minimum wage	$8,800	−$3,000	+$1,511	$3,500	$10,811
Full time at $5.00 per hour	$10,000	−$3,000	+1,185	$3,500	$11,685
Full time at $6.00 per hour	$12,000	−$3,000	+642	$3,500	$13,142

[a]Includes a refundable 30 percent child care credit, Social Security taxes of 7.15 percent, a 25 percent EITC up to $8,000 that is reduced by 20 cents for each dollar above that level.
[b]Assumes that mothers get the minimum benefit; many mothers would get more than the minimum.

The assured benefit is a critical part of this plan. Still, most child support checks would not be subsidized. If fathers of one child were expected to contribute 20 percent of their income in child support, then fathers with incomes over $8,700 would not be subsidized. If fathers of two children contributed 30 percent, they would not be subsidized if their earnings were over $11,700. The median income of married men is over $23,000, and only 13 percent earn less than $8,500. Even if absent parents earn considerably less than do married men, it seems safe to assume that most children would not need the government to pay anything in order to get child support payments at least as high as the minimum.

There would be a significant redistributive element in the minimum benefit in that children whose fathers were not earning enough to reach the minimum would be helped. Some critics have argued that the minimum benefit would be just another form of welfare. After all, many women who are now getting welfare would simply be getting the minimum benefit; thus, the child support check would be a substitute for the welfare check. To these critics, the plan is just a relabeling of welfare—not a replacement for it.

I think such arguments reflect a basic misunderstanding of the plan and an ignorance of many of the reasons why welfare can be so destructive. When a woman goes on welfare, she immediately loses control of much of her life. Administrators require information and verification; the welfare recipient can have virtually no assets. If she earns money, she must report it immediately. When she reports those earnings, her check is reduced or eliminated. If she moves, she must report it. If she starts sharing rent, she must report it. She uses food stamps at the market. She is labeled a "welfare" mother—one of "those welfare cheats."

However, under a child support system, a woman who worked part time could escape the welfare system. Her primary form of nonwage support would be child support payments—payments that would reflect the father's expected contribution to support of the children. This system would be sending checks to middle- and upper-income women as well as to disadvantaged ones. Indeed, most of the money collected would go to middle-class women. There would be no stigma, no failure, and no isolation under this system. When the check was partially or fully subsidized to reach the minimum, it would be a result of the *father's* failure to meet his reasonable responsibilities, not the result of the mother's failures.

A woman who received child support payments would thus avoid all the frustration, isolation, and loss of control of the welfare system. If she was willing to work half time, she could be in charge of her own life. When she worked, she would keep every dollar and would not lose one penny in support benefits. Child support payments would depend on what the father earned, subject to the minimum. They would be considered the children's right to a second source of support, not a grudging welfare benefit because the single mother had failed to support herself.

The extraordinary thing about this sort of plan is that, according to some estimates, if collection rates for absent fathers reached 80 percent and the minimum benefit were set at $2,000 per child, the cost of funding the assured benefit would be more than offset by the savings in AFDC and other welfare benefits.[26] In other words, if most absent fathers contributed the given percentages, the program would actually save money.

The proposal may seem ambitious, but such a program is already being tried in Wisconsin, and many other states, including New York, are planning to mount experiments of their own.[27] Child support assistance plans seem promising.

Questions and Answers

An assured child support system comes close to offering something for nothing. Still, there are some obvious problems and questions. Let me deal briefly with some of them.

Can We Really Find Every Father? Mothers who apply for AFDC are required to provide the names of the fathers of their children, and most have little difficulty doing so. According to Paul Jargowsky:

> In almost all cases the mother cooperates and identifies the father. Nationwide, 2,302 good cause exemptions were granted out of a total AFDC child support caseload of 6,135,571—less than ¹⁄₂₀th of one percent. An additional 1141 refused to cooperate and were not granted an exemption.
>
> In very unusual cases, the woman may cooperate fully yet not know the identity of the father. . . . [In New York] the cases are called "John Doe's" and account for a very small percentage of all AFDC cases. [In New York State] caseworkers estimate that about 1 percent of the cases they see are John Doe's. In our sample of 52 cases from upstate New York counties, only 1 case out of 52 did not have the name of the father listed.[28]

Unfortunately, when the mother has been out of contact with the father for more than a few years, it is often hard to find the father. Without a Social Security number, it is costly and time consuming to search for people.

A second problem is that when the government has been involved in finding fathers, it has usually done so through the welfare system. For both legal and logical reasons, the agencies have tended to concentrate on cases in which the cost of identifying the father and establishing paternity will be offset by welfare savings. And welfare mothers have little incentive to cooperate, since all but fifty dollars in collections will be deducted from their check.

Young men who father the children of women they do not marry often have low incomes initially. Thus, it makes little sense to drag them into court because only a minimal child support award will be made. Therefore, these fathers are rarely found and, if they are, they are not brought to court. Five years later, they may be earning decent money, but they have been lost to the system.

The establishment of paternity and child support simply cannot be allowed to languish on a narrow conception of costs and benefits that compares the short-run savings in welfare benefits to the costs of establishing paternity.[29] I am confident that, in the long run, both the money that is collected and the changes in behavior that may be induced by a more responsible policy will more than pay the costs. But this issue involves more than economics: it is a matter of right versus wrong.

If a more uniform system were put in place, if the establishment of paternity were required by law for all children (except in special cases), and if we committed more resources, we could do far better. Even under the current system, some states identify more than 60 percent of the fathers of children born out of wedlock, and others identify less than 2 percent.[30] There are large bureaucratic hurdles to be overcome. But fathers can be identified if we are willing to make the commitment.

Will Mothers Refuse to Cooperate? As I already noted, most women who apply for welfare identify their children's fathers—they are required to do so by law. Of course, men may try to pressure women to keep their identity secret if they know it will cost them money in the long run. If it were a legal obligation to record the identity of both parents, then a woman could easily argue that she had no choice. Moreover, a woman who did not identify the father would lose all child support payments. If there really was some danger to the mother or if special circumstances made a public revelation of the father dangerous or inappropriate, the courts could provide relief.

I have some worries that this requirement might put women in a vulnerable and pressured position, especially at first. Men may threaten women who reveal their identity, and this fear should be taken seriously and addressed thoughtfully. But we cannot let our children be held hostage by a few men who are unwilling to take responsibility. All fathers and mothers must know that if they parent a child, they will have financial responsibilities. If men really started to worry about their future obligations, they might be more careful about fathering children.

Will this Plan Cause a Man to Pressure the Woman to Get an Abortion or to Lie about his Identity? Certainly, an absent father would have much more reason to want the woman to get an abortion, just as he would have more incentive to pressure her to conceal his identity. I think that this is also a legitimate worry, although I do not know how serious the problem would be. Remember that a man would have much more incentive to be careful in the first place. The plan could reduce the number of abortions significantly by reducing the number of unwanted pregnancies.

What if a Father Denies his Responsibility?   Most experts report that with some sort of circumstantial evidence, current technology makes identification virtually certain. Some states still have arcane rules that make paternity harder to prove. For example, blood tests are not admissible in certain locales. These rules should be changed. Meanwhile, medical techniques continue to improve, so identification eventually will become almost foolproof.

What about a Father Who Is in Serious Financial Difficulty? Does this Plan Exacerbate his Situation?   The father's child support payments would be a percentage of his income, so if his income was low, his payments would be low. The minimum benefit offers some security for the custodial parent in such cases. It is true, however, that a poor absent father would be strapped if he had to share his income.

But a poor father who is living at home with his children is strapped now. His entire salary probably goes toward supporting himself and his family. Just being poor does not relieve a married father of his obligation to share whatever income he has with his children. Similarly, a father should not avoid his obligation just because he is not living at home. Remember that under the plan, a father owes nothing if he earns nothing, but he must share any income he has.

The plan may increase the incentive for absent fathers to work "off the books" or in the underground economy or otherwise hide their assets. And the plan will lower the rewards of work for absent parents. Such problems are present in any tax system, and the distortions generally are modest. But, again, this is not a matter of economic efficiency; it is a matter of right and wrong. Parents have obligations. The only way to avoid the obligations ought to be to avoid becoming a parent.

Finally, if we are concerned about the plight of the father, would not a far more logical and humane strategy be to help the absent parent become more productive by offering employment and training services? We should not relieve the absent father of obligations simply because he is having a hard time in the labor market. Rather, we should try to improve his capacity to help himself and his children.

Will this Plan Increase the Incentives to Form Single-Parent Families? One of the appealing features of this plan is that most of the money would come from the increased enforcement of the obligations of absent fathers, so men would have much less financial incentive to create single-parent families. Although child support would improve the situation of custodial parents, there is no evidence that welfare payments have had much of an influence on the formation of single-parent families, so it is doubtful that child support payments will have a significant influence. I suspect that the net effect of this plan would be to reduce the number of single-parent families.

What about Cases of Joint Custody or Remarriage? Joint custody payments would reflect the relative costs and responsibilities of each parent. Under the current law, the remarriage of either the absent or custodial parent does not end the absent parent's obligation for child support (unless the children are adopted by the new spouse). I see no reason for that part of the law to change. There will always be complicated situations that require the courts to modify the simple formula. But the basic idea that child support payments reflect a percentage of income and are collected like taxes ought to be preserved.

Any system that replaces total judicial discretion with much greater uniformity will create some inequities. Our tax system is loaded with them. Yet the inequity and irresponsibility fostered by our present system is surely far worse.

Child support assurance would be different from the present

system. It would be far more like Social Security than like welfare. Everyone would be in the system. Richer absent parents would pay more, and their children would get more. Money would be collected by the employer just like Social Security. There would be a minimum benefit, just as Social Security currently has a minimum benefit.

Social Security was designed when most single mothers were widows. It was clear then that families could not support themselves without earnings of fathers. So to protect widows without giving them welfare, survivors' benefits were created. In effect, men and women bought an insurance policy to ensure that their children would get some support if they were not around to help. The world has changed. The insecurity of single mothers is not usually caused by the death of their husbands, but their families are just as surely deprived of support. Today, women have more of a capacity to provide for their families, but if the only possible source of private support is the mothers' earnings, these families will be insecure. Would it not be sensible to extend the protection and uniformity of Social Security in light of these new circumstances? Do we really want most children in America to be at risk of going on welfare?

A child support assurance system comes close to providing a free lunch. It puts single mothers in a vastly more realistic position to become self-supporting and reduces the need for them to go on welfare. Moreover, it raises the standard of living of single parents, makes one of the main sources of support a mainstream insurance/protection system far more like Social Security than like AFDC, and simultaneously reinforces the responsibilities of absent fathers to support their children. The increased responsibilities may even deter some men from fathering children outside of marriage. And it does not cost more.

The Rest of the System

A child support assurance system would be of significant help to single parents by addressing the issue of dual responsibility. But labor market conditions and the nature of the welfare system also contribute greatly to the problems of single parents. In the last section, it looked possible for a single mother to work part time and still escape poverty with a child support assurance plan because I assumed that the proposals introduced in chapter 4 about medical care and making work pay had been adopted. I did not discuss what would become of the welfare system. To make a serious dent in the poverty of single parents, the same steps I suggested for the support of poor two-parent families ought to be taken for poor single parents:

- Ensure that everyone has medical protection.
- Make work pay.
- Replace AFDC and food stamps with transitional assistance of a limited duration.
- Provide jobs for those who have exhausted their transitional assistance.

By instituting these plans in combination with a child support assurance system, we can address most of the key problems of single mothers and have a system that is not only more helpful to single mothers but is more compatible with our basic values than is the current system. The use of the same elements for single parents and for two parents also has the appeal of creating a more uniform, equitable, and intelligible system for all concerned. Let me review these elements, looking specifically at how they would help single parents.

Medical Care

In chapter 4, I argued that some method of ensuring that everyone has medical protection was an essential part of any strategy to help the poor in a way that reinforces our values.

The prescription is doubly apt for single parents. Usually, single mothers who earn their way off welfare lose medical protection four or nine months later. The loss of protection can be a significant worry, especially for women in low-paying jobs that offer little or no medical protection. There is no reliable evidence on how many people on welfare choose not to work for fear of losing Medicaid, but anecdotal evidence suggests the number could be large.

Making Work Pay

Society needs to find a way to make work pay better if we hope to encourage work while diminishing poverty in two-parent families. The same ideas for making work pay would help single mothers: a higher minimum wage, an expanded EITC, and a refundable day care credit. Without the higher minimum wage implied in these policies, the examples in table 5.8 do not work nearly as well. Even with an assured child support benefit such as the one proposed, *full-time* work at the current minimum wage would not push mothers out of poverty if they had day care expenses like those shown in table 5.8. Part-time work would leave the family far short. Thus the make-work-pay measures have the appealing feature of helping not only working poor two-parent families but also single parents.

Let me return briefly to the question of day care. I noted previously that day care raises issues that reach far beyond the problems of the poor and deserve airing in a wider context. Still, one simply cannot ignore the fact that children need some sort of care if their mothers work. If the children are of school age and their mothers work part time, the problems are modest. But if the children are very young or their mothers work full time, then day care can be a critical problem.

In informal discussions with some operators of work-welfare programs I have been told that day care is not as important as its advocates claim. Often less day care money gets spent than is allocated. Some operators have suggested that mothers who really want to work can usually arrange something, often using more informal arrangements like relatives or friends. Lawrence M. Mead argued that day care is not a serious problem.[31] Others, including many welfare clients, the Children's Defense Fund, and advocates of day care argue that day care is essential—that unless massive new funds for day care are made available, little progress will be made.

I frankly do not know how to evaluate such claims. It is true that few working mothers (single or married) place their children in formal day care centers. As of 1985, only 28 percent of the working single mothers with children under age 5 used an organized child care facility and a third of these facilities were nursery-preschools.[32] Some 42 percent of the children were cared for by a relative, mainly their grandmothers. Most of the remaining children were cared for by nonrelatives.

Grandmothers and other relatives seem like a valuable resource, but they surely can only be counted on for care in a minority of cases, since almost two-thirds of the women aged 45–54 (the group who would be grandmothers) are themselves in the labor force.[33] Even when care is available from a relative, the mother often pays something for the service.[34] The other forms of care cost more, sometimes considerably more. And the share of children cared for in the more expensive settings seems to be growing rapidly. The fraction of children under age 5 in organized child care grew from 22 percent to the current 28 percent in just 2½ years.[35]

Without day care, many mothers simply cannot work. But formal institutional day care is expensive. The money spent on day care will probably reduce the money available for other forms of aid. Given the enormous expense and the uncertain need for government-provided day care on a massive scale, we should probably go slow and learn as much as we can about the need for more day care in helping single mothers work. I have already said that we should start by making the current 30 percent day care tax credit refundable. The failure to do so seems unfair and counterproductive. Why should we have day care credits only for the middle class? It would also make sense to increase the level of the credit further for the poor and to try other experimental programs.

One thing should be clear. If we want single parents to work, we must make it possible for them to support themselves and their families. Unless we make work pay better, we cannot expect to improve the independence and security of single mothers.

Transitional Assistance and Jobs

If we had child support assurance, if we ensured that people got medical protection, and if we made work pay, there would be far less need for welfare. Single parents could realistically support themselves at the poverty line if they were willing to work half time, even at jobs paying little more than the minimum wage. If they were willing to work full time, they could move well above the poverty line.

With this kind of support, I think one could easily contemplate major changes in welfare. There is clear evidence that many single parents have short-term transitional problems. It takes time to adjust to a divorce or separation or birth of a child. Often women spend a few years on welfare before remarrying or going to market work. Indeed, half those who go on AFDC have spells lasting two years or less.[36] The last thing that new single mothers need is immediate stress. They need help and support. If a woman has never worked, it will not be easy for her to move right into a new job. If she has young children, it may be undesirable and impractical to expect her to work right away. And even if a woman goes to work and gets out of poverty, economic fluctuations will inevitably create the kind of short-term job problems necessitating the same type of transitional program that I suggested for two-parent families.

Thus, the logic behind and need for a transitional support system are even stronger in the case of single parents. Single women certainly ought to have access to training, education, and job-search assistance if they are going to make the transition to work. Some will need such services as day care or transportation if they are to move toward supporting themselves.

Thus, I propose a transitional support system for single-parent families that would be similar to the one I proposed for two-parent families. As with the two-parent system, a wide variety of support and training services would be available, and the program would be limited in duration. There would be no confusion about the point of the program for beneficiaries, administrators, or the public. The program would be designed to help people achieve independence. In the case of single mothers, with child support and measures to make work pay, the realistic goal would be to get mothers part-time or full-time work.

The duration of assistance might be allowed to vary with the age of the youngest child. Generally, I favor making it last eighteen months to three years, depending on the age of the youngest child. But the key would be that this assistance would be *transitional.* Just as with the two-parent system, when benefits were used up, one would have to work some considerable amount of time before one could requalify for more. Although some child care and other services might be continued past the transitional period, the cash benefits would end. After the benefits ran out, the only alternative for support would be to supplement child support with work. One could not requalify for much more transitional assistance by having another baby or claiming that no jobs were available. The transitional program would be society's attempt to offer short-term aid and an opportunity for support and training. It would reflect the clear recognition that people often need help over a difficult period. It should be generous while limited in duration.

Obviously, some people will not be able to find work. Therefore, if the government is not willing to provide permanent income support, it must provide full- or part-time *jobs* so that people can support themselves. It is not possible to predict how many people would need these jobs. Half those who go on AFDC use it for more than two years, but they do so in a world where there is no way to work part time and escape poverty, where work does not pay well (because wages are often low and because welfare benefits fall as earnings rise), and where there is little help or incentive to move off welfare.

I surmise that only a tiny fraction would actually need these jobs if the other reforms were in place. Remember that single mothers with child support would not have to work more than half time to avoid poverty. Remember, too, that they would have had two or three years to adjust to their new situation, acquire training and transitional support, and move to a part-time job in the private sector. But for those who could not make it with child support, medical care, and transitional assistance, I think it is reasonable to say, "We have a job for you if you want it, but you cannot collect cash aid indefinitely."

As long as the government provides last-resort jobs and the level of work expected is reasonable, then it will be hard to argue that the system is unfair or that people do not have a chance to support themselves. No one who is willing to work half time will have an income below the poverty line. Just as in the case of two-parent families, there will be people who need special, intensive services but who do not qualify for disability programs, even though they cannot make it on their own. These people need to be treated on a case-by-case basis. They should not be allowed to shape the whole social welfare system.

It may seem harsh or unfair to offer only transitional assistance followed by jobs. One could implement the child support assurance plan, medical protection, and the proposals to make work pay without altering the current welfare system. But unless we replace the welfare system, we will not solve the problem that there is little aid, incentive, or pressure for single parents to work. We will not really have avoided the conundrums. Welfare will still be seen as the refuge for those who are not willing to work, and child support assurance will simply offset welfare benefits. Many single mothers will remain isolated. There must be both help and pressure for women to achieve real independence through their own efforts.

A transitional program followed by jobs bears some resemblance to many of the current welfare reform initiatives, such as California's GAIN program, which require job search or training followed by workfare for welfare recipients. These proposals may offer a workable alternative. They move in the right direction. Yet I believe that it is essential to make clear to all those concerned, both recipients and the public, that the core support program is a transitional one and the long-term support system is jobs.

The first few years of welfare are not now considered transitional assistance. The same demands, rules, obligations, and indignities are inflicted on new recipients as on old ones. The public does not perceive the difference between those who use welfare for temporary aid and those who use it for long-term assistance. They see all the money going to "welfare cheats." And so there is little dignity even in getting temporary help.

A system of transitional assistance would feel different from a welfare system with increasingly escalating rules and obligations. Transitional aid would clearly be designed to help recipients get on their feet. It would not be a program to punish people for misbehaving, nor would it offer the hope that manipulating the system would lead to permanent support. Transitional support would be a second chance, an opportunity to take advantage of special aid. However, since a woman would not get the training and other aid forever, it would be a chance to seize, not another burden to get through just to receive enough aid to get by.

Those who study management say that organizations with a clear goal are most successful. A welfare system that simultaneously tries to encourage self-support, demand work, help the working poor, and ensure that people have some minimal income has very mixed goals. Ensuring a minimal income is diametrically opposed to encouraging self-support. But the goal of a transitional support system would be clear: to help people help themselves.

After transitional support comes jobs. But is that not the same as workfare? I believe that there is something fundamentally different about "working off a welfare check" and working at a governmental job. In the first case, you seem to be working for free, since you are getting a welfare check and then told to go to work, but in the latter case, you are being paid for your work. Indeed, although participants in workfare programs express some satisfaction with the work, they think their employers are getting a good deal.[37] Similarly, when researchers recently asked welfare recipients about their attitudes toward workfare, they reported that recipients liked the idea that they would be working, but disliked the fact that they would still be on welfare.[38] To both the public and recipients, workfare is not jobs.

Finally, if they are separated, much more pressure will be placed on both the transitional program and on the employment program to do their jobs well. In a transitional program, it is easy to see how many people leave the program and when. It is also easy to check how many people end up in the employment program, since personnel have to certify that the recipients have completed transitional assistance before they can get the jobs. In a workfare program, if there are not enough jobs, recipients continue to receive welfare. In an employment program, there is an instant impetus to find more jobs if there are not enough of them. A true employment program will inevitably be more demanding than a workfare program. In workfare, one must go through an elaborate process of sanctions for people who fail to show up. In an employment program, people who do not work do not get paid.

Mead claimed that our goal ought to be to mimic the rules of the "outside" world "inside" the welfare system by imposing work.[39] I strongly disagree. The goal ought to be to get everyone into the "outside world." Helping people help themselves, providing a base of child support, and offering a job strikes me as far more reasonable and helpful than simply increasing the obligations of people in a welfare system that treats them with little dignity or respect.

A Chance to Make It Without Welfare

I have asserted that single parents face three problems: conditions in the job market, dual responsibilities, and the nature of the welfare system. Any plan that addresses only one or two of these problems will help. But only a plan that deals with all three can hope to make a large difference. Only a plan that corrects all three can allow us to replace our current system of unlimited duration yet inadequate and debasing welfare support. Only a plan that attacks the causes of the poverty of single parents can hope to provide aid in a way that reinforces rather than confounds our values of work, independence, family, and community.

The first and most crucial step is the child support assurance plan. There simply is no way that all single mothers can be expected to provide all the support to their families. If we do not provide income through a child support system, then the main alternative will be welfare. And many single parents will end up using welfare—at least part of the time. The welfare system will continue to discourage work, isolate recipients, and at least appear to promote the formation of single-parent families. Child support springs logically from the premise that both parents have responsibilities for their children. With child support, our compassion and our judgments about responsibility lead clearly to the same place. Welfare is accused of replacing the support of fathers. Child support, even with a supplement, will never be accused of such a substitution.

The minimum benefit is also crucial. Without it, women cannot count on a reliable nonwelfare source of support that they can supplement with their earnings. Without it, children have no protection when their absent fathers stop paying. Without it, we cannot expect most disadvantaged women to achieve any reasonable level of self-support outside the welfare system.

With a child support assurance plan, the measures proposed to help two-parent families will help single-parent families as well. With a base of child support, single parents will begin to look much like the working poor. The measures to ensure medical protection, to make work pay, and to provide transitional assistance and last-resort jobs could then solve most of the remaining job and welfare problems.

Just as for two-parent families, we would guarantee not a minimum income, but the opportunity for single-parent families to achieve real security and independence if the mothers are willing to work part time. Earnings plus child support allow every woman to reach the poverty line or near it. Transitional assistance helps people who are in a temporary crisis get through the early years of child rearing and offers training and support. Last-resort jobs mean that everyone can get long-term support by working.

Single-parent families can realistically gain control and independence over their lives, but not unless we recognize and address their problems. The current system is, at times, a cruel hoax that penalizes those who really try and debases those who have few options. But neither the liberal nor the conservative response to this problem has been helpful. Conservatives decry welfare but then make the absurd demand that all single mothers be responsible for their families' support or face new work obligations within the welfare system. Liberals offer tried-and-true claims that the lack of jobs, training, and day care are what holds people back. Welfare, they say, should be made more humane, not more demanding.

Making welfare either more demanding or more humane will not solve job problems, dual roles, or even the isolation and lack of incentives of welfare. I believe that the policies suggested here come much closer to reflecting and reinforcing the traditional American values than either the conservative or liberal plans. These proposals reward and encourage work by the poor, rather than frustrating it. They ensure that absent parents are held responsible for their children. They treat people with a good deal more dignity than does traditional welfare. The core support will come from a child support system and the tax system—systems that affect people of all incomes. Thus, the programs will integrate poor people rather than isolate them. Poor people will have a genuine chance to make it on their own. There will be no welfare dumping ground. There will be transitional support and jobs. More will be expected of people, but many more options will be available. People will have a chance to achieve real independence.

Appendix: Statistical Profile of Poor Female-Headed Families by Type of Situation (1984)

	Full-time Working Poor	Partially Employed Poor	Nonworking Poor	Disabled or Retired Poor	All Poor Female-Headed Families
RACE	100	100	100	100	100
White, non-Hispanic	38	50	36	40	42
Black, non-Hispanic	48	39	42	47	42
Hispanic	13	9	19	11	14
Other	1	2	3	2	2
FAMILY SIZE	100	100	100	100	100
Two	16	32	25	29	27
Three	31	31	31	26	30
Four	29	21	22	19	22
Five	11	7	11	12	10
Six or more	13	8	11	14	11
RESIDENCE	100	100	100	100	100
Central city	33	35	51	42	39
Suburban	35	26	24	23	29
Smaller town and rural	25	30	20	30	25
Unknown	7	9	5	5	7

	Full-time Working Poor	Partially Employed Poor	Nonworking Poor	Disabled or Retired Poor	All Poor Female-Headed Families
AGE OF HEAD	100	63	100	100	100
Under 20	0	2	3	0	2
20–29	24	38	41	6	33
30–39	39	15	30	17	32
40–49	26	5	16	20	17
50 and over	11	3	10	57	16
EDUCATION OF HEAD	100	100	100	100	100
Under 12 years	39	34	53	64	47
High school only	40	42	34	27	36
12–15 years	16	19	11	7	13
College or more	5	5	2	2	4
WORK CLASS OF HEAD[a]	100	100	—	—	100
Private industry	74	85	—	—	83
Farm	2	1	—	—	1
Nonfarm, self-employed	11	3	—	—	5
Government	13	11	—	—	11

Appendix (Continued)

MARITAL STATUS OF HEAD	Full-time Working Poor	Partially Employed Poor	Nonworking Poor	Disabled or Retired Poor	All Poor Female-Headed Families
	100	100	100	100	100
Divorced	34	33	26	28	29
Separated[b]	28	31	28	31	29
Never married	27	27	35	32	28
Widowed	11	9	11	9	14

[a]Work class is shown only for those who worked in the past year.
[b]Includes small number of female heads still classified as married.
SOURCE: Author's tabulations of data from U.S. Bureau of the Census, March 1985 Current Population Survey.

6

Ghetto Poverty

The "underclass" is the new synonym for the poor. It conveys many things to many people, but the essence is clear: it is a group apart from the rest of society. Ken Auletta described the underclass as a group that "feels excluded from society, rejects commonly accepted values, suffers from *behavioral* as well as *income* deficiencies. They don't just tend to be poor; to most Americans their behavior seems aberrant" (italics in the original).[1] Critics of our present welfare system always seem to turn to these images. And it is these same reflections of the poor that have shaken the faith of many 1960s liberals in the wisdom of our social policies.

This chapter examines the magnitude and causes of, and possible solutions to, the poverty of the so-called ghetto underclass. I see tremendous dangers in the current simplistic and usually ill-informed debate. The tendency to interpret the images of television or newspapers as being representative of the poor is to deny undeniable facts. The ghetto poor are but a tiny fraction of the poor overall. Moreover, the exasperated disgust with the welfare system expressed by conservatives and the "don't blame the victim" refrain of liberals trivialize a complex social phenomenon.

So far, this book has explored the causes of poverty for two-parent and single-parent families overall. For poor two-parent families, we saw that labor market problems are primary. The poverty of single parents is more involved, but it seems to reflect a combination of labor market problems, dual responsibilities, and an adverse welfare system. For the small subset of poor families who live in the ghetto, poverty is still more complicated. Important parts of the problem can, of course, be traced to the same forces that influence poor single-parent and two-parent families generally. Yet ghetto poverty seems to involve the joint effect of a large number of more serious economic and social troubles. As a result, people in the ghetto often seem to lack a clear direction or a sense that they are part of the larger society; they appear to have little hope for the future.

I think we know far more about what the problems are and what might be done to begin the process of reconstruction than most of the popular discussions suggest. We can do far better than simply to demand that ghetto residents on welfare be forced to work or that the government should step in and provide jobs. We can begin the process of rebuilding hope and control for those in the ghetto.

How Much Poverty Is Ghetto Poverty?

The term *underclass* has been applied to many different groups: long-term welfare recipients, the white rural poor in Appalachia, Native Americans, and others. But the most prominent images associated with the underclass are those of black ghetto residents. The old picture of the poor on television used to be of people desperately seeking a job, standing in line for food, or complaining of how the government was treating them.

Some of those shadows linger in pictures of the homeless or the hungry. But the searing silhouettes are of a different sort.

Now the place is the inner city. The values, culture, and attitudes seem distorted and perverse. On camera, young men brag about how many children they have fathered out of wedlock. Young women act as though having children outside marriage is inevitable and acceptable. Occasionally, murder is justified as an appropriate response by gangs whose honor was somehow challenged. Drugs and alcohol seem to be everywhere.[2]

White middle-class Americans recoil in horror from such images, which seem far worse than the old pictures of the underclass of Appalachia who were portrayed as physically isolated and unsophisticated, mired in an environment that offered little opportunity or outside contact, and whose tragedy was easier to understand and explain. People in this new "underclass" live in the biggest cities, yet seem to be in their own world. They seem to embrace values that the middle class cannot understand. And their very proximity makes them seem more foreign and more menacing than the earlier underclass who lived entirely in an Appalachian world few Americans would ever see. As our perception that the poor consist largely of the black ghetto underclass has grown, so, too, has our dissatisfaction with existing policies to help the poor. If America's willingness to help comes mainly from our desire for and sense of community, this image of a culture and class so far outside the mainstream would naturally choke off a part of our charitable instincts.

Academics have been unsuccessful in figuring out reliable ways to determine how many people (if any) are "socially dislocated," cut off from the mainstream and exhibiting antisocial and counterproductive behavior.[3] But they have found it easy to determine how many people live in areas of highly concentrated poverty. Since virtually all the underclass or "culture of poverty" theories emphasize that the problems seem to arise in areas where there is a concentration of social and economic problems, counting the number of people who live in concentrated areas of poverty seems like a logical starting point. The images provided by the press are invariably gathered from the worst parts of our major cities. Indeed, the terms *ghetto poor* and *underclass* are often used as synonyms, even among academic researchers.[4]

It should be understood that just being poor in a high-poverty area need not indicate that one suffers from behavioral or cultural deficiencies. The poor may be found concentrated together on the wrong side of the railroad tracks not because their poverty breeds new poverty, but because they are not allowed or financially able to live on the right side. Concentration would seem to be a necessary but not sufficient condition for the existence of a culture of poverty. Concentrated areas of poverty can be measured, but attitudes and values are much harder to examine.

The Bureau of the Census already has a designation for poverty areas. A poverty area in a metropolitan area is a "census tract" with a poverty rate of 20 percent or more. According to the Bureau of the Census, "when census tracts are established, they are designed to be homogeneous with respect to housing characteristics, economic status, and living conditions. Tracts generally have between 2,500 and 8,000 residents."[5] These are relatively small areas. The city of Chicago proper, for example, has some 860 tracts. Being so small, a census tract can be loosely seen as a neighborhood. There are no census tracts in rural areas, so in nonmetropolitan sections the census designates a whole county as a poverty area if the poverty rate exceeds 20 percent.

A neighborhood with a poverty rate of 20 percent hardly seems like a poor neighborhood. After all, the overall poverty rate for blacks is 30 percent, so predominantly black neighborhoods would be expected to have a poverty rate of 30 percent if there was *no* sorting by income. If there was any tendency for people of similar incomes and races to live together, one would expect virtually all poor black people to live in neighborhoods with poverty rates in excess of 20 percent. Even in white communities, where the overall average poverty rates are closer to 10 percent, one would probably expect that an even modest geographic sorting by income class would lead to a large proportion of poor persons living in such areas.

Amazingly enough, if we accept the loose census definition of poverty areas, less than 40 percent of all poor people lived in poor neighborhoods or poor counties in 1980.[6] Even slightly concentrated poverty is not much of an issue for at least three-fifths of the poor. But this definition of a poverty area is surely too broad. The people one sees on television or reads about in newspapers typically come from big-city neighborhoods that have poverty rates of 40 or even 80 percent. Thus, a more natural definition of a *ghetto poverty area* is a neighborhood with a poverty rate of 40 percent in a moderate-size or large city.

The census publishes a document that allows one to look at such neighborhoods in the 100 largest cities.[7] It reports that just 1.8 million of the 27.4 million poor people are found in high-poverty (40 percent or more poor) census tracts in the 100 largest cities. Thus, fewer than *7 percent* of the poor in 1980 lived in what might be called a big city ghetto. If we confined ourselves to the black ghetto poor, we would be looking at 5 percent of the overall population of poor people.

This definition of ghetto poverty has been used by several writers who have sought to estimate the potential size of the underclass.[8] It has been criticized as being too high because it looks only at concentrations of poverty, and those who live in poverty areas need not exhibit a high level of "behavioral deviancy."[9] It has been criticized as too being low because even nonpoor residents of ghetto areas may be part of an underclass and because there may be ghetto neighborhoods even in smaller cities. Erol Ricketts and Isabel Sawhill tried to remedy these problems in their study of the number of people (poor and nonpoor in all cities) who lived in census tracts in which there was a high degree of behavioral troubles, as measured by dropout levels, unemployed prime-age males, welfare recipients, and female heads of households. They concluded: "In 1980, using our definition of underclass areas, there were 2.6 million people . . . living in such areas. Not all of these people are poor, nor do all of them engage in underclass behaviors, but they all live in neighborhoods where such behaviors are common."[10] This 2.6 million figure is still less than 10 percent of the 27.4 million figure for the poor population in 1980.

These figures are surprising to many. The image of the ghetto poor person has been emphasized so heavily in the media and in recent books that even those who study poverty are surprised by what they have found. Figure 6.1 shows the distribution of poor people in America. It indicates that poor Americans are more often among us than isolated from us.

The ghettos contain the most visible and readily identifiable poor, but what one misses in them is the mass of people that we have been discussing in most of the book. The full-time working poor, the retired and disabled, divorced mothers struggling to get on their feet, unemployed workers, rural farmers, young families who are starting out—these are much closer to the true faces of American poverty. Policy makers who see only

Figure 6.1
Geographic Distribution of the Poor in 1980

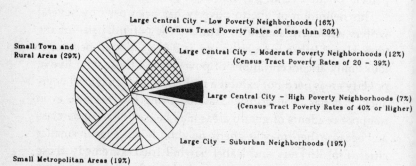

Large Central City – Low Poverty Neighborhoods (16%)
(Census Tract Poverty Rates of less than 20%)

Small Town and
Rural Areas (29%)

Large Central City – Moderate Poverty Neighborhoods (12%)
(Census Tract Poverty Rates of 20 – 39%)

Large Central City – High Poverty Neighborhoods (7%)
(Census Tract Poverty Rates of 40% or Higher)

Large City – Suburban Neighborhoods (19%)

Small Metropolitan Areas (19%)

NOTE: Large cities are the one hundred largest central cities.
SOURCES: U.S. Bureau of the Census, *General Social and Economic Characteristics, United States Summary, 1980 Census of Population* (Washington, D.C.: U.S. Government Printing Office, 1983), table 119, pp. 1–90; U.S. Bureau of the Census, *Poverty Areas in Large Cities, 1980 Census of Population*. Vol. 2, *Subject Reports* (Washington, D.C.: Government Printing Office, 1985), table S-1, p. 1, and table 1, p. 45.

the black faces in Harlem are committing as grave a sin as those who ignore these faces altogether. Even among poor blacks, fewer than 20 percent live in large cities in ghetto neighborhoods where at least 40 percent of the residents are poor.

The images on television and in the newspapers are drawn from the most desperate 5 percent or 10 percent of the poor. And, even then, reporters are prone to select the most outrageous and provocative cases. For example, Auletta discussed the case of "Jean Madison," who said she had eight children by the time she was 14, and twenty-nine children by the time she was 38. Auletta suggested that he believed her.[11] Even if the story is true, it is wildly unrepresentative. In 1982, only 1.6 percent of the AFDC families had six or more children, and 75 percent of the recipients had only one or two children.[12]

But if the ghetto poor represent less than 10 percent of the poor, they are visible enough and troubled enough to justify special consideration. And they would surely represent a larger percentage of the long-term poor. So in the remainder of this chapter, I will examine the problems of the poor who are concentrated in the ghettos. Over 75 percent of the residents of ghetto neighborhoods are black; most of the rest are drawn from other minority groups. I wish I could offer information on all these groups, but the Census' definitions of Hispanics and other minorities have gone through so many iterations over the years that the historical statistics that I would want to use simply are not available. Thus, I will explore only the problem of blacks in high-poverty urban neighborhoods.

"Situational" vs. "Cultural" Causes of Ghetto Poverty

The debate over the existence and nature of a culture of poverty has one of the most confused and perplexing intellectual histories of any topic related to the disadvantaged. The notion that

a high degree of "social dislocation" or "social disorganization"
existed in the nation's cities received considerable attention in
the early and mid-1960s. Kenneth Clark, Michael Harrington,
Herbert Gans, and Oscar Lewis all described worlds of isolated
and concentrated poverty.[13] Their message was that the desperation of the ghetto needed to be understood and remedied, not
that ghetto residents were inevitably trapped by their own culture. Even Lewis, who is seen as the strongest proponent of the
view that culture becomes independent of current circumstance, believed that a revolution could change all that he saw
for the better. According to William Julius Wilson:

What was both unique and important about these earlier studies
was that the discussions of the experiences of inequality were
closely tied to discussions of the structure of inequality in an attempt to explain how the economic and social situations into which
so many disadvantaged blacks are born produce modes of adapta-
tion and create norms of behavior that take the form of a "self-
perpetuating pathology."[14]

At first, this vision galvanized people to action. Something
had to be done to correct the conditions that bred such problems. But with the attacks on the Moynihan report[15] and an
increasing sense that analysts were blaming the victim, liberal
scholars "shied away from researching behavior construed as
unflattering or stigmatizing to particular racial minorities."[16]
According to Wilson, liberals tended either to deny that underclass behavior existed or to lay the blame entirely on a lack of
opportunity or on racism.

Work on these matters practically ceased until the 1980s,
when the problems of the ghetto reemerged in popular debates.
But in its later iteration, the culture of poverty seems to have
been embraced by conservatives rather than liberals. Those on
the right argued that the poor suffered not from a lack of opportunity but from bad values. To the extent that external forces
played a role, they were the adverse incentives created by an
overly generous and misguided set of social policies.

Until recently, the policy debate that surrounded these issues has been exceptionally simplistic. Conservatives seemed to blame all poverty on bad values. Ghetto poverty was "cultural" and so conservatives offered only those solutions that they thought would bring values back in line—workfare or the elimination of welfare. Liberals blamed poverty entirely on racism and the lack of opportunity. They believed that poverty was "situational," so the key was equal opportunity and training and jobs. The fact that those on all sides of the debate have pointed to ghetto poverty to justify their preferred action suggests that the discussion has often been superficial.

Any sensible model of behavior emphasizes the role of opportunities along with values and motivation. Two people who have the same opportunities will make different choices because their background and abilities lead them to have different goals and expectations. But, according to the sociologist Lee Rainwater, anthropological conceptions of values and culture usually treat them as reflective of or reactive to the environmental, social, and economic forces in the community.[17] And, as the anthropologist Ulf Hannerz said, "It is anthropological common sense that any culture is adaptive."[18] Back in 1968, Herbert Gans argued:

Behavior is thus a mixture of situational responses and cultural patterns, that is, behavioral norms and aspirations. Some situational responses are strictly ad hoc reactions to a current situation; they exist because of that situation and will disappear if it changes or disappears. Other situational responses are internalized and become behavior norms that are an intrinsic part of the person and of the groups in which he moves.[19]

Culture and values develop as ways of understanding and coping with the world in which people find themselves. Culture is never static unless conditions are static and unless the culture successfully helps people deal with the world around them. When the culture is put under stress, it adjusts in some fashion. Again, as Gans noted, "A new situation will initially be met with available norms; only when these norms turn out to be inapplicable or damaging will people change; first, their behavior, and then the norms upholding that behavior."[20] Just how dynamic the culture is and what the response will be to changed environmental conditions is hard to judge.

Actually, it is clear that conservatives believe values and culture are strongly affected by external forces. Charles Murray stated:

Three conditions promote this state of affairs in a community of poor people: (1) insularity, the isolation of a community from intercourse with mainstream society, (2) expectation of failure, conditioning that leads to fragile self-confidence (independently of real abilities); (3) official sanction to reject personal responsibility for one's actions.[21]

Thus, the behaviors one observes are the direct result of isolation, failure, and, most important for Murray, a social welfare system that penalizes rather than rewards responsibility. It is ironic that Murray uses these observations to support a conservative agenda, for his words echo those of the left who argued for integration and desegregation in the 1960s and 1970s—to correct the "insularity" problem. And the notion that people learn to fail is another favorite of liberals. Only the argument about the influence of the social welfare system makes it conservative.

Lawrence M. Mead called for workfare with the argument that values have gone astray and that changed policies or conditions can reverse them.[22] Indeed, this view that only strict rules about work can change the ghetto culture is often used to justify a work-oriented support system.[23] The important message of the current conservative thinkers is that values and culture adjust to and reflect the environment, opportunities, history, and incentives that people face; that is why welfare is such a big part of the problem. These conservatives claim that it changes values.

On the liberal side, few really argue that the poverty in ghettos is purely situational in the sense that the elimination of racism and the rapid expansion of jobs would instantaneously alter behavior. According to Rainwater:

The argument developed . . . is that the ethnographic evidence, which is the kind of evidence most appropriate to cultural concepts does not support the extreme version of the culture of poverty hypothesis [that culture is passed on through families and unchanged by altered environmental and social conditions]. . . .

But I have argued that an assessment of the ethnographic evidence also does not provide support for the so called "situational" view. . . . In fact those who have argued this view have been very unclear as to exactly how they believe the impact of social structure forces are translated into "situational behavior" on the part of lower class individuals. They simply assert that the responses of lower class individuals are in some sense "natural" or predictable. But that is exactly the view argued by those who have proposed the usefulness of the concept of lower class sub-culture. . . .[24]

Clearly, people on all sides of the debate implicitly acknowledge that motivation and culture play an important role but that these are strongly influenced by forces around them. The main arguments are over the relative importance of different forces, the ways in which behavior can be changed, and the speed with which changed circumstances have an impact. But most agree that environment, opportunity, incentives, circumstance, attitudes, and expectations all play a critical role.

How far, then, does the culture-versus-situation debate take us in understanding the causes of ghetto poverty? By itself, not far. Opportunity and incentives influence culture, which influences behavior, which influences opportunity, which influences culture, ad infinitum. A far more productive approach seems to be the one suggested by Wilson, who argues for putting aside the culture/situation debate and trying to understand the forces that shape the behavior, attitudes, and expectations of ghetto residents.[25]

Negative Forces That Influence Ghetto Residents

What one finds in the ghetto is a frightening array of negative forces: deprivation, concentration, isolation, discrimination, poor education, and the movement of jobs away from central cities. Add crime, drugs and alcohol, the underground economy, and welfare to these forces, and you have a combination of factors that would be hard for even the strongest and most concerned parents to fight.

Deprivation

Black children generally, not just those who live in ghettos, suffer far more economic deprivation than do white children. Family structure and labor market performance were shown earlier to be the two biggest factors that influence the poverty of families. Black families are much more likely to be female headed, and the earnings of black men are still much lower than those of white men. It should come as no surprise, therefore, that black children typically fare much worse economically than do white children. The magnitude of the differences is shocking nonetheless.

Figure 6.2 shows the number of years of poverty that black children and white children, who were born between 1967 and 1973, experienced from birth to age 10.[26] The majority of black children had four years or more of poverty in the first ten years of life. Only 8 percent of the white children were poor for four or more years. One black child in three was poor in at least seven of his or her first ten years, compared to only one white child in thirty-three. Think about the implications of these simple statistics. Only 8 percent of white children will know as much economic deprivation as the typical black child. Although long-term poverty is rare for whites, it is a fact of life for a large minority of blacks.

If you knew nothing else about two groups except that as children their economic conditions were this divergent, would

Figure 6.2
Years of Pretransfer Poverty from Birth to Age 10 for Children, by Race

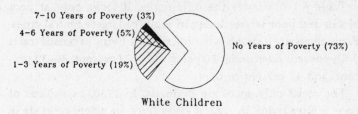

7–10 Years of Poverty (3%)

4–6 Years of Poverty (5%)

1–3 Years of Poverty (19%)

No Years of Poverty (73%)

White Children

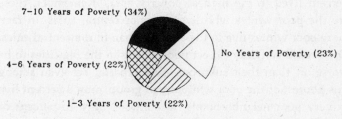

7–10 Years of Poverty (34%)

4–6 Years of Poverty (22%)

1–3 Years of Poverty (22%)

No Years of Poverty (23%)

Black Children

SOURCE: Author's tabulations of survey data from the Panel Study of Income Dynamics. See note 2 in chapter 4.

you not expect sizable differences in the children's futures? It is not just the money, although the lack of money surely can be a direct source of deprivation and stress. A family who is poor is often troubled by something else: the lack of a job, low-paying or menial work, only one parent, or personal tragedy.

Worse yet, these are the figures for all black children, not the minority who live in the ghetto.[27] Ghetto poverty and deprivation must be significantly worse on average. One can reasonably hypothesize that ghetto children can count on growing up poor.

Concentration

Poor whites rarely live in areas of concentrated poverty. They live in or near areas where others are not poor. Poor blacks, however, often are surrounded by other poor blacks. And things seem to have gotten worse over time.

Table 6.1 illustrates the differences. It looks only at poor blacks and poor whites living in the fifty largest central cities. For each group, it shows what fraction are living in census tracts with poverty rates under 20 percent, 20–29 percent, 30–39 percent, and 40 percent or over.

The racial differences are dramatic. In 1980, two-thirds of poor whites living in central cities lived in neighborhoods in which the poverty rate was less than 20 percent, and only 8 percent lived in the highest poverty areas. Remember, these are the poor whites who live in major central cities. In fact, more poor whites live in the suburbs than in the central cities. One would certainly expect poor whites in the big cities to be worse off than their suburban counterparts. Yet even among this poorest of the poor white urban group, only 8 percent live in very poor neighborhoods. In contrast, only 16 percent of poor blacks in these cities live in neighborhoods in which the poverty rate is under 20 percent; in 1980, over one-third of them lived in areas in which the poverty rate exceeded 40 percent.

TABLE 6.1

Distribution of Poor Whites and Poor Blacks Living in the Fifty Largest Central Cities, by Poverty Rate in the Census Tract of Residence 1970 and 1980 (Percentage)

Percentage in Poverty in the Census Tract	Poor Whites		Poor Blacks	
	1970	1980	1970	1980
Under 20	64	66	20	16
20–29	18	17	26	21
30–39	10	9	27	27
40 and over	8	8	27	36

SOURCES: U.S. Bureau of the Census, *Poverty Areas in Large Cities,* Vol. 2 of *1980 Census of the Population, Subject Reports* (Washington, D.C.: U.S. Government Printing Office, 1985), table 1, p. 45; and U.S. Bureau of the Census, *Low Income Areas in Large Cities, 1970 Census of the Population, Subject Reports* (Washington, D.C.: U.S. Government Printing Office, 1973), table 1.

Moreover, things seem to be getting worse. The fraction of poor blacks living in very poor ghetto neighborhoods grew from just over one-quarter in 1970 to over one-third in just ten years, even though the overall poverty rate for blacks fell somewhat between 1970 and 1980. The worsening situation is dramatic in some areas. For example, in New York City in 1970, "just" 15 percent of poor blacks were in high poverty neighborhoods (40 percent or more poor); by 1980, the figure had jumped to 45 percent. In Chicago, the fraction moved from 25 percent to nearly 50 percent.[28] So blacks are not only poor much more often than are whites, they are much more often surrounded by poverty.

Isolation

Several contemporary observers, most notably Wilson, have claimed that the oppressive discrimination in housing and the labor markets in the earlier days forced blacks of different classes and backgrounds to live together or at least in close proximity. More recently, as new opportunities opened to educated and professional blacks, many fled the ghetto neighborhoods. Wilson believes that with them went many of the traditional mainstream role models, the people who make it in spite of the adversity around them. What was left was a vacuum where practically the only economically successful people who remained were the drug dealers, the pimps, and the petty thieves—those who feed off the ghetto's desperation.

According to Wilson:

Indeed, in the 1930s, 1940s, and 1950s such communities featured a vertical integration of different segments of the urban black population. Lower class, working class, and middle class black families all lived in more or less the same communities (albeit in different neighborhoods), sent their children to the same schools, availed themselves of the same recreational facilities, and shopped at the same stores. . . . In the earlier years, the black middle and working classes were confined by restrictive covenants to communities also inhabited by the lower class, and their very presence provided stability to inner-city neighborhoods and reinforced and perpetuated mainstream patterns of behavior.

This is not the situation of the 1980s. Today's ghetto neighborhoods are populated almost exclusively by the most disadvantaged segments of the black urban community; that heterogeneous grouping of families and individuals who are outside the mainstream of the American occupational system. Included in this group are individuals who lack training or skills and either experience long-term unemployment or are not part of the labor force, individuals engaged in street criminal activity and other forms of aberrant behavior, and families who experience long-term spells of poverty and/or welfare dependency.[29]

The departure of the black middle class could mean more than a loss of role models. It probably led to the loss of connections and networks. If successfully employed persons do not live nearby, then the informal methods of information and search methods by which one worker tells someone else of a job and recommends him or her to the employer are lost.

Those left behind in the ghettos are surrounded by disadvantage. In the worst areas of our cities, over two-thirds of the children are living in single-parent families. According to the 1980 census, the median income for these female-headed families was under $5,000 in 1980, even after counting governmental cash transfers. In addition, the census found one-third more adult women than adult men in these areas. Of the adult men who were found, only 48 percent were working at at all; 31 percent of the adult women worked. Dropping out of school is common. Even among young (under age 21) black high school graduates, only one person in four has a job. Some 40 percent of all families report income from public assistance.[30]

Education

Since the early 1960s, the overall enrollment of black students in high schools has increased dramatically. Even as late as 1970, only 58 percent of the blacks aged 25–29 had completed four or more years of high school—well below the rate for whites of 78 percent. By 1984, the figure was up to 79 percent—close to the rate for whites of 86 percent.[31] Yet, in spite of this narrowed gap in enrollment, the achievement by blacks and whites, as measured by standardized tests, remains different. According to Gordon Berlin and Andrew Sum, the National Assessment of Educational Progress shows that the average black 17 year old reads at the same level as the average white 13 year old. They also report that black high school graduates usually do not score as well as white high school dropouts on the Armed Forces Qualification Test (AFQT)—a test that measures basic skills and educational attainment.[32]

Big-city schools seem to have a particularly large problem. Drop-out rates in some major school systems are extremely high. In Chicago, for example, 43 percent of the freshman class of 1978 had not graduated by 1984; one all-black high school had a drop-out rate of 63 percent. In Miami, the dropout rate was 30 percent overall and 34 percent for blacks.[33] Just maintaining order is difficult in some schools. Glenn Loury noted that in the 1984–85 school year, 288 shootings resulted in 25 fatalities "in and around Detroit public schools."[34]

Whether the educational achievements and the problems of big-city schools are a cause or an effect of poverty, the reality is that children in poorer areas of big-city school systems must try to learn in a hostile environment. And there is no question that black children in general and ghetto children in particular enter the job market far less well prepared than their white counterparts. With such different educational outcomes, young blacks must be in a far worse position to compete in the labor market.

Collapsing Opportunity

In addition to the deprivation, concentration, isolation, and poor education, ghetto residents face collapsing labor market opportunities. We have already noted the lack of growth in wages and the rising level of unemployment among all men from the late 1970s to the mid-1980s. What economic growth there was went to putting women and some in-school youths to work, often in service industries.

Jobs for black men, particularly the high-paying jobs, have traditionally been blue collar. In 1970, almost 60 percent of employed black men were craftsmen, operators, fabricators, or laborers.[35] These are the types of jobs that have been hit hardest in recent years. Between 1970 and 1980, total employment (of all races and sexes) grew by nearly 30 percent, but employment in these four occupations grew by just 13 percent. And the employment of black men in these same jobs grew by just 5 percent. Meanwhile, during this decade, the number of black men in the population grew by 30 percent.

These job changes are particularly damaging because they mean that older blacks cannot help younger ones with connections in the labor market. Jobs that require moderate skills in industry are traditionally filled through informal job networks.[36] Employers hire people they know or who have been recommended by other workers. Older black workers could thus help younger ones get a foot in the door. When the door is locked and workers are trying to avoid being pushed out themselves, they can do little for their younger counterparts.

Worse yet, the changes have been greatest in our major cities, particularly in the North. John Kasarda, of the University of North Carolina, examined industrial changes in a variety of cities by the level of educational preparation required on the job. His basic conclusion was that "black males in northern cities are still most concentrated in the [employment category] . . . where employment opportunities declined fastest and are least represented in that category where northern central city employment has expanded since 1970."[37] Kasarda also noted that "essentially all of the national growth in entry level and other low education requisite jobs have accrued in the suburbs, exurbs, and nonmetropolitan areas far removed from the growing concentrations of poorly educated minorities."[38]

Some time ago, I looked in detail at job changes in Chicago.

I found a clear pattern of the outmigration of jobs requiring low skills.[39] Indeed, high-skill workers commuted in and low-skill workers commuted out. Low-skill blacks were spending a longer and longer time commuting to their jobs. I was skeptical that this fact alone accounted for the differential labor market outcomes of black and white men, but the pattern of increasing disadvantage was clear.

There is considerable controversy over just how difficult it is for young blacks to get jobs. One hears press reports of employers saying that they cannot find people to work. Such claims are difficult to evaluate. I believe that the shortage of jobs is a major contributor to the problems of young black men. Let me offer three bits of evidence.

The United States military offers good jobs, but the working conditions are severe. Only those who are willing to accept a highly structured and authoritarian work environment would even think of applying. Yet, even in the best economic times, vastly more blacks attempt to join the military than are accepted. Furthermore, many more blacks get hired by the military when economic times are *good* than when they are bad. This fact seems counterintuitive. You would expect people to want to join the army when conditions were bad. The paradox is explained by the fact that blacks tend to score much lower on average than do whites on the Armed Forces Qualification Test. In good times, higher-scoring (and disproportionately white) recruits are less interested in joining the military, so more room is available for blacks.[40]

Second, a variety of youth employment programs provide jobs for youths. If plenty of jobs were available, then each youth hired by the government should diminish the number of blacks working in the private sector, since black youths would substitute public work for private jobs. Yet recent evidence suggests that governmental jobs represent a substantial net increase in employment for blacks, which indicates that the recruits were formerly unemployed or that the jobs they left were filled by unemployed youths.[41]

Finally in Boston, where the economy is booming, the unemployment rate of black males was just 5.6 percent in 1985, compared to the national rate of 15.3 percent. Perhaps even more telling is the fact that 71 percent of black men of all ages were working, a percentage far higher than the national average of 60 percent. Indeed, the unemployment rate and employment percentage for blacks in Boston were nearly identical to the national averages for whites of 6.1 percent and 72 percent, respectively.[42]

These three pieces of evidence all suggest that more blacks would like to work than are currently being accommodated. Apparently, in our stagnant economy, which has had to absorb a large number of new workers, blacks are often left off the ladder because they lack the necessary skills, do not have the appropriate connections, or are victims of discrimination. Only when the economy booms and labor is in short supply do blacks fare better.

Crime, Drugs, and the Underground Economy

According to governmental figures, the odds of being robbed are twice as high for low-income blacks as for low-income whites and they are three to four times higher than for middle-income whites.[43] Rapes are far more common in the low-income black community than elsewhere. And in the worst areas of our major cities, the incidence of crime and victimization is much worse.

Wilson reported that in 1980 the Robert Taylor Homes public housing project, which housed just half of one percent of Chicago's population, witnessed "11 percent of the city's murders, 9 percent of its rapes, and 10 percent of its aggravated assaults."[44] The next year in Cabrini-Green, another housing project, he noted that over "a nine week period . . . 10 Cabrini-Green residents were murdered; 35 were wounded by gunshots, including random sniping."[45]

A National Bureau of Economic Research (NBER) study surveyed black male youths, aged 16–24, in ghetto areas in three cities: Boston, Chicago, and Philadelphia in 1979. The study directors Richard B. Freeman and Harry J. Holzer reported that, "with respect to 'socially deviant behavior,' 16 percent of the NBER survey group reported having engaged in crimes; 26 reported drug use beyond marijuana."[46] W. Kip Viscusi estimated that after adjusting for underreporting, roughly one-quarter of all income reported by the youths came from criminal sources.[47] He stated that more than half the youths may have engaged in crime. Crime, it would seem, is both a source of danger and insecurity and an alternative to employment in many cases.

Welfare and Public Assistance

It is clear that the desperation and troubles of the ghetto predate the current preoccupation with welfare as the major underminer of values and responsibility. It is interesting to read the older research on the ghettos of the early 1960s because the world of the ghetto depicted then had much in common with the world depicted today. Yet, many observers believe that conditions have worsened significantly in the past decade, and they lay the blame largely on welfare.

Few studies have looked systematically at the impact of welfare on the behavior of ghetto residents per se. The statistical evidence cited in chapter 3, which found only minor links between welfare and the structure of families, was for all persons, not just for the small fraction who live in the ghettos. But some of the same arguments apply to ghetto residents.

Welfare benefits rose sharply until about 1973, but they have been falling since then. Adjusted for inflation, the combined AFDC and food stamp benefits are now only slightly higher than they were in 1960 (although other benefits such as Medicaid and some housing assistance are now available). Many observers trace the real decay of the ghettos to the past decade or so, a period when welfare was decreasing. And only 40 percent of the residents in poor neighborhoods report that they get welfare.

Still it is clear that the welfare system described in chapter 5 does nothing to reinforce, reward, or encourage work (except by making welfare unpleasant). And it does nothing to reinforce paternal responsibility. It does not open up options for single mothers. Indeed, it creates a situation in which the most logical choice for a poorly educated mother may be to remain indefinitely on welfare. A world in which many, many children are being raised in families who rely on welfare is one in which there are few working persons who offer role models and connections. Welfare may not have created the problem, but it surely has done nothing to solve it.

Discrimination

On top of all these factors there remains discrimination. Although some have announced that racism has been largely banished, discrimination in the housing market has been proved over and over again in our cities. Controlled experiments in which blacks and whites with similar incomes are sent to the same realtor have found that blacks simply are not shown certain types of properties.[48] Racist incidents continue to occur with alarming frequency all over the country.

Racism cannot be blamed for the apparently worsening situation of many inner-city residents since the 1960s and early 1970s, for virtually no contemporary observer would deny that there have been significant achievements in reducing barriers to opportunity. The civil rights movement, affirmative action programs, and increased awareness all seem to have contributed to an opening up of opportunity for educated and professional blacks. Doubts remain, however, about whether there have been any great strides in reducing discrimination for those at the lower end of the education and skills spectrum.

With overt discrimination legally banished, there is no easy way to judge how much discrimination exists in the labor market, but the discrimination that remains is surely worse for ghetto residents. A black person who talks strangely and dresses unusually and who has little work experience will surely be regarded with a jaundiced eye by the white (and the black) public. When stereotypes are strong and information is weak, discrimination is likely to be more severe.

The Combined Impact—The Human Side

Imagine the world of the ghetto through the eyes of its children. The children are surrounded by poverty. They are likely to spend their whole lives poor, as are virtually all their friends. Few around them are working at solid, traditional, even moderately well-paying jobs, since anyone who could afford to get out of this environment has done so. The children attend schools that seem to offer little real education or encouragement. They grow up with considerable fear and little trust. Can such children dare to think that they will someday be a part of middle America? Do they have much opportunity to join the wealthy mainstream paraded so visibly on television?

And imagine this world through the eyes of their parents. Even if parents were determined to raise their children right—to motivate them, to see to it that they achieved their potential, to give them the chance to better themselves—what would be their chances of success? Placed in a similar situation, how many middle-class people could pull it off, instilling the hope, the dreams, the drive, the motivation, the skills, the ambition, and the confidence? And what if the parents themselves are a product of this environment? It is easy to see why middle- and working-class black families have left these neighborhoods. They have done what any sensible person would do who had a choice. They have left to protect themselves and their children.

Yet, there still are people with initiative, energy, and determination in the ghetto. Some of the best accounts of the ghetto are from people who started there and escaped. Claude Brown, author of *Manchild in the Promised Land*, went back to Harlem twenty years later and described the desperation he saw.[49] Sylvester Monroe, now a reporter for *Newsweek*, grew up in the Robert Taylor Homes in Chicago and recently wrote a story about what happened to his friends and associates.[50]

But what comes through sharply in most of these stories is

that relatively few people seem to make it. Those who do usually had a strong determination and some significant figure in their life who guided them and encouraged them to rise above their world. The tragedy is that success is achieved by so few.

Some of the most vivid images of the ghetto appeared in a series of articles by Leon Dash that appeared in the *Washington Post*. [51] Dash spent a year living in one of the most troubled areas in Washington, D.C., and focused his series on teenage pregnancy. He described one girl who got pregnant in the hope of keeping her boyfriend. (She had become moody following her mother's death from cancer). But her boyfriend (who later went to prison) was not pleased. "During the next 2 years, Sherita moved 16 times, shunted back and forth between her grandmother . . . , an aunt of a boyfriend and friends of her brother."[52] In desperation, she eventually asked her welfare social workers for help. They did little. Finally she called a television reporter and shortly she received a call from the city's Commissioner of Social Services. The city found her a shelter but said that because she was a minor, her child would probably have to be put in foster care. She left immediately. The girl eventually went to live with the mother of her half sister.

Another girl told Dash she did not want to have a baby because

. . . there is so much love I want to give my child. So much love. So much attention. I'm not financially fit. I don't really have an education, I can't get out of my mother's house. To me that's like bringing a child into a world that all he's going to see is a lot of pain.[53]

But a major tragedy in her life sent her into a depression. She started skipping school and quarreled frequently with her family. She was unhappy at home, but she had been involved in a satisfying relationship with a boyfriend and she thought a baby might pull her out of her depression. She got pregnant, but lost the baby. Both she and her boyfriend dropped out of school and have worked off and on since then. The girl found a job at

McDonalds one summer, but she quit in December. Her boy-friend was laid off a construction job and then got a job at the same McDonalds. According to Dash, "She said she made a mistake by dropping out of school but added, 'I don't think it was a big mistake. I see girls and guys who finished school and they still can't find a job.' "[54]

A third couple in Dash's series had a baby and hoped to marry soon. But the boy lost a job that paid $150 per week, was out of work for three months, and finally got a $60-a-week job as a delivery boy. Recently, he found a new job paying $130 per week. The girl remains hopeful, but she "knows one thing for certain: she wants to move out of Washington Highlands. 'The neighborhood . . . is treacherous. You have to look both ways. . . . I'm looking for drug addicts. I'm looking for police. I'm looking for people stampeding over my baby.' "[55]

The real tragedy is that most of the young people who appear in the ghetto documentaries clearly have some cleverness and initiative. A few are gang members and drug pushers. But in most, you see evidence of the values of autonomy/independence, work, family, and even community. Nonetheless, these young people do not look like they are going to escape from a world that does not offer them much direction. In the words of one counselor on Bill Moyers's television special, "The Vanishing Family: Crisis in Black America" (broadcast on January 26, 1986), they are kids "on a trip without a road map."

These are people with a hard life and few mainstream options or role models. Who do they know who can get them good jobs? And what would they bring to such jobs? What evidence is there that hard work pays off, that commitments are critical, or that responsibility is rewarded? One is led to ask, Who would we expect to escape this world? Ghetto residents are often accused of thinking only of the present and ignoring the future. It is hard to see how looking to the future would give them more initiative or drive, since the future does not look much different from the past.

In a context such as this, questions of why young girls get

pregnant or why couples do not marry or why people do not work more seem trite. For a young girl who sees no chance of joining the mainstream, few ways to control her hostile environment, few opportunities to marry an employed and responsible man, having a child may seem a desirable thing, giving her a source of love and control. Even if work were available, it would seem to offer little immediate chance for escape. Why should a youngster who sees the past as a series of happenstance events expect his or her actions to change the future?

It is not hard to see that both the conservative and liberal treatments of the ghetto poor contain insights as well as oversimplifications. Murray's argument that isolation and failure breed disdain and alienation rings true.[56] But his emphasis on the welfare system as the primary force whose elimination would do considerable good seems to trivialize a complex and multifaceted problem. Similarly, in accordance with the liberal view, situational factors clearly are important, but the notion that only jobs and opportunity are the issues rings false. The lack of real control, the hostility of the environment, and the perception of impotence and failure contribute to a host of potentially destructive values and behavior.

One of the most plausible explanations for what one sees in ghettos may be found in a recent article by Thomas Kane.[57] Kane points out that according to theories of social psychology when people are put in an environment in which they are faced with a large number of uncontrollable circumstances, in which their actions seem to have little direct influence on their destiny, you can expect them to respond in one of two ways: "reactance" and learned helplessness. Reactance represents an aggressive attempt to exert control over the environment in whatever ways one can. Learned helplessness is a kind of resignation that leads to passivity, limited motivation, and nonresponsive behavior. America's ghettos seem to offer clear examples of both types of behavior.

What seems lacking in the ghetto is a direction—a sense of

options, opportunity, and hope. The obvious place to start is by providing clear, direct routes into the mainstream.

Searching For Answers

Consider the efforts of Eugene Lang. According to a *New York Times* report by William Geist,

Sitting on the dais, Eugene Lang, multimillionaire industrialist, suddenly realized the commencement speech he was about to deliver was complete balderdash, to put it nicely.

He was about to tell 61 sixth-graders in a warm Harlem auditorium that he had also attended P.S. 121, a half century ago, that he had worked hard and made a lot of money, and that—quick, the No-Doz!—if they worked hard maybe they could be successful too.

Instead, Mr. Lang, a magnate with a no-nonsense style, stepped to the podium and told the graduates that if they stayed in school he would pay the college tuitions for each and every one of them: college educations on the house!

There was a stunned silence, peppered with a few audible gasps. Then students, parents, and teachers cheered and mobbed him. "I have never kissed so many strangers," Mr. Lang recalled.[58]

Lang did much more than offer college. He hired a social worker named Johnny Rivera, who works at the Youth Action Program in East Harlem, to look after the children. He encouraged the students to visit him to talk and held frequent Saturday afternoon sessions with them. Over the years, he has spent perhaps $250,000 on tutors, counselors, support.[59]

Apparently both teachers and parents have responded. One student said, "My junior high school teachers were always after me to keep my grades up." One boy said his mother told him, "If you blow this opportunity, I'll kill you!" The members of this class report that other students are jealous of them and tease them.

For other students in this area, "dropping out is normal." As one student put it, "Around here, you are big and important if you drop out." Yet these students did not drop out. All of the 51 students who remained in the New York area are expected to graduate from high school, and 40 of them are expected to go to college.[60] What is incredible is that Lang's offer to pay for their college education was not really necessary. Many got sizable scholarships. And they all could have gone to tuition-free or nearly tuition-free schools in the area.

It is obvious this is a unique and special story without any clear message for policy, since the government cannot create millions of Eugene Langs. But the story does offer something of a vision. What Lang seems to have offered these children was hope, along with services and direction. He made the children aware, from a young age, that there was another route, another alternative. He made them special and gave them dignity and attention. He made sure that someone looked after them and offered help and guidance. And they responded; they became success stories, not lost souls trapped in their environment.

Could they have done it on their own if they were strong enough and committed enough? Some surely could have. But many would not have tried, for they would not have seen the options, they would not think they could make it, and they would not see any real future. They are surrounded by failure and despair. Why should they have expected anything different? But Lang got them working toward a dream in sixth grade. Now it looks like they can achieve it.

The lesson I take from this story is that somehow we need to let people know that they can make it, that there are real options, that hard work pays off, that they are special, and that there is hope for the future. But we will also have to find a way to provide the tutoring and direction that Lang and Rivera seemed to provide. These words are easy to say but they are much harder to implement.

A Starting Point: Replace Welfare

Murray claims much of the despair of people who live in the ghettos is the result of the elite liberal wisdom that brought us welfare rights and a "don't-blame-the-victim" mentality.[61] Murray has a solution. Cut off the lifeline. Force them to swim.

In the face of this combination of negative forces, such a conclusion seems ludicrous. At most welfare helps sustain the community even though only 40 percent of the families in these areas report receiving public assistance.

Eliminating welfare would have some impact on the ghetto poor. But it is not clear what the effect would be. Fewer people might have babies, but those who had children would be truly desperate. Murray's idea is just a variant of the common conservative theme that these people have been coddled for too long and what they need is a good swift kick in the pants. I suspect that is about all that life has offered most ghetto residents so far. Helplessness is born of a system in which the motivated do not succeed—a system that offers a swift kick to all who come by.

Few policy makers seriously contemplate eliminating the entire social welfare system. But they continue to talk about cutting it back. In the ghetto world, welfare is only one bit player in a drama with many major actors. Reducing welfare benefits will just make these mixed-up lives more difficult.

Still one must worry about a system that allows people to stay on welfare for ten or even twenty years. One must be concerned about a situation in which welfare benefits outstrip the money from the low-wage jobs that are available nearby. One can disagree about whether welfare is a major cause of the problems, but, surely, there can be no disagreement that welfare does little to help people gain control and independence. It certainly does not improve their confidence or self-esteem or reward initiative. It does not give most recipients a chance to live even a remotely decent life or offer any routes to self-support. Welfare does not provide a chance to make it and it penalizes those who try.

The primary message of this book is that the welfare system does not reflect and reinforce our commonly held values and expectations. If we want to change the environment and the attitudes, hopes, and expectations of the ghetto poor, replacing the welfare system seems the obvious and important place to start.

I have spent the previous two chapters discussing how we might replace the welfare system and why we should do it. I drew those lessons without much reference to the ghetto precisely because I believe that ghetto poverty is not the major part of the poverty problem. I contend, however, that the logic for replacing the welfare system applies doubly well in the ghetto.

The changes I have recommended are an attempt to give people a genuine chance and an incentive to make it. Welfare gives no hope at all. It is hard to see how a woman from the ghetto, who is a high school dropout and has a child, will ever be able to get a job good enough to enable her to leave welfare, to give up the medical protection, and to make it on her own. She might try it, but it will be a long and difficult road, and she is likely to fail.

By making work pay, by guaranteeing medical protection, and by offering a base of support in the form of guaranteed child support, we can make it much easier for people to achieve some measure of independence and security. Even a half-time job at the minimum wage would put a woman and two children above the poverty line. And if the woman eventually worked full time, she would earn considerably more than the poverty line. She might even be able to move out of the neighborhood. She would have a reasonable chance to make it on her own, even if she could find a job only at McDonalds.

If a parent did not feel ready to work right away, there would be a transitional assistance program with an emphasis on training and services to help the parent develop some skills and the capacity to move into a decent job. Transitional assistance would not be like the welfare program that cannot decide whether its role is to offer long-term support or to help people establish some independence. There would be no ambiguity. The program would help people move up, and it would not offer them the option of long-term receipt.

Finally, even if parents could find no work after the transitional program, they could still get a governmental job—not a great job, but a job. And because of the expanded earned income tax credit, medical protection, and child support, single mothers would have to work only half time to live far better than they did on welfare while still having more independence and control than before. There can be no doubt that if single mothers were willing to work half time, they could achieve at least an income above poverty.

Things would look most different for two-parent families. Now such families often get no support. Under the proposed system, two-parent families would know that they would be able to support their families through work. They also would have more medical protection, higher effective wages, transitional support, and even a guaranteed job at the minimum wage after they exhausted the other options. Marriage would make more sense. And if parents split up or never married in the first place, the absent parent would still have child support obligations. These are all forces that would strengthen and support two-parent families without the conflicts and contradictions of welfare.

People would have more options, but they would have more responsibilities as well. Any parent would know that when he or she had an income, some of it would have to be shared with the child. I cannot accept the image of Timothy in Bill Moyers 1986 television special "The Vanishing Family: Crisis in Black America." Timothy fathered six children but felt no responsibility to support them. He said, "That's on them. . . . I ain't gonna let no woman stand in the way of my pleasures." I think there is no excuse for Timothy or a system that allows him not to pay child support. Someone like Timothy needs to know that whenever he has income, he will automatically have to share it with his children. If Timothy never finds a real job, we may never collect much child support, but anytime he earns any money that the government can find, he ought to be obligated to share it. Then, maybe Timothy will not father a seventh child.

Because public assistance will not be available to support people indefinitely, work will be the only option for permanent security. Any family will be able to make it through work. The system will be generous with people as they try to get on their feet. But eventually, the people will have to work if they want added help from the government.

These policies do not offer the promise, the special attention, the real direction that Eugene Lang offered. Thus, they would not be enough by themselves. Still, they seem a reasonable place to start. People would have a chance to make it, not into the true middle class, but at least out of poverty, through their own work and energies. There would be more hope than before. Moreover, the options of doing nothing to help an absent child (if you have earnings), of taking no responsibility for support of the family, or of simply collecting welfare for years and years will not be available.

Other Options

Replacing welfare will not be enough, even though it would be a start. The complex problems of the ghetto must be attacked on many fronts. Policy makers will have to weave together a multifaceted approach to help. I will not try to offer a comprehensive plan of aid. Instead, I will briefly summarize some of the other directions that have been suggested and comment on their plausibility and potential.

Education and Training. I have already noted that the educational system seems to leave blacks in a disadvantaged position in the labor market. Others have offered prescriptions for the educational shambles that persists in many of our cities. In the long run, unless people come out of the educational system better trained and motivated, there is little chance that the tragedy of the ghetto will be reversed. Indeed, that is one significant feature of the Lang story: he reached children early enough that they had time to learn.

One area of considerable promise is preschool education. For example, the careful long-term study of a special program in Ypsilanti, Michigan, found that just one to two years of preschool training led to major changes in the lives of disadvantaged black youngsters who were compared to a randomized control group. High school graduation rates were 67 percent, versus 49 percent for the control group.[62] Arrest rates were cut by 40 percent, and the rate of teenage pregnancy was cut almost in half. Unfortunately, only about 120 children were studied (half of whom received the preschool education). It is dangerous to draw conclusions about what might work for the whole country on the basis of such a select study, but other studies have also shown positive results.[63]

Benefits exceeded costs by seven to one in Ypsilanti. Even if the actual results are just one-fifth of those found in this study, preschool education is an investment well worth making. Moreover, preschool education can free parents of child care responsibilities and thus make work more of an option.

Another idea that deserves closer scrutiny is to keep children in school more of the time. There is evidence that poor children lose far more of their learning over the summer than do rich ones. If children were kept in school over the summer, they might learn more, forget less, spend less time on the streets, and be less of a strain on their mothers who are interested in working.

Programs for older children have tried to link schoolwork with jobs in the private sector. For example, under the Boston Compact, "business, university, and union leaders have signed separate agreements with the schools establishing measurable goals for progress in the schools, youth employment, and higher education."[64] The Boston Compact has sought to coordinate existing resources and create new ones. Businesses provide summer jobs and help place young people in more permanent work. Schools have career counselors with links to business. And a special program provides financial aid for tuition for those who need it to enter or continue in college.

Finally, employment and training programs for young adults who are out of school have had some impact, although it is hard to make definitive judgments because few programs have been carefully evaluated.[65] The Supported Work program showed some promise. In that program, gradually escalating expectations and demands were placed on participants in a workplace setting. The participants were selected from among long-term welfare recipients, ex-offenders, and youths. The program seemed to work well for the welfare recipients, but less well for the youths.[66] The Job Corps, which trains youngsters outside their home environment, seems to improve the earnings of those who go through it. The total benefits exceed the costs, even though the program only makes a modest dent on the problems.[67]

As we think about training programs, it is particularly important to keep in mind that we want to ensure that the motivated and responsible children really succeed. Too often in the past, we have been reluctant to "cream" our programs in these areas, wanting to serve the most disadvantaged. But one way to encourage initiative and responsibility is to ensure that the motivated do better than those who are not willing to try.

We can make some difference with training and educational programs. But even a modest impact requires intensive and serious help. The earlier and more intensively one intervenes, the more likely the program will be successful. It is foolhardy to assume that a ten-week training program for young adults is going to solve the problems accumulated from a childhood in the ghetto.

Direct Creation of Jobs. A strong hypothesis for why so few blacks get married is that there are few jobs for black men. If welfare was replaced with transitional support and jobs, married men would be guaranteed transitional help and last-resort jobs. I think that would be a major step forward and it could make marriage more attractive. In the ghettos, however, something more than last-resort jobs is needed. Anything that can be done to open up new private jobs could help. Reasonably well-paying governmental jobs that are given to the best people who qualify might be one more avenue for making it. If we are serious about strengthening the black family, we must find a way for young men (and women) to get decent work.

The Reagan administration has repeatedly proposed setting up "free enterprise zones"—areas in which the government would provide the infrastructure and some tax breaks to private businesses to relocate in ghetto areas. The proposals continue to be greeted with justifiable skepticism, since there is no real guarantee that the businesses would hire local residents, and similar state plans have had a spotty record.[68]

I think it is worth experimenting with comprehensive governmental and private jobs programs in a few cities to determine what difference a system that offered a real chance to work would make. Such programs can be expensive and they are controversial. But the ghetto economies offer so few options that much stronger medicine is needed than we have tried so far.

Empowerment.   Empowering the poor used to be the battle cry of the left, particularly the radical left. But lately it is used to rally the right. The idea that poor people will do better if they take the control of their lives away from the bureaucrats now appeals to those who want to get the government off the backs of people in general. There are a few impressive stories of how people have taken control of a housing project and "turned things around."[69]

Another way in which people can be given more control over their lives is the controversial idea of educational vouchers. Under such a system, parents would be given vouchers that they could use to enroll their children in any nearby school. This proposal is appealing in that it would give parents a chance to make decisions and exert some control over the schools their children attend. Some worry that such a plan would severely hurt public education, and others claim that it could save public education. Surely, the proposal deserves some serious experimentation.

The notion that people need control over their lives seems to appeal to both ends of the political spectrum, but the consensus is thin. Conservatives are willing to give tenants control over their housing projects but not over their landlords. Radicals want to organize the poor to demand their rights from the government and the private sector, whereas conservatives decry the welfare rights movement. When people organize and demand control, not everyone believes it is the right kind of empowerment.

The ghetto seems to offer people only a perverse control over their environment. There certainly are ways to ensure that people have more control. And increased control in one realm may inspire them with confidence to enter other realms.

Teach Responsibility and Values. Loury has been prominent in proclaiming that the black community should do more to condemn illegitimacy, to demand responsibility, and to instill middle-class values. He offers a now-familiar but powerful message: the overwhelming tendency to blame behavioral problems on a corrupting system robs blacks of individual initiative and responsibility. According to Loury:

It is difficult to overemphasize the self-defeating dynamic at work here. The dictates of political advocacy require that personal inadequacies be attributed to "the system," and that emphasis by black leaders on self-improvement be denounced as irrelevant, self-serving, dishonest. Individual black men and women simply cannot fail on their own, they must be seen as never given a chance. But where failure at a personal level is impossible, there can be no personal successes. For a black to embrace the Horatio Alger myth, to assert as a guide to *personal* action that "there is opportunity in America" becomes a *politically* repugnant act. For each would-be Horatio Alger indicts as inadequate, or incomplete, the deeply entrenched (and quite useful) notion that individual effort can never overcome "the inheritance of race." Yet where there can be no Horatio Algers to celebrate, sustaining an ethos of responsibility which might serve to extract maximal effort from the individual in the face of hardship becomes impossible as well.[70]

Loury went on to say:

For too many blacks, dedication to the cause of reform has been allowed to supplant the demand for individual accountability; race, and the historic crimes associated with it, has become the single lens through which to view social experience; the infinite potential of real human beings has been surrendered on the altar of protest. In this way does the prophesy of failure . . . fulfill itself: "Loyalty to the race" in the struggle to be free of oppression requires the sacrifice of the primary instrument through which genuine freedom might be obtained.[71]

These are powerful arguments. Blaming the system means that people have no personal responsibility. There is no point in striving or working hard because doing so will not make a difference.

Just how important is the rhetoric versus the reality? Do black children fail to believe that their own initiative will not get them ahead because liberal leaders have proclaimed it is so, or do they believe it because it often is true? As the girl in the Dash article put it, "I see girls and guys who finished school and they still can't find a job."[72] One of the boys in the same article wanted to start his own business, but now he is only working at McDonald's. Will he fail to start his own business because he has been told that black businesses always fail or because the chances of ever accumulating any capital are nil when one earns $100 a week and has to support a family?

Surely Loury is right that we must avoid telling people that they are not responsible for their actions. Blaming only the system is both condescending and counterproductive. But I find myself also swayed by the arguments of many sociologists that if one gives people a real and tangible chance to make it, their behavior and attitudes will change. It is much easier even for long-term poor white children to believe in

Horatio Alger because they can see that their situation is different from that of other whites (some thirty-two out of thirty-three white children are different from him). Poor white children rarely grow up surrounded by poverty; they see evidence of the success of other people all around them. Black children in the ghettos do not have these same perceptions because their peers are all growing up poor. Escape may seem to come more from athletics and underground activity than from education or business acumen.

The danger of a thesis like Loury's is that it will be used by those who want to stop doing everything possible to open up clear and attainable routes out of the ghetto. The hope is that it will be joined with attempts to offer real alternatives. We need to work both sides of the street. Expect a lot of people, but show them that their hard work will pay off. Exhort and exhibit. We must find a way to reward responsibility and initiative. Then we can talk about Horatio Alger.

Impose Obligations. A related but conceptually different approach is to enforce certain responsibilities and obligations on the underclass. Mickey Kaus is the most explicit advocate of this approach. According to him, "only work works"[73] in breaking the "culture of single-motherhood."[74]

The notion of mutual responsibility is not controversial any more. It seems that in both the liberal and conservative policy-making communities, there is widespread acceptance of the notion that it is legitimate to ask people to fulfill some obligations and that, in exchange, the government must provide some training, jobs, or other programs.

If we stay within the confines of the current welfare system, imposed obligations could play a positive role. One administrator of a mandatory program in Chicago told me that many of the clients he served are understandably cynical about any new program. He claimed that many recipients had been victims of scams by vocational and technical schools in which the schools arranged for and collected federal grants or loans for the students but gave the students minimal training and no jobs. He said many would simply not come in unless they were required to do so.

I witnessed a session in one office on Chicago's south side. Recipients were expected to show up at 9:00 A.M. sharp for a session. Many looked surly and angry at having to jump through yet another hoop. Then a dynamic and exciting instructor took over. Whenever anyone asked a question, she asked what kind of work they had done before. Then she said something like, "Gee, we had a job come in just last week that you could probably get. You're not going to be on welfare long." By the end, people crowded around her, excited by the job prospects she promised.

But in another session on the same day, conducted by a far less effective instructor, I saw the other side of mandatory programs. The instructor asked people to read out of a book. The people appeared to feel silly and some were embarrassed by their inability to read well. The teacher offered no real hope. At the end of the session, the people looked more angry and frustrated than before. Once again, they were being intimidated and humiliated.

Simply imposing burdens on people is likely to do little to improve attitudes or expectations. But expecting them to act in a certain way while giving them hope that something may come of the experience can be a real motivating device. If people do not believe that working at a low-paying and low-skill job will lead to much of a future, it is hard to see how forcing them to work in a government-provided job that clearly has *no* future will change their attitudes and expectations. But opening up new options and giving people a chance to do some work that they regard as worthwhile can help.

Generally, though, I remain skeptical of the capacity of imposed work to alter values and attitudes. One can surely insist that a welfare policy send the proper "moral signal," as Loury put it, "by affirming that certain modes of behavior are more comfortable with societal norms than others."[75] But, as Loury continued, it is certainly proper to insist that reasonable obligations be placed on those in need, obligations consistent with our expectations for the behavior of all citizens, and, one hopes, sufficient to induce behavior in recipients which will enhance the chance they will become independent. Yet, it is another thing altogether to believe that the imposition of constraints and requirements of the sort which can be implemented through public agencies will be adequate to replace the myriad and profound influences on character which occur within the home, the religious group, the local community of peers.[76]

There is not a shred of evidence to justify the claim that imposed work changes attitudes and expectations for the better.

Much of my discussion and much of what both conservatives and liberals have written about the ghetto suggest that ghetto residents do not see where their efforts will lead, do not have control over their lives, and do not have real employment options. The imposition of work within the welfare system is not likely to give people in the ghetto a sense that they have more hope or more options or that hard work pays off. Rather, it will give them the feeling that they have one more burden to bear.

Desegregation and Integration. Every convincing analysis of the ghetto that I have read suggests that isolation and concentration are a large part of the problem. It would seem that the obvious solution to that problem is integration. One should move poor people into rich neighborhoods and send black children to better schools elsewhere in the city.

Integration has been a big part of the government's efforts to help the poor in general and blacks in particular. When it has been done successfully, integration of and busing to schools seems to have helped the disadvantaged students.[77] But many people still resist desegregation, especially if it means busing. To many whites, the people who look sinister in the ghetto look downright dangerous in their local schools. People want to be able to select their neighbors, not have them imposed on them. The remarkable book *Common Ground* tells the story of several Bostonians on different sides of the desegregation issue.[78] It shows that desegregation of the Boston schools was a struggle on all sides.

True integration really might be the best answer if the society would allow it. The tragedy is that too often the anger, hatred, and resistance that integration breeds may seem worse than the segregation it replaced. But we cannot give up such efforts, since they continue to hold promise.

A Long Journey in Small Steps

Life in the ghetto is not the good life on the dole. It is not calculated abuse of the system. Nor is it the life of complete helplessness. It is a story of complexity and some strength. But, mostly, it is a story of adversity with little hope and few obvious routes into the mainstream.

I do not pretend to have offered a complete strategy for dealing with America's ghettos. There is no one answer. Instead, I have tried to suggest that the best hope lies in hope itself. People need to believe that they have options. With options go responsibilities: for oneself, one's children, and one's community. I am skeptical of those who argue that we just need to be tougher on ghetto residents so they will shape up. We can and should expect more. But high expectations must go hand in hand with genuine opportunities and alternatives.

The story of the ghetto provides the strongest case of all that we need a social welfare system that reflects and reinforces the values of autonomy/responsibility, work, family, and community. A great many forces work against these values in America's ghettos. A set of social policies that ensure that all families who are willing to work a reasonable level will be secure, autonomous, and responsible for their own decisions seems essential if we are to begin the process of healing the desperation in America's inner cities.

We must not stop there. Education, empowerment, jobs, the teaching of values and responsibility, and one-on-one services all must be a part of a larger strategy to give people a genuine sense of options for the future, a sense of control, and a feeling of being part of, not isolated from, the larger society.

None of these steps will quickly eliminate the ongoing tragedy of the ghetto. However, from those attempts, more answers should emerge. People in the ghetto are neither helpless nor hopeless. Offering help and hope, though, does seem like an obvious place to start.

7

Choosing a Future

America needs to decide what role it wants social policy to play in the lives of the poor. If the main goal of policy is to relieve some of the burden caused by the failures and misfortunes of both society and individuals, then our social welfare system might be given passing marks. Current social policies have helped people who might otherwise have been destitute, and the policies have not done a great deal of damage. But if our hope is that social policy will address some of the real causes of poverty, if the goal is to use it as a tool for integrating people and aiding them to become more independent and more responsible, and if our desire is to help the poor help themselves, then the current system must be judged more harshly.

Four Problem Areas

The evidence in this book clearly suggests the the major causes of poverty have not been addressed well by social policy. As a result, we are confronted with numerous contradictions and dilemmas as we look at the situation of the poor. Let me single out four problem areas:

- Many families remain poor although at least one parent is working full time. They are often without medical protection and get little governmental support. They are trying to make it on their own, but they are failing. After governmental transfers, the full-time working poor are among the poorest of the poor. Furthermore, many others are suffering from temporary unemployment; they want to work but cannot seem to find jobs.

The particular tragedy of the working poor is that they are the group who ought to command our greatest sympathy and respect, yet they get virtually no help. The group consists mainly of two-parent families. Indeed, the poverty of two-parent families is the poverty of low wages and unemployment. In an era in which the public is worried about family stability and work among the poor, it seems perverse to ignore the plight of this group while we focus attention on single mothers who are on welfare. By leaving working families out in the cold, particularly when single-parent families with no working members get welfare and medical protection, the system seems to mock the serious efforts these families are making.

But the fact that welfare is available to single mothers does not mean they are being aided sympathetically or effectively.

- Single parents are forced to choose between two difficult options: work full time or be supported by welfare. If they choose the former, they will be forced to deal with difficult questions concerning the proper care and nurturing of their children. They will have to find ways to deal with crises, such as illness or disciplinary problems, and even school holidays. And they may still be poor. If they choose welfare, they put themselves and their children in a system that often treats them with suspicion and disdain, that forces them to deal with a wide variety of rules and bureaucracies, and that does little to reward or encourage work, and they will be stigmatized as "welfare mothers."

Full-time work is the only route out of poverty and welfare for single parents, but even that is not always enough. Moreover, full-time work outside the home is hard for any mother. Only about one-quarter of *married* mothers work full time all year. And married mothers usually have additional support—material, logistical, and psychological—from their husbands that may ease the difficulty of working fully. Furthermore, with the welfare system, it often makes little sense to work unless a woman can make $5 per hour or more and has low child care costs. In spite of the difficulties, over 40 percent of single mothers do work all the time. It is not surprising that those who work full time all year are typically the best-educated women with the least child care responsibilities.

For the others, there is only welfare. Few single parents get any child support and when they do, it is often sporadic and unreliable. And welfare seems designed to discourage and penalize work. Part-time work rarely makes sense. The women's total income is raised little, since their welfare benefits are cut, and the women are still forced to cope with the frustrations of the welfare system. As a result, few women on welfare are working.

As long as there are no additional sources of support, as long as single mothers must choose between specializing in work or child rearing, many will choose welfare, in spite of its stigma and poor treatment. Some mothers and their children will be dependent on welfare for many years. And each year, they may be in a worse position to compete in the job market. Meanwhile, an increasingly frustrated and angry public will push for more rules and lower benefits.

This situation is particularly troubling because the majority of children born in America today will spend time in a single-parent home. Virtually every one of their mothers will have to confront the same hard choices: full-time work or welfare. Each will face the decision at a time of real stress—from divorce or separation or the birth of a child. Recognizing that all families must fulfill the dual roles of nurturer and provider, do we really want the typical child and single parent left with only these options?

Almost every child has two living parents. So an obvious place to look for additional support for single-parent families is the absent parents. Unfortunately, we are not doing so now.

- Absent parents usually provide little financial support for their children. Less than half the divorced fathers are paying any child support. A man who fathers a child out of wedlock knows that he will not be forced to bear any financial responsibility for the child almost without exception. Single parents who want child support must usually pay the economic and psychological costs of fighting for it. Child support can become a battleground on which both parties can express the bitterness of a relationship gone astray.

Child support policies say a lot, both economically and symbolically, about parental responsibilities and children's rights. The current system's message is clear: only the custodial parent (almost always the mother) has responsibility. Child support is a problem for all single parents and it is most serious when a child is born out of wedlock. At times, it seems that these children have no fathers. When we are troubled by changes in the family structure throughout our society and out-of-wedlock births in particular, expecting absent fathers to take on so little responsibility is foolhardy and unjust.

Ideally, both parents would share the nurturing and provider responsibilities, as usually happens in some fashion in two-parent homes. But anger, bitterness, limited incomes, or simple indifference make shared roles difficult when the parents are living apart. Shared nurturing can be stressful, and shared financial responsibility, infuriating and complicated. However, these are issues that must be resolved as the structures of our families become less traditional. Furthermore, child support simply cannot be allowed to languish in the judicial system, closely linked to the emotions and actions of the custodial and absent parents. Child support should not be yet another source of tension in the lives of children and parents. If we want to support families and children and promote responsibility, both parents must be held accountable for their children.

Finally, let us turn our attention to the small but troubled group that lives in the worst sections of our nation's inner cities: the ghetto poor.

- Families and children in big-city ghettos live in a world without hope or a future. They live with deprivation, isolation, concentrated poverty, the departure of jobs, and discrimination. They grow up in an environment in which most people who have had enough success to afford better get out. It is a world of few traditional role models and few apparent mainstream routes to middle-class security. As the result of all this, one finds disturbing, often counterproductive, behavior.

The greatest tragedies of poverty are found in America's ghettos, where the American dream seems not just deferred but demolished. The behavior of a teenager who bears a child out of wedlock is far easier to understand when one realizes that she may see limited opportunities to control her life and few options that lead to middle-class security. And the social welfare system does virtually nothing to help. Welfare may sustain the community, but it certainly does not promote or reinforce independence. It is far more likely to hinder work and autonomy than to promote them, even though it may prevent financial desperation.

Looking over the situation, I think it is easy to see why the two women on the Oprah Winfrey show (mentioned in chapter 1) were so angry and why their anger was directed toward each other. Each thought she was trying hard to do the right thing for herself and her family under adverse conditions. Each felt that the system did not really help or understand her struggles. Each felt belittled by the behavior and attitude of the other. The working mother saw the woman on welfare living off the system and avoiding all the frustrations of work. The welfare mother felt that her life was filled with frustration of a different sort, arising from welfare and from the day-to-day struggle to protect and raise a family with too little money. Yet she found nothing but disdain from her employed counterpart.

Surely, we do not want a set of policies for the poor that leaves the working poor insecure, that isolates people who are struggling with legitimate difficulties in a welfare system that begrudgingly offers money to people whom society then judges as unmotivated and irresponsible. We can and must develop a system that tackles the real causes of poverty and reinforces our values of autonomy, work, family, and community.

What Can We Do?

Both liberals and conservatives have offered their visions of the future. Conservatives call for a strong economy so that trickle-down will allow the poor more opportunities. They would correct the long-term dependence on welfare by abolishing the welfare system or by replacing it with workfare. Liberals want to make major investments in people, to break down discriminatory barriers, to humanize the welfare system, to offer governmental jobs, and even to reform the economy.

There is wisdom in both visions, but there is naivete and oversimplification as well. Trickle-down really does help the working poor. Education and antidiscrimination policies must be a part of any long-term strategy. Long-term dependence on welfare is a serious problem that needs attention. The welfare system is often inhumane. But abolishing welfare or forcing people to work for their benefits will not help the working poor, it will not help single mothers balance their dual roles, it will not make fathers more accountable, and it will not give hope to those in the ghetto. And short-term education and training for adults has had only a modest impact. No matter how much educating we do, there will still be low-paying jobs and families will still split apart.

Whether the proposals come from the left or the right, I am skeptical that any welfare-based solution—whether it be mixing work and welfare, instituting workfare, making welfare more humane, or providing training to welfare recipients—will ever take us far. Long-term cash-based welfare for the healthy is inherently flawed. It inevitably reduces the incentive to work, it inevitably supports mostly single parents, and it automatically isolates and stigmatizes. Humane welfare will never be realized; too many suspicions and conflicts are built into the system. And even though I strongly dispute the conservative claims that welfare has been a large part of the problem, I agree that it has never been a big part of the long-term solution for those who are healthy and who could work at least part time. Conservatives are right when they assert that welfare does not reflect and reinforce our basic values.

But the proposals of conservatives usually create just as much conflict with values as those of the liberals. Their solutions suggest that laziness and inertia are the chief causes of poverty. The conservatives often ignore our sense of community, our capacity to help and understand, our recognition that a capitalist system inevitably leads to both high and low wages and to economic dislocation. They ignore the fact that we care not just whether a child is living in a family on welfare but whether the child is being nurtured and protected.

The best hope is to understand the real causes of poverty and to address them directly. The goal ought to be to ensure that everyone who behaves responsibly will avoid poverty and welfare. The big challenges to be tackled involve supporting the working poor, resolving the dual role of single parents, helping people over temporary difficulties, and offering hope to all people that they can get a job if they are willing to work.

We could go a long way toward improving the plight of the poor by creating a system that encourages and rewards work and responsibility. I recommend adopting five significant reforms:

- *Ensure that everyone has medical protection.* There are many alternatives. My favorite is for the government to offer a last-resort medical plan for the uninsured with premiums collected through taxes and varied by income level.
- *Make work pay so that working families are not poor.* I would expand the earned income tax credit, raise the minimum wage, make the child care tax credit refundable, and possibly add other tax-based support.
- *Adopt a uniform child support assurance system.* All absent parents ought to be identified. All single mothers ought to be part of a Social Security-like system that requires absent parents to pay a percentage of their income for child support and that automatically collects this money like taxes. The government ought to ensure that each month the custodial parent gets at least some minimum child support benefit even if collections from the absent parent fall short.
- *Convert welfare into a transitional system designed to provide serious but short-term financial, educational, and social support for people who are trying to cope with a temporary setback.* Welfare could be replaced by a transitional support system whose duration might vary from eighteen months to three years, depending on the situation. Both single-parent and two-parent families ought to be eligible for this transitional assistance.
- *Provide minimum-wage jobs to persons who have exhausted their transitional support.* If welfare is going to be transitional, then we must provide some way for people to provide for themselves once their benefits are exhausted.

Compare the situation of several different types of families under the current situation and under this proposal. Take, for example, a two-parent family with two children in which one parent is working full time at a minimum-wage job. Presently, the earnings of such a family would leave them at least $4,000 below the poverty line, and the family probably would be without medical protection. The family qualifies only for food stamps, which require a considerable hassle, the disclosure of income and assets, and the use of stigmatizing coupons.

But if a plan similar to my proposal were adopted, the effective wage for the worker in this family would be raised dramatically—high enough that the family's income would reach the poverty level. And unlike a welfare-based system, the much higher effective wage would mean that work is rewarded more, not penalized. Any two-parent family which had one adult who was willing to work full time (or two adults willing to work half time) would be able to support itself adequately.

And what if the same family suffered unemployment or temporary illness or disability? If they did not get enough unemployment insurance, they would qualify for transitional assistance designed to help them over their short-term difficulties. There would be no danger, though, that the family would become dependent on this program, because benefits would run out. But even if the benefits were exhausted, the family could still support itself with one of the governmental jobs available for those who exhausted transitional assistance.

Consider the situation of single parents. Today, when a single-parent family is formed, the mother is faced with the choice of full-time work or welfare when she is under considerable stress. The father usually pays nothing. Under my proposed program, a mother would have access to transitional assistance that she could use to get her life in order. She would be able to support her family in the long run through a combination of part-time work and child support. If she worked full time, she would be even better off. There would be no long-term welfare program to struggle under or that would make work a pointless and unattractive proposition. With a modest amount of work, the single mother could gain independence and control over her life.

The absent father would know that, as long as his children were minors, a portion of his wages would automatically be collected for child support payments that would be given to the mother and their children. Even if the collections from the father fell below some minimum level because the father earned little in some month, the mother and children could count on some guaranteed child support payment from the government.

The change might be particularly important for never-married mothers and the fathers of their children. Because they usually have very young children and a poor education, these mothers often consider full-time work to be impossible. It is not surprising, therefore, that long-term dependence on welfare is common among this group. Under this proposal, the mothers would know that they could count on some guaranteed child support but that eventually they would have to work at least part time to contribute to their family's support. Once they did so, the women could avoid the current welfare system. Every dollar they earned would make their families better off. And they could use half-time work as a stepping stone to better jobs. At the same time, the absent fathers would finally be held to some account. Under the new plan, the fathers would know that whenever they had earnings, they would automatically pay some child support.

This proposal ought to provide somewhat more hope even in the ghettos because families in which one member was willing to work could escape poverty and be closer to the mainstream. People would have more of a chance to make it on their own and more responsibility to do so. Of course, if we really want to change the ghettos, we must ensure that the government undertakes intensive additional efforts, such as education and job training, empowerment, and antidiscrimination policies. But even without such efforts, we would have a social welfare system that integrated people and rewarded their efforts, rather than isolating them and destroying their incentives.

If we made work pay, provided child support assurance, and made welfare transitional, then we would go far toward replacing the welfare system with one that would integrate and support people in the lowest income strata by rewarding their efforts. The system would offer better support, but it would also give the poor greater personal responsibility.

Under such a plan, the two women on the Oprah Winfrey show would have nothing to argue about because they would both be part of the same system with common supports and responsibilities. In the long term, although both would be expected to work, both would be assured medical, tax, and child support so that they could genuinely make it through work—even part-time work.

I regret that I cannot give a reliable estimate of how much these measures would cost. They may cost well over $20 or even $30 billion to do everything right. That seems like a great deal of money given the current budget deficit. But is it? Is it worth less than 1 percent of the gross national product to change our approach from salving problems with cash to solving them by helping people support themselves? Many are willing to spend over $1 trillion to protect us from Soviet missiles. Can we not spare a little for social policies that give the poor a real chance to make it without welfare?

Is Real Change Feasible?

Welfare reform proposals seem to come and go. The greater the changes proposed, the less likely they are to be adopted. But few of these proposals have tapped into our American values. Instead, they have often brought these values into conflict. Indeed, their proponents have misled the public about the nature of the proposals, claiming they supported work or family when they did not.

I have tried to suggest a system that reinforces American values about autonomy, work, family, and community. Compromises always have to be made, but a program that focuses explicitly on the causes of poverty looks far more promising than does the current array of programs. This proposal involves a variety of specific policies that can be woven together to form a coherent whole.

Each of the policies individually represents only modest change. Certainly, none of the ideas is original. Medical protection has been a major topic of discussion since the mid-1960s. Even during the Reagan years, the groups that were granted Medicaid protection were expanded. Proposals to make work pay have been around for decades. Recent tax reforms already expanded tax-based aid to the working poor. The minimum wage may be raised before this book is published. The child support plan is being tested in Wisconsin and several other states, and most states are moving toward a more uniform and universal child support system. Making welfare a transitional program followed by work is the essence if not the letter of several state and federal initiatives.

Many recent task forces on poverty have urged the adoption of significant parts of these programs. Governor Mario Cuomo of New York set up a poverty commission that proposed a plan that is similar to this one.[1] Another commission set up by the conservative American Enterprise Institute endorsed the idea of transitional support.[2]

Changes such as those proposed here could be accomplished in small steps, but they would ultimately yield a system that is fundamentally different from the current one that often emphasizes welfare. Welfare needs to be replaced, not reformed.

Hope for the Future

In the end, it is not the details or the cost of the plan that is the issue. My message is simple. Policies to alleviate poverty often are presented as a set of hopeless tradeoffs and dilemmas with the underlying message that nothing can make much difference. I am more optimistic. If we are willing to decide what is expected of citizens and then look carefully at the poor, we can understand a great deal about why people are poor. By understanding that, we can design a set of social policies that will reinforce our values by encouraging and supporting the efforts of the poor. Our system of support for the poor can be something more than a holding ground for people who are not making it on their own. It can address the real causes of poverty and be the basis of hope.

NOTES

Chapter 1

1. Hugh Heclo, "The Political Foundations of Anti-Poverty Policy," in *Fighting Poverty: What Works and What Doesn't?* edited by Sheldon Danziger and Daniel Weinberg (Cambridge, Mass.: Harvard University Press, 1986), 330.

2. Daniel Patrick Moynihan, "Report's Error Would Make Beneficial Law," *USA Today,* November 21, 1986.

3. Working Group on the Family, *The Family: Preserving America's Future* (Washington, D.C.: White House Domestic Policy Council, November 1986), 34. The report noted that common sense and anecdotal evidence suggested there was some effect.

4. Charles Murray, *Losing Ground: American Social Policy, 1950–1980* (New York: Basic Books, 1984), 236.

5. Lawrence M. Mead, *Beyond Entitlement: The Social Obligations of Citizenship* (New York: Free Press, 1986), 3.

6. D. Pacholczyk, "Linn Yann Spells Success," *Reader's Digest* (November 1984): 107–111.

Chapter 2

1. National Conference of Catholic Bishops, *Economic Justice for All: Pastoral Letter on Catholic Social Teaching and the U.S. Economy* (Washington, D.C.: Office of Publishing & Promotion Services, 1986). The first two "principal themes" listed in the letter are, "Every economic decision and institution must be judged in light of whether it protects or undermines the dignity of the human person" and "Human dignity can be realized and protected only in community" (p. ix).

2. See, for example, Michael Barth, George Carcagno, and John Palmer, *Towards an Effective Income Support System* (Madison: Institute for Research on Poverty, University of Wisconsin, 1974).

3. Charles Murray, *Losing Ground: American Social Policy, 1950–1980* (New York: Basic Books, 1984).

4. Lawrence M. Mead, *Beyond Entitlement: The Social Obligations of Citizenship* (New York: Free Press, 1986).

5. Daniel Patrick Moynihan, *Family and Nation* (San Diego, Calif.: Harcourt Brace Jovanovich, 1986).

6. William Morris, ed., *The American Heritage Dictionary of the English Language* (New York: American Heritage Publishing Co., 1971), 290.

7. Robert Moffitt, "Dependency and Labor Supply: A Review of the Literature," paper prepared for the U.S. Department of Health and Human Services (Providence, R.I.: Brown University, 1987).

8. Gary Burtless, "The Work Response to a Guaranteed Income: A Survey of Experimental Evidence," in *The Income Maintenance Experiments: Lessons for Welfare Reform,* edited by Alicia Munnell (Boston: Federal Reserve Bank, 1987). Although Burtless's results are an accurate reflection of what was found, there are many reasons to be skeptical about their interpretation. Those persons who participated in the negative income tax experiments had reason to underreport their earnings, since their benefits depended on their having a low income (so people may have lied about their earnings when they were eligible for benefits). Yet, the short-term nature of the experiment is usually thought to have understated the change in work which might have been expected in a permanent system.

9. U.S. Bureau of the Census, *Statistical Abstract of the United States, 1987* (Washington, D.C.: U.S. Government Printing Office, 1986), table 746, p. 443.

10. George Gilder, *Wealth and Poverty* (New York: Basic Books, 1981), 122.

11. I. A. Lewis and William Schneider, "Hard Times: The Public on Poverty," *Public Opinion* 7 (June/July 1985): 2–7.

12. Gary Burtless, "Are Targeted Wage Subsidies Harmful? Evidence From a Wage Voucher Experiment," *Industrial and Labor Relations Review* 39 (October 1985): 105–114. An alternative interpretation, of which Burtless is skeptical, is that employers saw the voucher program as involving so much hassle and governmental red tape that they avoided workers who had vouchers.

13. For a more serious and complete history of social policy, see, for example, James Patterson, *America's Struggle Against Poverty, 1900–1980* (Cambridge, Mass.: Harvard University Press, 1981).

14. As quoted in Arthur M. Schlesinger, Jr., *The Coming of the New Deal* (Boston: Houghton Mifflin Co., 1959), 308.

15. *Social Security and Similar Benefits:* U.S. Bureau of the Census, *Statistical Abstract of the United States, 1979* (Washington, D.C.: U.S. Government Printing Office, 1979), table 528, p. 331, and table 530, p. 332; U.S. Bureau of the Census, *Statistical Abstract of the United States, 1987* (Washington, D.C.: U.S. Government Printing Office, 1986), table 577, p. 342, and table 581, p. 345; U.S. Social Security Administration, *Social Security Bulletin, Annual Statistical Supplement, 1986* (December 1986), table 15, p. 81, table 16, p. 82, and table 165, p. 252; U.S. Social Security Administration, unpublished data.

Employment-related Benefits: U.S. Bureau of the Census, *Statistical Abstract of the United States, 1979* (Washington, D.C.: U.S. Government Printing Office, 1979), table 528, p. 331, and table 530, p. 332; U.S. Bureau of the Census, *Statistical Abstract of the United States, 1987* (Washington, D.C.: U.S. Government Printing

Office, 1986), table 577, p. 342, and table 581, p. 345; U.S. Bureau of the Census, *Statistical Abstract of the United States, 1986* (Washington, D.C.: U.S. Government Printing Office, 1985), table 639, p. 376; U.S. Social Security Administration, *Social Security Bulletin, Annual Statistical Supplement, 1986* (December 1986), table 165, p. 252; Ann Bixby, "Social Welfare Expenditures, 1981 and 1982," *Social Security Bulletin* 47 (December 1984), table 2, p. 15.

Means-tested Nonmedical Benefits: U.S. Bureau of the Census, *Statistical Abstract of the United States, 1979* (Washington, D.C.: U.S. Government Printing Office, 1979), tables 528, p. 331, and table 522, p. 326; U.S. Bureau of the Census, *Statistical Abstract of the United States, 1981* (Washington, D.C.: U.S. Government Printing Office, 1981), table 523, p. 322; U.S. Bureau of the Census, *Statistical Abstract of the United States, 1987* (Washington, D.C.: U.S. Government Printing Office, 1986), table 577, p. 342, and table 580, p. 344; U.S. Department of Commerce, Bureau of Economic Analysis, unpublished data on General Assistance spending for 1984; Ann Bixby, "Public Social Welfare Expenditures, FY 1984," *Social Security Bulletin* 50 (June 1987), table 1, p. 50; U.S. Bureau of the Census, *Historical Statistics of the U.S., Colonial Times to 1970, Bicentennial Edition* (Washington, D.C.: U.S. Government Printing Office, 1975), p. 356; U.S. Social Security Administration, *Social Security Bulletin, Annual Statistical Supplement, 1986* (December 1986), table 282, p. 205; U.S. Social Security Administration, *Social Security Bulletin, Annual Statistical Supplement, 1984–85* (December 1985), table 175, p. 241.

Medical Benefits: U.S. Bureau of the Census, *Statistical Abstract of the United States, 1979* (Washington, D.C.: U.S. Government Printing Office, 1979), table 522, p. 326; U.S. Health Care Financing Administration, unpublished data on estimated Medicare disbursements for the elderly and disabled for calendar years 1976 and 1984; Ann Bixby, "Public Social Welfare Expenditures, FY 1984," *Social Security Bulletin* 50 (June 1987), table 1, p. 50; Ann Bixby, "Social Welfare Expenditures, 1981 and 1982," *Social Security Bulletin* 47 (December 1984), table 2, p. 15; U.S. Bureau of the Census, *Historical Statistics of the U.S., Colonial Times to 1970, Bicentennial Edition* (Washington, D.C.: U.S. Government Printing Office, 1975), p. 356; U.S. Social Security Administration, *Social Security Bulletin, Annual Statistical Supplement, 1984–85* (December 1985), table 155, p. 222.

Employment and Training and Social Services: U.S. Bureau of the Census, *Statistical Abstract of the United States, 1979* (Washington, D.C.: U.S. Government Printing Office, 1979), table 522, p. 326; U.S. Department of Commerce, Bureau of Economic Analysis, *National Income and Product Accounts of the United States, 1929–82, Statistical Tables* (Washington, D.C.: U.S. Government Printing Office, 1986), table 3.15, p. 171, and table 3.16, p. 182; U.S. Department of Commerce, Bureau of Economic Analysis, *Survey of Current Business* 67 (July 1987), table 3.15, p. 44, and table 3.16, p. 45; Ann Bixby, "Public Social Welfare Expenditures, FY 1984," *Social Security Bulletin* 50 (June 1987), table 1, p. 50.

16. As quoted in Moynihan, *Family and Nation,* 5–6.

17. Peter F. Drucker, "Three Unforeseen Jobs for the Coming Administration," *Harper's* 221 (July 1960): 46.

18. Lawrence Friedman, "The Social and Political Context of the War on Poverty: An Overview," in *A Decade of Federal Antipoverty Programs: Achievements, Failures, and Lessons,* edited by Robert Haveman (New York: Academic Press, 1977), 35.

19. Daniel Patrick Moynihan, "America's Poor: What Is to Be Done?" Address delivered at Harvard University, Cambridge, Mass., September 4, 1986.

20. Michael Harrington, *The Other America* (New York: Macmillan Co., 1962); and Kenneth B. Clark, *The Dark Ghetto: Dilemmas of Social Power* (New York: Harper & Row, 1965).

21. Henry Aaron, *Politics and the Professors: Studies in Social Economics* (Washington, D.C.: The Brookings Institution, 1978), 27.

22. Dennis Coyle and Aaron Wildavsky, "Requisites of Radical Change: Income Maintenance Versus Tax Reform," *Journal of Policy Analysis and Management* 7 (Fall 1987): 10.

23. Committee on Ways and Means, U.S. House of Representatives, *Background Material and Data on Programs within the Jurisdiction of the Committee on Ways and Means* (Washington, D.C.: U.S. Government Printing Office, 1987), table 11, p. 414.

24. For the most recent review, see Burtless, "The Work Response to a Guaranteed Income."

25. Glen G. Cain, "Negative Income Tax Experiments and the Issues of Marital Stability and Family Composition," in *The Income Maintenance Experiments: Lessons for Welfare Reform,* edited by Alicia Munnell (Boston: Federal Reserve Bank, 1987).

26. "Opinion Roundup: Poverty in America," *Public Opinion* 7 (June/July 1985): 27.

Chapter 3

1. U.S. Bureau of the Census, *Statistical Abstract of the United States, 1980* (Washington, D.C.: U.S. Government Printing Office, 1980), table 72, p. 51.

2. U.S. Bureau of the Census, *Statistical Abstract of the United States, 1987* (Washington, D.C.: U.S. Government Printing Office, 1986), table 68, p. 49.

3. See, for example, Mary Jo Bane, "Household Composition and Poverty," in *Fighting Poverty: What Works and What Doesn't,* edited by Sheldon Danziger and Daniel Weinberg (Cambridge, Mass.: Harvard University Press, 1986), 209–231; and Victor R. Fuchs, "Feminization of Poverty?" working paper, Stanford University, April 1986.

4. For a review of this literature, see two reports from the National Research Council, National Academy of Science: *Children of Working Parents* (Washington, D.C.: National Academy Press, 1983); and *Families that Work: Children in a Changing World* (Washington, D.C.: National Academy Press, 1982).

5. Victor R. Fuchs, "Sex Differences in Economic Well-Being," *Science* 232 (April 25, 1986): 459–464.

6. See, for example, Carl Degler, *At Odds: Women and the Family from the Revolution to the Present* (Oxford, England: Oxford University Press, 1980), chap. 18.

7. Jerry Falwell, *Listen America!* (Garden City, N.Y.: Doubleday & Co., 1980), 124.

8. Betty Friedan, *The Second Stage* (New York: Summit Books, 1981), 65.

9. Sam H. Preston and Alan T. Richards, "The Influence of Women's Work Opportunities on Marriage Rates," *Demography* 12 (1975): 209–222.

10. See, for example, Ron C. Kessler and James McRae, Jr., "The Effects of Wives' Employment on the Mental Health of Married Men and Women," *American Sociological Review* 47 (1982): 216–227.

11. Catherine Ross, John Mirowsky, and John Huber, "Marriage Patterns and Depression," *American Sociological Review* 48 (1983): 809–823.

12. Heather Ross and Isabel Sawhill, *Time of Transition: The Growth of Families Headed by Women* (Washington, D.C.: Urban Institute Press, 1975).

13. As quoted in Falwell, *Listen America!* p. 125.

14. Frank Levy, *Dollars and Dreams: The Changing American Income Distribution* (New York: Russell Sage Foundation/Basic Books, 1987), 80.

15. Daniel Patrick Moynihan, *The Negro Family: The Case for National Action* (Washington, D.C.: U.S. Department of Labor, March 1965).

16. William Julius Wilson and Katherine M. Neckerman, "Poverty and Family Structure: The Widening Gap between Evidence and Public Policy Issues," in *Fighting Poverty: What Works and What Doesn't,* edited by Sheldon Danziger and Daniel Weinberg (Cambridge, Mass.: Harvard University Press, 1986), 232–259.

17. See, for example, Robert Aponte, Katherine Neckerman, and William J. Wilson, "Race, Family Structure, and Social Policy," University of Chicago, Working Paper No. 7 (Chicago: Project on the Federal Social Role, 1985).

18. For a careful review of the literature, see Irwin Garfinkel and Sara McLanahan, *Single Mothers and Their Children* (Washington, D.C.: The Urban Institute, 1986), 55–63; and Wilson and Neckerman, "Poverty and Family Structure."

19. All these figures were taken from the extraordinarily helpful report of the Committee on Way and Means, U.S. House of Representatives, *Background Material and Data on Programs within the Jurisdiction of the Committee on Ways and Means* (Washington, D.C.: U.S. Government Printing Office, 1986), 578. All the figures have been adjusted for inflation and put into 1984 dollars.

20. Charles Murray, *Losing Ground: American Social Policy, 1950–1980* (New York: Basic Books, 1984).

21. Indeed even these figures misstate the fall. During this period, the average family size was also declining, from four persons per case to three. Since benefits are adjusted to the size of families, the actual decrease in money received was considerably greater.

22. Inferred from table 15, U.S. Bureau of the Census, *Money Income and Poverty Status of Families and Persons in the United States: 1984 (advance data from the March 1985 Current Population Survey), Current Population Reports,* Series P-60, No. 149 (Washington, D.C.: U.S. Government Printing Office, 1985).

23. Committee on Way and Means, U.S. House of Representatives, *Background Material and Data on Programs within the Jurisdiction of the Committee on Ways and Means* (Washington, D.C.: U.S. Government Printing Office, 1987), table 21, pp. 429–430.

24. Inferred from table 15, U.S. Bureau of the Census, *Money Income and Poverty Status of Families and Persons in the United States: 1984.* The number of poor children increased by 20 percent.

25. Inferred from tables 21 and 22, Committee on Way and Means, *Background Material and Data on Programs within the Jurisdiction of the Committee on Ways and Means 1987,* assuming that the size of black and white families is identical and that the proportion of the caseload that was black in 1972 was identical to the proportion that was black in January 1973.

26. Betty Friedan, *The Feminine Mystique* (New York: W. W. Norton & Co., 1963), 255–256.

27. Garfinkel and McLanahan, *Single Mothers and Their Children,* 82.

28. U.S. Bureau of the Census, *Statistical Abstract of the United States, 1987,* table 99, p. 64.

29. *The General Mills American Family Report 1980–1981: Families at Work,* con-

ducted by Louis Harris and Associates, 66; *The 1985 Virginia Slims American Women's Poll,* conducted by The Roper Organization, 105.

30. See, for example, Melvin Zelnick, John Kanter, and Kathleen Ford, *Sex and Pregnancy in Adolescents* (Beverly Hills, Calif.: Sage Publications, 1981).

31. *The 1985 Virginia Slims American Women's Poll,* 105.

32. Andrew J. Cherlin, *Marriage, Divorce, Remarriage* (Cambridge, Mass.: Harvard University Press, 1981), 48.

33. *The 1985 Virginia Slims American Women's Poll,* 49.

34. Barbara Ehrenreich, *The Hearts of Men* (Garden City, N.Y.: Anchor Press/ Doubleday, 1983), 169.

35. See, for example, Garfinkel and McLanahan, *Single Mothers and Their Children,* 78–79.

36. U.S. Bureau of the Census, *Statistical Abstract of the United States, 1986,* table 124, p. 79, and unpublished data.

37. U.S. Bureau of the Census, *Statistical Abstract of the United States, 1987,* table 82, p. 59.

38. U.S. Bureau of the Census, *Statistical Abstract of the United States, 1986,* table 124, p. 79.

39. See, for example, Mary Jo Bane and David T. Ellwood, "The Dynamics of Children's Living Arrangements," unpublished paper, Harvard University, 1985.

40. Ibid.

41. Figures inferred from tables 83 and 94, U.S. Bureau of the Census, *Statistical Abstract of the United States, 1986,* 57, 62.

42. U.S. Bureau of the Census, *Statistical Abstract of the United States, 1987,* table 86, p. 61.

43. Ibid.

44. Wilson and Neckerman, "Poverty and Family Structure."

45. U.S. Bureau of the Census, *Statistical Abstract of the United States, 1986,* table 66, p. 45. Figures for nonwhites were gotten by subtracting the figures for whites from totals.

46. This estimate is created by subtracting the reported age of the family's oldest child from the age of the mother in single-parent families with children. Unfortunately, the age of the oldest child only goes up to 25, so mothers who still have children in the home under age 18 but whose oldest child is over age 25 may not get counted properly.

47. See, for example, K. A. Moore and M. R. Burt, *Private Crisis, Public Cost: Perspectives on Teenage Childbearing* (Washington, D.C.: The Urban Institute, 1982).

48. All these numbers are from Cheryl D. Hayes, ed., *Risking the Future: Adolescent Sexuality, Pregnancy, and Childbearing,* National Research Council Panel on Adolescent Pregnancy and Childbearing (Washington, D.C.: National Academy Press, 1987). Many of the numbers were quoted from M. Zelnick and J. F. Kanter, "Sexual Activity, Contraceptive Use, and Pregnancy Among Metropolitan-Area Teenagers: 1971–1979," *Family Planning Perspectives* 12 (September/ October 1980), 230–237.

49. *The 1985 Virginia Slims American Women's Poll,* 66.

50. "Changing Attitudes," *New York Times,* November 23, 1986, sec. 4, p. 26.

51. *The 1985 Virginia Slims American Women's Poll,* 86.

52. Sheldon Danziger, Robert Haveman, and Robert Plotnick, "How Income Transfers Affect Work, Savings, and the Income Distribution: A Critical Review," *Journal of Economic Literature* 19 (1981): 975–1028.

53. Bureau of Labor Statistics, *Geographic Profile of Employment and Unemployment, 1985,* U.S. Department of Labor (Washington, D.C.: U.S. Government Printing Office, 1986), 40.

54. For an excellent summary of these studies and reports, see Cheryl D. Hayes, ed., *Risking the Future.*

55. The Children's Defense Fund has a variety of useful publications that explore what can be done to help.

56. *The 1985 Virginia Slims American Women's Poll,* 55.

Chapter 4

1. See U.S. Bureau of the Census, *Statistical Abstract of the United States, 1986* (Washington, D.C.: U.S. Government Printing Office, 1985), table 743, p. 446.

2. These data come from tabulations of the Panel Study of Income Dynamics (PSID)—a longitudinal survey that, since 1967, has followed the experiences of all the persons in a representative sample of 5,000 American families. The children shown in figure 4.1 were born between 1967 and 1972 and they and their families were followed over the next 10 years. Readers should realize, however, that even though the PSID is supposedly a representative sample, it consistently shows lower levels of poverty than does the annual Current Population Survey, which the government uses to determine the official poverty statistics. The differences have never been fully explained. One possibility is that the PSID sample misses some low-income people. An alternative is that the more detailed income questions in the PSID and the frequency with which people in the PSID survey are questioned may lead to more accurate information on income. The important point here is that in relation to the official governmental statistics, the picture of children painted here is actually too rosy.

3. Working Group on the Family, *The Family: Preserving America's Future* (Washington, D.C.: White House Domestic Policy Council, November 1986), 24.

4. U.S. Bureau of the Census, *Current Population Reports,* Series P-60, No. 124, *Characteristics of the Population Below the Poverty Level, 1978* (Washington, D.C.: U.S. Government Printing Office, 1980), table 27, p. 122; U.S. Bureau of the Census, *Current Population Reports,* Series P-60, No. 147, *Characteristics of the Population Below the Poverty Line, 1983* (Washington, D.C.: U.S. Government Printing Office, 1985), table 26, p. 107. Unlike most of the other numbers reported in this chapter, these figures are for the officially defined poor, the only ones available from published data. In the official definition of poverty, governmental transfers are added before comparing family income to the poverty line.

5. Sheldon Danziger and Peter Gottschalk, "Unemployment Insurance and the Safety Net for the Unemployed," working paper, May 1986.

6. Unpublished data from Social Security Administration, Office of Disability. The average time from first claim to determination in May–July 1987 was 82 days. Checks typically arrive a week or two later.

7. The actual poverty rate is the posttransfer poverty rate, not the pretransfer rate usually used in this book. I would prefer the pretransfer rate, but such data are not available for all years, and since two-parent families get relatively modest benefits, the two patterns are likely to be close.

8. See, for example, Charles Murray, *Losing Ground: American Social Policy, 1950–1980* (New York: Basic Books, 1984).

9. Actually, growth seems to narrow the distribution of income somewhat. See, for example, Rebecca M. Blank and Alan S. Blinder, "Macroeconomics, Income Distribution, and Poverty," in *Fighting Poverty: What Works and What Doesn't,* edited by Sheldon Danziger and Daniel Weinberg (Cambridge, Mass.: Harvard University Press, 1986), 180–208.

10. Based on author's tabulations of data from U.S. Bureau of the Census, March 1985 Current Population Survey.

11. The AFDC-unemployed parent program is available in twenty-eight states for families with an unemployed parent with past work experience. *Background Material and Data on Programs within the Jurisdiction of the Committee on Ways and Means 1987,* 401.

12. In my tabulations, only 27 percent of fully working poor families reported getting food stamps.

13. Roughly 10 percent of the work force is not working in covered employment. Those who work in very small businesses, some agricultural workers, and the self-employed are not covered. Some 16 percent of those who were part-year workers in poor families were self-employed, and 40 percent worked in rural areas.

14. Generally, benefits run out after six months of unemployment.

15. There is evidence that workers in some kinds of industries (such as construction and manufacturing) are far more likely to collect benefits than those in other industries (such as service and trade). See, for example, Tom Kane, "What Happened to Unemployment Insurance," working paper, Harvard University, 1987.

16. Sheldon Danziger and Peter Gottschalk, "Unemployment Insurance and the Safety Net for the Unemployed." Danziger and Gottschalk actually use a weekly earnings figure that translates to between five and six dollars per hour, assuming that one works full time.

17. *Background Material and Data on Programs within the Jurisdiction of the Committee on Ways and Means 1987,* table 4, p. 330. Here, too, no one really understands why. Gary Burtless and Daniel Saks ("The Decline in Insured Unemployment During the 1980s" [Washington, D.C.: The Brookings Institution, 1984]) argued that state crackdowns are largely to blame. Thomas Kane ("What Happened to Unemployment Insurance") claimed that administrative changes are unlikely to be the cause.

18. Indeed, one of the most serious flaws in the poverty statistics is that they take no account of taxes or work expenses, even though the poverty line was specifically designed to be an after-tax, disposable-income measure.

19. See Robert Reischauer, testimony before the Subcommittee on Social Security and Family Policy of the Committee on Finance, U.S. Senate, February 23, 1987. Reischauer showed that a married couple with two children and a poverty-level income will pay a net of $250 in taxes in 1987. A poverty-level family with four children will pay almost $1,000 in taxes. Starting in 1988, the situation improves somewhat due to tax law changes.

20. Author's tabulations show that, for full-time, working two-parent families, 42 percent report employer group protection, 19 percent report other insurance, and 36 percent report getting nothing. (Figures add to more than 100 percent because some families have more than one source of protection.) For the partially employed and unemployed, the figures are 21 percent, 42 percent, 8 percent, and 38 percent for employer coverage, government coverage, other

coverage, and no coverage, respectively. For two-parent families with a disabled or elderly person, the respective figures are 8 percent, 75 percent, 17 percent, and 16 percent.

21. Gary Burtless, "The Work Response to a Guaranteed Income: A Survey of Experimental Evidence," in *The Income Maintenance Experiments: Lessons for Welfare Reform,* edited by Alicia Munnell (Boston: Federal Reserve Bank, 1987). For discussion see note 8 in chapter 2.

22. Marilyn P. Rymer and Brian O. Burwell, "Medicaid Eligibility: Analysis of Trends and Special Population Groups," Medicaid Program Evaluation Working Paper 5.6 (Washington, D.C.: Department of Health and Human Services, February 1987).

23. Many variations on this sort of plan have been proposed. For an excellent recent discussion of issues surrounding health insurance, see Sara Rosenbaum, "Children and Private Health Insurance," in *Children in a Changing Health Care System,* edited by Mark Schlesinger and Leon Eisenberg (Baltimore: Johns Hopkins University Press, in press); and Gail Wilensky, "Viable Strategies for Dealing with the Uninsured," *Health Affairs* 6 (Spring 1987): 33–46. Recent proposed legislation that provides for residual public health insurance includes the Med America act proposed by Senator John Chafee.

24. This is really just a variation on the many Medicaid buyout plans offered from time to time.

25. This discussion draws heavily on the work of Robert Reischauer, particularly his paper, "Welfare Reform and the Working Poor," in *Reducing Poverty and Dependency,* Center for National Policy (Washington, D.C.: National Academy Press, 1987); and on Eugene Steurle and Paul Wilson, "The Taxation of Poor and Lower Income Workers," in *Ladders Out of Poverty,* report of the Project on the Welfare of Families, edited by Jack Meyer (Washington, D.C.: American Horizons, December 1986).

26. For a recent review of the impact of training programs see Burt S. Barnow, "The Impact on Earnings: A Review of the Literature," *Journal of Human Resources* 22 (Spring 1987): 187–193.

27. Reischauer, "Welfare Reform and the Working Poor," quoted from the manuscript, p. 21. This figure probably understates the change, since nonwage benefits expanded greatly over this period for higher paid workers.

28. Ralph Smith and Bruce Vavrichek, "The Minimum Wage: Its Relationship to Incomes and Poverty," staff working paper (Washington, D.C.: Congressional Budget Office, June 1986). Near-poor is below 150 percent of the poverty line.

29. *Report of the Minimum Wage Study Commission, Vol. 1* (Washington, D.C.: Government Printing Office, 1981), 38; Gary Solon, "The Minimum Wage and Teenage Employment: A Reanalysis with Attention to Serial Correlation and Seasonality," *The Journal of Human Resources* 20 (Spring 1985): 292–297.

30. Robert H. Meyer and David A. Wise, "The Effects of the Minimum Wage on the Employment and Earnings of Youth," *Journal of Labor Economics* 1 (January 1983): 66–100.

31. See, for example, Robert H. Haveman and John L. Palmer, eds., *Jobs for Disadvantaged Workers: The Economics of Employment Subsidies* (Washington, D.C.: The Brookings Institution, 1982).

32. Robert I. Lerman, "Separating Income Support from Income Supplementation," *Journal of the Institute for Socioeconomic Studies* 10 (Autumn 1985): 101–125.

33. For a recent discussion, see John Bishop, "Targeted Jobs Tax Credit: Findings from Employer Surveys" (Columbus: National Center for Research in Vocational Education, Ohio State University, 1985).

34. If the program was not universal or if not all employers would or could take advantage of the credit, then employers might just use a subsidy to help them pay the market wage.

35. Because the credit is "refundable," which means that a family may get a larger refund than it paid in taxes, some have spoken loosely of the EITC as being like a "negative income tax." If "negative income tax" is meant to connote something similar to the earlier negative income tax proposals, the comment is totally misleading. An EITC rewards work for low-paid workers; a negative income tax penalizes it. An EITC benefit starts at nothing and grows as earnings grow up to some limit; a negative income tax starts high and is reduced as earnings grow. A negative income tax is a guaranteed minimum income in disguise; an EITC is a wage subsidy in disguise.

36. Steurle and Wilson, "The Taxation of Poor and Lower Income Workers."

37. Some estimates of the total impact of an EITC show a modest negative effect overall, but changes are trivial compared to the work reductions for the poor under a guaranteed annual income or so-called negative income tax scheme.

38. This is still quite different from a negative income tax plan, as discussed in note 35. For any family who gets the EITC, the total return to work is higher (if you work you get more compared to not working) than before. But in the phase-out region the marginal gain from an additional dollar of earnings is reduced.

39. Committee on Ways and Means, U.S. House of Representatives, *Background Material and Data on Programs within the Jurisdiction of the Committee on Ways and Means,* (Washington, D.C.: U.S. Government Printing Office, 1987), 586.

40. One could imagine a child care credit targeted to the poor, but as it was phased out for higher incomes, one would again be raising the effective tax on each additional dollar of income for moderate-income persons. Adding both a significantly expanded EITC and a highly targeted child care deduction could create a high effective tax rate for middle-income families. If I had to choose, I would favor an expansion of the EITC, since it has the advantage of helping all low-income working families, not just those who must pay for day care. I think it makes sense to expand the current more uniform credit while making it refundable.

41. Alfred Kahn and Sheila B. Kamerman, *Income Transfers for Families with Children: An Eight-Country Study* (Philadelphia: Temple University Press, 1983). Note that the data in this book are for 1979.

42. A refundable tax credit means that every family gets $500 credited against the taxes it owes. A $2,000 deduction is taken off income before taxes are paid. Thus, at a 25 percent average tax rate, a $2,000 deduction is worth a $500 credit.

43. What happens to families of other sizes depends on how much the EITC is allowed to vary by family size. To get a family of five up to the poverty line requires an effective hourly wage of roughly $6.50. A minimum of $4.40 would imply an EITC for this size family of close to 50 percent. I do not think that the government ought to subsidize wages to the point where effective wages fully compensate for the cost of extra children, since childbearing has a large voluntary component. But a minimum wage of $4.40 and EITC rates of say 18 percent for a family of two, 24 percent for a family of three, 30 percent for a

family of four, and 35 percent for a family of five or more would come close to removing all but the largest working families from poverty.

44. Committee on Ways and Means, *Background Material and Data on Programs within the Jurisdiction of the Committee on Ways and Means,* table 27, p. 610.

45. On the one hand, we are more than doubling the benefits for most families. On the other hand, we are raising the minimum wage, which will reduce the number of families in this part of the income distribution. And expenditures now provided through food stamps and welfare to these groups would be saved, although such expenditures are modest. Note that there also would be some increase in Social Security taxes.

46. I believe there should be no attempt to build work incentives into the transitional assistance program. Work incentives alone have never done much good in welfare programs. (See, for example, Robert Moffitt, "Work Incentives in Transfer Programs [Revisited]: A Study of the AFDC Program," *Research in Labor Economics* 8 [1986]: 384–439.) If someone in the family is working, there is no need for aid. With an EITC and a higher minimum wage and medical protection, we would have assured that work pays. The incentive to work is to avoid using up the transitional assistance protection that one starts with.

Chapter 5

1. Excluding Alaska, monthly AFDC benefits for a family of three in January 1987 ranged from $118 in Alabama to $617 in California. Benefits in the median state were $354. See Committee on Ways and Means, U.S. House of Representatives, *Background Material and Data on Programs within the Jurisdiction of the Committee on Ways and Means* (Washington, D.C.: U.S. Government Printing Office, 1987), 409.

2. If she works half time, she must pay for 1,000 hours of care for the toddler. If she works full time, she must pay for 2,000 hours of care for the toddler and 1,000 hours of after-school care for the older child. These figures are, if anything, optimistic. The report of the U.S. Bureau of the Census, *Who's Minding the Kids? Child Care Arrangements, Winter 1984–85 (Current Population Reports, Household Economic Studies,* Series P-70, No. 9 [Washington, D.C.: U.S. Government Printing Office, 1987]), shows that the median day care payment for women with *one* child who work part time is $25 per week ($1,300 per year) and $43 per week ($2,236 per year) for those who work full time. Moreover, a significant proportion of the women who pay for day care (over 20 percent) are paying a relative to do the care, and they typically pay small amounts, which brings down the median.

3. As of this writing, the WIN program was due to expire in Fall 1987.

4. These wage rates are inferred by dividing the total earnings by the number of weeks and the usual hours worked. This method is the only available on the Current Population Survey, but it is not very reliable. Also it means that a calculated wage is not available for nonworkers.

5. Half the nonpoor part-year workers had child support payments. The average payment per family who received payments and avoided poverty was $4,800.

6. It is easy to get the impression in these annual figures that many people are mixing work and welfare. In fact, it appears that what is happening is that

these women work part of the year and are out of work and on welfare for the remainder of the year. In a typical month in 1984, only 5 percent of those on AFDC reported they were working. In contrast, a wide variety of studies have shown that many women who leave welfare for work return to the program quickly. Finally, only 5 percent of poor single mothers report that they worked all year at a part-time job (as opposed to part of the year at a full-time job).

7. All these facts are derived from David T. Ellwood, "Targeting the Would-Be Long Term Recipient: Who Should Be Served?" report to the U.S. Department of Health and Human Services (Princeton, N.J.: Mathematica Policy Research, 1986); and Mary Jo Bane and David T. Ellwood, "The Dynamics of Dependence: The Routes to Self-Sufficiency," report to the U.S. Department of Health and Human Services (Cambridge, Mass.: Urban Systems Research & Engineering, 1983).

8. All these facts are derived from Ellwood, "Targeting the Would-Be Long Term Recipient: Who Should Be Served?"

9. Based on author's tabulations of U.S. Bureau of the Census, Current Population Survey, March 1985.

10. Barbara Goldman, Daniel Friedlander, and David Long, *Final Report on the San Diego Job Search and Work Experience Demonstration* (New York: Manpower Demonstration Research Corp., 1986).

11. For a summary of many of these programs, see Judith Gueron, *Work Initiatives for Welfare Recipients: Lessons from a Multi-State Experiment* (New York: Manpower Demonstration Research Corp., 1986).

12. Goldman et al., *Final Report on the San Diego Job Search and Work Experience Demonstration.*

13. Gueron, *Work Initiatives for Welfare Recipients: Lessons from a Multi-State Experiment.*

14. See, for example, Mickey Kaus, "The Work Ethic State: The Only Way to Cure the Culture of Poverty," *The New Republic* (July 7, 1986): 22–33.

15. Jean Baldwin Grossman, Rebecca Maynard, and Judith Roberts, "Reanalysis of the Effects of Selected Employment and Training Programs for Welfare Recipients," report prepared for the U.S. Department of Health and Human Services (Princeton, N.J.: Mathematica Policy Research, 1985).

16. *The 1985 Virginia Slims American Women's Poll,* conducted by the Roper Organization, table 3.21, p. 55.

17. For an excellent review, see Lenore J. Weitzman, "Child Support: The National Disgrace," in L. Weitzman, *The Divorce Revolution* (New York: Free Press, 1985), chap. 9.

18. The Massachusetts formula is complicated. Awards for men whose incomes are less than $200 per week are left to the discretion of judges. Men with incomes of $200–500 pay 28 percent for two children. Those with incomes above $500 pay 30 percent. On top of these percentages, there is a 10 percent increase if the oldest child is between 7 and 12, and a 15 percent increase if the oldest child is over 13. Finally, the child support award is adjusted downward if the custodial parent earns more than $15,000 after day care expenses.

19. U.S. Bureau of the Census, *Money Income of Households, Families and Persons in the United States: 1985, Current Population Reports,* Series P-60, No. 156 (Washington, D.C.: U.S. Government Printing Office, 1987), table 33, p. 118. Figures are for married men aged 25–64 with wives present.

20. See, for example, Bush Institute for Child and Family Policy, *Estimates of Child Support Collections Potential and the Income of Female Headed Families* (Washington,

D.C.: U.S. Department of Health & Human Services, 1985); Irwin Garfinkel and Donald Oellerich, "Noncustodial Fathers' Ability to Pay Child Support," Discussion Paper No. 815-86 (Madison: Institute for Research on Poverty, University of Wisconsin, 1986); and Mark X. Cronin and Paul A. Jargowsky, "Child Support in New York State: Making the System Work," unpublished paper, Harvard University, 1986.

21. State welfare departments will pursue the absent fathers of the children of AFDC recipients, but the women usually gain little if the men start paying, since all but $50 per month is deducted from their welfare checks.

22. Lenore J. Weitzman, *The Divorce Revolution* (New York: Free Press, 1985), 321.

23. Actually the bill had some new incentives for awards.

24. The next two sections draw heavily on the work of Irwin Garfinkel, notably Garfinkel and Elizabeth Uhr, "A New Approach to Child Support," *The Public Interest* 75 (Spring 1984): 111–122; and Garfinkel, "Child Support Assurance: A New Tool for Achieving Social Security," unpublished paper, University of Wisconsin, October 1985.

25. For a discussion of this point, see Robert Lerman, "Child Support and Welfare Dependency," unpublished paper, Brandeis University, February 1987.

26. Irwin Garfinkel, "Child Support Assurance," table 1, p. 18. The table gives figures in 1983 dollars and shows net savings with a collection rate of 80 percent, a first-child assured benefit of $2,500, a second-child benefit of $1,500, and smaller benefits for additional children. The figures are based on the Wisconsin child support collection formulas.

27. And Sweden has a system of child support assurance. Courts set child support levels and then government automatically pays that level and takes on the job of collecting the payments. Children are guaranteed the money whether or not the government is successful in collecting the money. See Alfred Kahn and Sheila B. Kamerman, *Income Transfers for Families With Children: An Eight-Country Study* (Philadelphia: Temple University Press, 1983).

28. Paul Jargowsky, "Going After Fathers: Can We Really Collect Child Support?" unpublished paper, Harvard University, May 1986, 23.

29. Note that even under these narrow cost-benefit terms, expanded efforts seem to pay off quickly. See Center for Health and Social Services Research, *Costs and Benefits of Paternity Establishment,* report to the U.S. Department of Health & Human Services (Washington, D.C.: U.S. Government Printing Office, 1985).

30. John Treacy, "Analysis of Selected Paternity Establishment Issues," unpublished paper, December 1985. Treacy works in the Federal Office of Child Support Enforcement.

31. Lawrence M. Mead, *Beyond Entitlement: The Social Obligations of Citizenship* (New York: Free Press, 1986), 3.

32. See U.S. Bureau of the Census, *Who's Minding the Kids?* table 1, p. 13.

33. U.S. Department of Labor, *Handbook of Labor Statistics* (Washington, D.C.: U.S. Government Printing Office, 1985), table 5, p. 19. For women aged 35–44, the participation rate is even higher.

34. The U.S. Bureau of the Census report *Who's Minding the Kids?* table G, p. 11, shows that almost 40 percent of mothers with one child who use a relative for care pay for the care.

35. Ibid., table 3, p. 15.

36. See Bane and Ellwood, "The Dynamics of Dependence."

37. Goldman et al., *Final Report on the San Diego Job Search and Work Experience Demonstration.*

38. Susan Rees, "How the Poor Would Remedy Poverty: Summary of Results," report to the Ford Foundation (Washington, D.C.: Coalition on Human Needs, Summer 1986), 2.

39. Mead, *Beyond Entitlement,* 4.

Chapter 6

1. Ken Auletta, *The Underclass* (New York: Random House, 1982), xiii.

2. See, for example, Bill Moyers's television special "The Vanishing Family: Crisis in Black America," as well as Leon Dash's series of articles in the *Washington Post,* January 1986: "Children's Children," January 26, 1986, A1; "Motherhood the Hard Way," January 27, 1986, A1; "When Outcomes Collide with Desire," January 29, 1986, A1; "Mario, I Want a Baby," January 30, 1986, A1; "Breaking the Hold of a 'Choke Chain,'" January 31, 1986, A1; and "The American Millstone" series in *Chicago Tribune,* sec. 5, December 1–11, 1985.

3. See, for example, Mary Corcoran et al., "Myth and Reality: The Causes and Persistence of Poverty," *Journal of Policy Analysis and Management* 4 (Summer 1985): 516–536, for one review that discusses the direct influence of culture and motivation. My reading of the literature is that attitudes and motivation are difficult to measure.

4. See, for example, William Julius Wilson, "The Ghetto Underclass and the Social Transformation of the Inner City," Plenary Lecture, Annual Meeting of the American Association for the Advancement of Science, Chicago, February 1987; Sheldon Danziger and Peter Gottschalk, "Earnings Inequality, the Spatial Concentration of Poverty, and the Underclass," *American Economic Review, Papers and Proceedings* (May 1987): 211–215; and Richard Nathan, "The Underclass—Will It Always Be With Us?" paper prepared for a symposium at the New School for Social Research (New York City), Princeton, N.J., November 1986.

5. U.S. Bureau of the Census, *Poverty Areas in Large Cities, 1980 Census of the Population,* Vol. 2, *Subject Reports* (Washington, D.C.: U.S. Government Printing Office, 1985), A-2.

6. Robert Reischauer, "The Geographic Distribution of Poverty: What Do We Know?" working paper (Washington, D.C.: The Brookings Institution, 1987).

7. U.S. Bureau of the Census, *Poverty Areas in Large Cities,* table 1, p. 45.

8. See, for example, Wilson, "The Ghetto Underclass and the Social Transformation of the Inner City"; Danziger and Gottschalk, "Earnings Inequality, the Spatial Concentration of Poverty, and the Underclass"; and Nathan, "The Underclass—Will It Always Be With Us?"

9. This term is from Erol Ricketts and Isabel Sawhill, "Defining and Measuring the Underclass," paper presented at the American Economic Association meetings, December 1986.

10. Ibid., 7.

11. Regarding the credibility of Jean Madison's childbearing, Auletta reported: "Ultimately like any reporter, I relied on my sniffer. Mine told me these people generally were pretty straight, certainly a lot straighter than many politicians I interview." See Auletta, *The Underclass*, xv.

12. U.S. Bureau of the Census, *Statistical Abstract of the United States, 1986* (Washington, D.C.: U.S. Government Printing Office, 1985), table 647, p. 382.

13. See Kenneth B. Clark, *The Dark Ghetto: Dilemmas of Social Power* (New York: Harper & Row, 1967); Michael Harrington, *The Other America* (New York: Macmillan Co., 1962); Herbert J. Gans, *Urban Villagers: Group and Class in the Life of Italian-Americans* (New York: Free Press, 1962); and Oscar Lewis, *La Vida* (New York: Panther, 1965).

14. William Julius Wilson, "Cycles of Deprivation and the Underclass Debate," *Social Service Review* 59 (December 1985): 242.

15. Daniel Patrick Moynihan, *The Negro Family: The Case for National Action* (Washington, D.C.: U.S. Department of Labor, March 1965).

16. Wilson, "Cycles of Deprivation and the Underclass Debate."

17. Lee Rainwater, "Class, Culture, Poverty, and Welfare," unpublished manuscript, Harvard University, 1987.

18. Ulf Hannerz, *Soulside* (New York: Columbia University Press, 1969), 183.

19. Herbert J. Gans, "Culture and Class in the Study of Poverty: An Approach to Anti-Poverty Research," in *On Understanding Poverty: Perspectives from the Social Sciences*, edited by Daniel P. Moynihan (New York: Basic Books, 1968), 211.

20. Ibid.

21. Charles Murray, *Losing Ground: American Social Policy, 1950–1980* (New York: Basic Books, 1984), 189.

22. Lawrence M. Mead, *Beyond Entitlement: The Social Obligations of Citizenship* (New York: Free Press, 1986).

23. See for example Mickey Kaus, "The Work Ethic State: The Only Way to Cure the Culture of Poverty," *The New Republic* (July 7, 1986): 22–33.

24. Rainwater, "Class, Culture, Poverty, and Welfare."

25. Wilson, "Cycles of Deprivation and the Underclass Debate."

26. See note 2 in chapter 4 for a discussion of the methods of the Panel Study of Income Dynamics (PSID).

27. The PSID data, the source of these tabulations, do not allow a determination of whether people live in ghettos.

28. U.S. Bureau of the Census, *Poverty Areas in Large Cities*, table 1, p. 45; and U.S. Bureau of the Census, *Low Income Areas in Large Cities, 1970 Census of the Population, Subject Reports* (Washington, D.C.: U.S. Government Printing Office, 1973), table 1.

29. Wilson, "Cycles of Deprivation and the Underclass Debate," 242.

30. U.S. Bureau of the Census, *Poverty Areas in Large Cities*, table 1, p. 45.

31. U.S. Bureau of the Census, *Education in the United States: 1940–1983, Special Demographic Analysis* (Washington, D.C.: U.S. Government Printing Office, 1985), table A-2, p. 47.

32. Gordon Berlin and Andrew Sum, "Toward a More Perfect Union: Basic Skills, Poor Families, and Our Economic Future," Project on Social Welfare and the American Future, Occasional Paper 3 (New York: The Ford Foundation, in press).

33. All these dropout figures come from Floyd Morgan Hammack, "Large School Systems' Dropout Reports: An Analysis of Definitions, Procedures, and Findings," *Teachers College Record* 87 (Spring 1986): 324–341.

34. Glenn C. Loury, "Race and Poverty: The Problem of Dependency in a Pluralistic Society," paper prepared for the Working Seminar on the Family and American Welfare Policy, American Enterprise Institute, Washington, D.C., November 1986.

35. All these figures are taken from Bureau of the Census, *1980 Census of Population, General Social and Economic Characteristics, U.S. Summary* (Washington, D.C.: U.S. Government Printing Office, 1983), table 89, p. 45, and table 87, p. 31.

36. See, for example, Al Rees and George Shultz, *Workers and Wages in an Urban Labor Market* (Chicago: University of Chicago Press, 1970).

37. John D. Kasarda, "The Regional and Urban Redistribution of People and Jobs in the U.S.," paper prepared for the Committee on National Urban Policy, National Acadamy of Science, 1986.

38. Ibid.

39. David T. Ellwood, "The Spatial Mismatch Hypothesis: Are There Teenage Jobs Missing in the Ghetto?" in *The Black Youth Unemployment Problem,* edited by Richard Freeman and Harry J. Holzer (Chicago: University of Chicago Press, 1986), 147–185. I also concluded that this increasing disadvantage did not seem to be the primary reason why blacks and whites fared so differently.

40. David T. Ellwood and David A. Wise, "Uncle Sam Wants You—Sometimes," in *Public Sector Payrolls,* edited by David A. Wise (Chicago: University of Chicago Press, 1987), 97–118.

41. See Jon Crane and David T. Ellwood, "The Youth Employment Program: Job Supplement or Job Substitute?" unpublished manuscript, Harvard University, 1986.

42. Bureau of Labor Statistics, *Geographical Profile of Employment and Unemployment, 1985* (Washington, D.C.: U.S. Government Printing Office, 1986), tables 1, pp. 3, 23, and 88.

43. Bureau of Justice Statistics, *Sourcebook of Criminal Justice Statistics, 1981* (Washington, D.C.: U.S. Government Printing Office, 1982), table 3.12, p. 258.

44. William Julius Wilson, "The Urban Underclass," in *Minority Report: What Has Happened to Blacks, Hispanics, American Indians, and Other Minorities,* edited by Leslie W. Dunbar (New York: Pantheon Books, 1984), 84.

45. Ibid.

46. Richard B. Freeman and Harry J. Holzer, "The Black Youth Employment Crisis: Summary of Findings," in *The Black Youth Employment Crisis,* edited by Freeman and Holzer (Chicago: University of Chicago Press, 1986), 8.

47. W. Kip Viscusi, "Market Incentives for Criminal Behavior," in *The Black Youth Employment Crisis,* edited by Richard B. Freeman and Harry J. Holzer (Chicago: University of Chicago Press, 1986), 343.

48. See for example, John Yinger, "Measuring Discrimination with Fair Housing Audits: Caught in the Act," *The American Economic Review* 76 (December 1986): 881–893.

49. Claude Brown, *Manchild in the Promised Land* (New York: Macmillian Co., 1965); and Brown, "Manchild in Harlem," *The New York Times Magazine* (September 16, 1984): 36–44, 54, and 76–77.

50. Sylvester Monroe, "Brothers: A Vivid Portrait of Black Men in America," *Newsweek* (March 23, 1987): 54–86.

51. Leon Dash, *Washington Post,* January 26–31, 1986. (See note 2 for full listing.)

52. Dash, "Motherhood the Hard Way."

53. Dash, "When Outcomes Collide with Desire."

54. Ibid.

55. Dash, "Mario, I Want a Baby."

56. Murray, *Losing Ground.*

57. Thomas Kane, "Giving Back Control: A New Perspective on Long-Term Poverty and Motivation," *Social Science Review* 61 (September 1987): 405–419.

58. William E. Geist, "One Man's Gift: College for 52 in Harlem," *The New York Times,* October 19, 1985, pp. 1 and 50.

59. Conversation with Johnny Rivera, June 1987.

60. Conversation with Johnny Rivera, June 1987.

61. Murray, *Losing Ground.*

62. John R. Berrueta-Clement et al., *Changed Lives: The Effects of the Perry Preschool Program on Youths Through Age 19* (Ypsilanti, Mich.: High/Scope Press, 1984), table 1, p. 2.

63. See ibid., pp. 95–115, for one review.

64. For more details, see William J. Spring, "Youth Unemployment and the Transition from School to Work," *New England Economic Review* (March/April 1987): 11.

65. For a comprehensive review, see Charles Betsey, Robinson Hollister, and Mary Papageorgiou, eds., *Youth Employment and Training Programs,* National Research Council, National Academy of Sciences (Washington, D.C.: National Academy Press, 1985).

66. Peter Kemper, David Long, and Craig Thornton, *The Supported Work Evaluation: Final Benefit Cost Analysis* (New York: Manpower Demonstration Research Corp., 1981).

67. Charles Mallar et al., "Evaluation of the Impact of the Job Corps Program: Third Follow-Up Review" (Princeton, N.J.: Mathematica Policy Research, 1982).

68. See, for example, Mark Laponte, "The Connecticut Enterprise Zone Program: An Evaluation," policy analysis exercise, John F. Kennedy School of Government, Harvard University, April 1984; and Dick Cowden and Gerald Bonetto, "Enterprise Zone Activity in the States: Summary of Findings" (Washington, D.C.: The Sabre Foundation, November 1983).

69. For some examples, see Executive Office of the President, Office of Policy Development, *Up From Dependency: A New National Public Assistance Strategy, Supplement 3, A Self-Help Catalogue* (Washington, D.C.: U.S. Government Printing Office, 1986).

70. Loury, "Race and Poverty," 25.

71. Ibid., 28 and 29.

72. Dash, "When Outcomes Collide with Desires."

73. Mickey Kaus, "The Work Ethic State," 30.

74. Mickey Kaus, reply, in "Welfare and Work: A Symposium," *The New Republic* (October 6, 1986): 23.

75. Loury, "Race and Poverty," 14.

76. Ibid.

77. See, for example, Robert L. Crain et al., "A Longitudinal Study of a Voluntary Metropolitan Desegregation Plan," unpublished paper, National Institute of Education, October 1984.

78. J. Anthony Lukas, *Common Ground: A Turbulent Decade in the Lives of Three American Families* (New York: Alfred A. Knopf, 1985).

Chapter 7

1. Report of the Task Force on Poverty and Welfare, *A New Social Contract: Rethinking the Nature and Purpose of Public Assistance* (Albany: Executive Chamber, State of New York, 1986).

2. Michael Novak, *The New Consensus on Family and Welfare* (Washington, D.C.: American Enterprise Institute, 1987).

INDEX

Aaron, Henry, 35

Abortion: child support and, 171–72; teenage pregnancy and, 72

Absent parents, 78, 79, 234, 239–40; expectations of, 156–58; *see also* Child support

Affirmative action, 34, 35, 210

Aged, the, 4, 5, 30, 39, 42–43; Medicaid and, 106; Medicare and, 106; SSI and, 37; two-parent families and, 88; welfare system and, 100, 102; *see also* Social Security

AIDS, 74, 75

Aid to Families with Dependent Children (AFDC), 20, 31; benefits determined by state, 38, 61; children on, 59–60; contraction of, 40, 59–61; expansion of, 37–38, 58–59; goals of, 44; Medicaid and, 103, 106; two-parent families and, 38, 39

American values, 15–18, 26–27, 236, 243; altered by welfare, 5; causes of poverty and, 5–10; children's allowance and, 118; EITC and, 115, 116, 120; ghetto poor and, 224–28, 229; medical protection and, 108; Social Security and, 27–28, 35; two-parent families and, 81, 88, 126, 127; unemployment

insurance and, 35; *see also specific values*

Antidiscrimination programs, 34–35, 210, 228–29, 236

Armed Forces Qualification Test (AFQT), 205, 207

Assistance-family structure conundrum, 20–23, 41, 42, 57–61

Auletta, Ken, 189, 195

Autonomy of the individual, 6, 16

Berlin, Gordon, 205

Birthrate: 1960–83, 66; for nonwhite women, 67–70; for teenage women, 71–72

Blacks: economic conditions and, 207, 208; education and, 204–5; family structure of, 56–57, 70, 74, 200, 222–23; governmental policies and, 74, 207; marriage rates among, 57, 70, 222–23; middle class, 204; single-parent families among, 57, 60; unemployment and, 205–8; United States military jobs and, 207; white children compared to black, 200–1; *see also* Antidiscrimination programs; Ghetto poor

51 78